Reactive Voting in Danish General Elections 1971 - 1979

Peter Nannestad

REACTIVE VOTING IN DANISH GENERAL ELECTIONS 1971 - 1979

A REVISIONIST INTERPRETATION

AARHUS UNIVERSITY PRESS
1989

Published with financial support from the
Danish Social Science Research Council

Printed by AKA-PRINT
Cover by Inga Friis

ISBN 87-7288-243 3

AARHUS UNIVERSITY PRESS
University of Aarhus
DK8000 Aarhus C
Denmark

Table of contents

0. Preface

The impetus to conduct a study and write a book like the present one may come from many sources. Curiosity, ambitions, frustrations etc. combine into an intricate web of motivations. I certainly do not intend to bore or embarrass anybody by trying to unravel its texture.

Nevertheless there is one important source of intellectual inspiration I should like to mention and acknowledge explicitly. In late 1986 I was made to read a manuscript titled "Complementarity and political science. An essay on fundamentals of political science theory and research strategy",* written by Erik Rasmussen, one of the "founding fathers" of the discipline of political science in Denmark. It did not meet with the approval of all Bohr experts, but especially its discussion of the problem of determinism versus voluntarism in electoral research did influence my own way of thinking about voters, elections, and electoral research. I would hardly have gone through writing this book without this inspiration.

Furthermore I do want to gratefully acknowledge the assistance so generously provided to me by a number of my colleagues in the finishing stages of this work. Erik Damgaard, Jørgen Elklit, Øystein Gaasholt, Ingemar Glans, and (once more) Erik Rasmussen from the Institute of Political Science, and Manfred Holler, Peter Jensen, and Martin Paldam from the Institute of Economics at the University of Aarhus all read parts and versions of the manuscript. I have profited greatly from their critique and comments, and I certainly owe them to stress that they are the last to be blamed for whatever shortcomings remain. They probably did their best to draw my attention to them.

Finally my thanks are due to the Danish Social Science Research Council for supporting the publication of this book through a grant, and to Tønnes Bekker-Nielsen from Aarhus University Press who took care of many practical details during its production.

---

* Published in 1987 under the same title by Odense University Press.

1. Introduction: Setting the stage

1.1. The big bang: The 4th of December 1973

The 8th of November 1973 Erhard Jakobsen, a long-standing member of the Danish parliament (the Folketing) and a widely known and popular mayor of the Copenhagian suburb Gladsaxe, reportedly ran out of gas while on his way to the afternoon session in the Folketing. He did not arrive on time that day.

Two days earlier he, who had been a party member since the early thirties, had broken away from the Socialdemocrats (SD), protesting the party's alleged turn to the left under the new party leader, Anker Jørgensen. The following day, he had founded his own party, the Center-Democrats (Centrum-Demokraterne, CD). On both occasions however, he had pledged his continued support to the Socialdemocratic government, except on some issues of taxation, and especially the taxation of house owners.

The Socialdemocratic minority government was critically dependent on Erhard Jakobsen's continued support. Together with the Socialist Peoples' Party (SF), the Socialdemocrats held 87 of the 179 seats in the Folketing elected in 1971. The opposition, consisting of the Radical Liberals (RV), the Agrarians (V) and the Conservatives (KF), held 88 seats. Only by including one of the two members of the Folketing elected on the Faeroe Islands, who happened to be a Socialdemocrat, as well as one of the two members elected on Greenland, who was made Minister of Greenland in return, the government could marshall a threadbare 89:88 majority, provided the two other members elected on the Faeroe Islands and on Greenland, respectively, both abstained from voting which they could usually be expected to do on issues of no relevance to their home regions. Obviously, the defection of just one member could thus prove fatal to the government's life.

Up to the referendum on October 2nd, 1972, on Denmark's entry into the EEC the parliamentary situation had been remarkably stable, despite the government's somewhat precarious parliamentary basis. The opposition which agreed with the official government position of recommending membership of the EEC had not shown much interest in creating difficulties for the government. Given the widespread skepticism and in some quarters even outright hostility towards Danish membership of the EEC in the Socialdemocratic rank and file as well as in some of the major trade unions, it was clearly seen as tactically advantageous to the opposition to have a Socialdemocratic government dealing with these problems.

But as soon as the EEC-question had been decided upon (64 pct. voting for Denmark's entry into the EEC), the parliamentary situation started to grow more tense. The new prime minister and leader of the Socialdemocratic party, Anker Jørgensen, a former trade union leader, who had replaced J.O. Krag in both functions when Krag decided to step down just after the referendum, intensified the cooperation with the Socialist Peoples' Party. In June 1973 it culminated in a "deal" on the future housing-policy between the two parties, excluding the opposition from influence on this central policy-issue. Two months later, Anker Jørgensen publicly declared his party's proper place in Danish politics to be "left of the center". The opposition,suspecting that Anker Jørgensen intended to rule with the support of SF only, answered back by challenging his ability to lead his party as well as the country and over and over again demanded new elections.[1]

When Erhard Jakobsen failed to turn up in the Folketing on the 8th of November, the roll call division on a government bill concerning some adjustments in the taxation of wealth produced a draw (86:86) and the bill was thus defeated. The government, finding the situation untenable, decided to call for new elections, to take place on December 4th, 1973.

The opinion polls held ominous forebodings. Since the beginning of 1973 the Progress Party (Frp), founded in 1972 by the tax lawyer Mogens Glistrup, had shown unprecedented strength in various "trial elections", reaching a peak of 25 pct. of the "votes" during the spring of 1973. After that time, its strength had declined somewhat, but had continued to run around 15 pct., far above the normal level of support for new parties in the Danish party system. The Center-Democrats too made a strong appearance in the polls, oscillating around 8-10 pct.. A number of smaller parties which had all been represented in the Folketing at some time in the past - Communists (DKP), Left Socialists (VS) and the Justice Party (DR) - were waiting in the wings, ready for a come back, together with the Christian Peoples' Party (Krf), founded in 1970, which had come very close to gaining representation in 1971.

Altogether, the voters could pick from among 11 parties. In itself, this was not an unusual high number for a Danish election. The unusual was that - judged from the opinion polls - all of these parties stood a realistic chance of passing the threshold of the Danish electoral law[2] and to gain seats in the Folketing. Moreover, two of the new parties - Glistrup's Progress Party and Erhard Jakobsen's Center-Democrats - together were approaching 20 pct. of the vote, and obviously popular support for the "old" parties - i.e. the parties already represented in the Folketing: SD, RV, KF, SF, and V - had decreased dramatically. Neither the socialist bloc, consisting of SD and SF, nor the liberal-conservative bloc, consisting of RV, KF and V, could look forward to obtain a majority in the new Folketing. Speculations on who would be able to form a government with whom became a prominent theme during the campaign, and there was no shortage of admonitions to the voters not to create an unstable parliamentary situation.

---

[1]For example, the Agrarians' former foreign minister, Hartling, declared that Anker Jørgensen would do his party and the country a favor by calling new elections , cf. Avisårbogen (1973, p.22).

[2] Danish electoral law contains three thresholds for representation, one of which must be passed. In practice the "critical" one is a 2 pct. share of the votes cast.

When the polling stations closed in the evening of the 4th of December, it quickly became clear that the voters had not heeded the advice. Of the 11 parties running, only the Left Socialists did not gain seats in the new Folketing. The "old" parties had taken a severe beating, SD and KF suffering the heaviest losses. Table 1.1. below summarizes the outcome, together with the 1971-results for comparison.

Thus overnight the number of parties in the Folketing had doubled from five to ten. More important, the percentage of the vote received by the five "old" parties had dropped to an all-time low point of 64.3 pct. as against the "normal" level of well above 90 pct.. Never since 1920 had there been such a degree of fractionalization in the Folketing.[3] The Danish party system which had existed almost unchanged since the first decade of this century[4] (with the addition of the Socialist Peoples' Party in 1960 as the only lasting innovation) was shattered. The leaders of the "old" parties were shocked. Observers - foreign and Danish alike - were stunned.

Table 1.1.: Electoral results 1971 and 1973 (Pct. of votes cast)

Party	21.9.1971	4.12.1973
SD	37.3	25.6
RV	14.4	11.2
KF	16.7	9.2
DR	1.7	2.9
SF	9.1	6.0
DKP	1.4	3.6
CD	-	7.8
Krf	2.0	4.0
V	15.6	12.3
VS	1.6	1.5
Frp	-	15.9

The day after the election, the Socialdemocratic government resigned. After two weeks of protracted negotiations, former foreign minister Poul Hartling (V) formed a minority government, based solely on the Agrarians' 22 seats. It was the weakest minority government since the introduction of parliamentarism, and it had to find its support from case to case by bargaining with other parties.

When the recession in the wake of the first oil crisis hit Denmark about six months later, thus adding an economic dimension to the crisis, the scene was set for a period of political instability and unrest which was to last through the remaining part of the decade.

---

[3] Measured by Rae's index of fractionalization, it reached a value of 0.85, cf. Damgaard (1977, pp.92-93).
[4] See Elklit (1984) for a historical account on the genesis of the "classical" Danish party system.

1.2. Shock-waves in electoral research

The outcome of the 1973-election with its massive defections from the established parties stunned and shocked the politicians. It also left the experts on electoral behavior in considerable bewilderment and in disagreement as to how to account for this "landslide" and for the unprecedented electoral volatility that developed in its wake.

The reason was probably not so much that these developments had not been foreseen before they had become manifest[5] - political scientists usually develop a rather detached attitude to errors of prediction, the sheer magnitude of which would send professionals in other fields (with the possible exception of meteorologists) looking for alternative ways of making a living - but rather the fact that they posed a serious challenge to two theoretical frameworks which were jointly dominating Danish electoral research at that time (as, in fact, they still are today). These were the social-psychological and the structural theory of voting, respectively.

The social-psychological theory of voting had been imported to Denmark from Michigan in the late sixties, complete with the questionnaires from the SRC-surveys.[6] From that time, the social-psychological theory of voting in Danish electoral research had largely become synonymous with the "Michigan school" or "Michigan model", as originated by Campbell, Converse, Miller and Stokes (1960).[7]

In short, the Michigan school sees the individual act of voting as a conditioned choice, the main conditioning agent being party identification. Party identification expresses the voters' affective orientation towards a party, i.e. his or her feeling of psychologically "belonging to" the party as a group, rather than the mere support for a political party based on its perceived closeness to the voter with respect to certain issues or to specific political means or ends. Hence the essence of party identification is emotional, not cognitive, and in that respect party identification can be seen as quite analogous to identification with other groups the voter may have emotional ties with, like religious or ethnic groups.

---

[5] The only analysis of the 1971-election to appear before - and hence untainted by - the election of 1973 was Borre and Katz (1973). It interprets the 1971-election as a "normal" (maintaining) election alongside the elections of 1964 and 1966 and as opposed to the "realignment" election of 1960 and the "deviating" election of 1968. As will be shown below, it was only on the surface the 1971-election resembled a return to "normality". Beneath that surface, the ferments were already brewing that exploded the party system in 1973.

[6] The 1971-election was the first Danish election to be covered by a nationwide mass-survey. The inspiration from the SRC-surveys is obvious.

[7] There are numerous accounts available of what the Michigan model stands for. The original works by Campbell and his associates may still be the best source for a complete understanding and appraisal. For Danish readers, Borre (1984a) gives a short and fair, though mainly sympathetic, overview. Tonsgaard (1984) adds some important question marks. The key concept in the Michigan theory is extensively discussed in Budge, Crewe and Farlie (1976).

Party identification is supposed to be acquired mainly through socialization processes in the family, neighborhood, place of work and other peer-groups. Although the individual may change its party identification during his or her life-span, it will normally be stable over long periods of time. Hence voting behavior is not "free", but is largely determined by forces beyond the control of the voters. Basically voting is an a-rational choice.

The Michigan theory of voting quickly became a prominent paradigm in electoral research both inside and outside the U.S. Especially party identification rose to the rank of a near-ubiquitous concept in the vocabulary of political science and has been put to use in innumerable studies of electoral behavior.

There are several obvious reasons for the theory's strong success (besides the intellectual brilliance of its originators). For one thing, the Michigan theory ties voting neatly into broader small group-theories. It thus provides a theory of voting which is consistent with theories in another, important sub-field of social science.

But for those who tend to consider the cumulative aspects of theory-building a dispensable aesthetic quality, the Michigan theory of voting offers some more "tangible" advantages as well. The power of the measure of party identification as a predictor of the actual vote has been demonstrated repeatedly. It has also been demonstrated to be a good predictor of, i.a., the level of political interest and involvement in Denmark (Borre and Katz, 1973).

Moreover, the concept of party identification appears to offer an explanation to at least two of the more puzzling empirical findings which seem to emerge almost invariably from electoral studies in Western democracies.

One of these empirical results is the "gyroscopic stability" (Borre and Katz, 1973) in the electoral support for parties or groups of parties, when seen over a time period of sufficient length.[8] By this is meant the parties' tendency to finally revert to some stable level of strength, even after heavy losses or gains in a series of elections. Here the concept of party identification as a long-term vote disposition - which however can be occasionally offset by short-term factors like a specific issue or the special appeal of a party leader - seems to offer a plausible explanation. The phenomenon of safe seats or of party strongholds in specific geographical regions (Borre and Stehouwer, 1968) can be explained analogously by resorting to the concept of party identification.

Besides that, party identification also seems to explain why and how people manage to vote in a non-random fashion despite the fact - more or less confirmed in study upon study - that the vast majority of voters can be divided into two groups: Those who know near to nothing, and those who

---

[8] In some cases, however, it can be quite difficult to decide whether this "gyroscopic stability" is in the numbers or in the eyes of the beholder. For an example see Borre (1977, pp.12-13).

know absolutely nothing about the issues of the campaign or the parties' stands on these issues, and that many of them do not care, either.

In importing the Michigan model and making it one of the corner stones in electoral research from the start of the seventies onwards, Danish political science was then just following an international trend.[9] Given i.a. the "gyroscopic stability" so characteristic of Danish electoral behavior since about 1920, the theory certainly looked plausible at that time, and its very first application appeared promising.[10]

The social-psychological (or Michigan) theory of voting has not reigned unchallenged in Danish electoral research, however. Its prime alternative has always been various structural theories of voting behavior. Due to the traditionally strong correlation between social class and voting in Denmark and the absence of strong religious, ethnic or regional cleavages,[11] structural theory in Danish electoral research has been largely synonymous with a (Marxist or non-Marxist) class theory of voting. The neo-Marxist renaissance in Danish social science in the late sixties and early seventies lent further strength to this tendency.

According to class theory, the individual's voting behavior is determined by class membership, or - in neo-Marxist terminology - by the individual's position in the social division of labor. Elections are just expressions of the democratic class struggle (Lipset, 1960, p.230). The mechanism by which class membership is turned into a voting decision is usually left unspecified. Structural theory is strictly a macrotheory[12] of voting.

The important thing to notice here is that the individual act of voting is considered a conditioned choice within the framework of structural theory as much as it is within the framework of social-psychological theory. In structural theory, too, forces largely outside the control of the individual voter determine how (s)he votes. The main conditioning agent, however, now becomes (objective) class membership.

Despite numerous differences, the social-psychological and the structural theory of voting can hence be seen to share one basic assumption about the

---

[9] There appears to have been remarkable little theoretical discussion of the Michigan model when it was first introduced in Denmark. In part this may be attributable to a general tendency in Danish electoral research to softpedal theoretical questions altogether. In most publications on Danish electoral behavior, theoretical positions and assumptions are simply not made explicit or discussed. In that respect Worre (1987) is just the most recent, but in no way a singular, example of a trait already noted in Nannestad and Gaasholt (1982, p.135).

[10] See note 5 above.

[11] With the exception of a German minority in Southern Jutland.

[12] The "missing link" between macro-phenomena in society and the individual act of voting is often made a main point of criticism against structural theory, notably by scholars working from social-psychological assumptions, cf. Borre (1984a, p.85). In his work on the applicability of the Bohrian notion of complementarity to political science, Rasmussen (1987) arrives at the interesting conclusion that if macro- and microtheory of voting behavior can be considered complementary in the sense of Bohr, then macrotheory cannot be required to be able to account for phenomena on the micro level. If accepted, this result renders criticism as to the missing macro-micro link void.

voter and the act of voting: The voter is conditioned by outside forces to vote for one party or another. In this respect both theoretical frameworks are firmly premised on determinism. They are - disagreement as to who pulls the strings notwithstanding - both "puppet-programs" (Poulsen, 1979, pp.121-149).

Thus we have a long-standing and strong tradition in Danish electoral research for a deterministic or "puppet"-view of the voter and of the act of voting. The alternative, voluntaristic viewpoint (as embedded in classical democratic theory) which sees the voter as a rational individual making an informed choice between alternatives as to optimally further his or her personal interest has largely been relegated to economists. Paldam and Schneider (1980) e.g., working with Gallup-data from the period between 1957 and 1978, have demonstrated how inflation, unemployment, real income, and level of taxation have influenced voter support for the main parties in the Danish party system. Basically the reactions found agree with what would have been expected, if it is assumed that voters vote from (economic) self-interest. For example, under a Socialdemocratic government the liberal and conservative opposition parties gain when prices and taxes go up, while the Socialist Peoples' Party is the main beneficiary when unemployment rises. Paldam (1979) has also shown an electoral cycle (or political business cycle) to exist in the Danish economy.

Both findings, together with a largely parallel one reported by Madsen (1980), support the "responsibility"-hypothesis, i.e. the notion that the electorate tends to keep the party in government responsible for the state of the economy and to punish or reward it on election day, depending on the state of the economy. This suggests that the vote decision may be rational, and that it may be reactive, passing a verdict on prior performance. So far, such findings apparently have not led to a serious reappraisal of the merits of the "puppet"-view of voters and voting as the foundation of established electoral research, however.

It seems to be just this insistence on the deterministic nature of electoral choice that lies at the bottom of the difficulties in accounting for the outcome of the 1973-election and the subsequent electoral volatility solely within the framework of the Michigan-model or of structural theory (or of some pragmatic combination of pieces from both). Both theories view electoral choice as conditioned by outside forces which must be assumed to be relatively stable. Class relations typically tend to change at a slow pace (except for revolutionary situations); due to its basic role in the structure of the self, party identification must also be assumed to be quite stable and the distribution of party identification in the electorate to change only slowly (except, once more, in revolutionary situations or under the impact of major crises or other traumatic experiences). Hence electoral stability or slow, measured change is most easily accounted for within both frameworks. In contrast, short-term fluctuations above a certain size pose problems.

Class theory requires us to account for electoral changes in terms of changes in class relations (the class struggle). There has been no shortage of attempts to do just that for the 1973-election and its successors (Rasmussen, 1976; Wickman, 1977; Fryklund and Peterson, 1981; Hansen, 1981a; 1981b). Invariably, these attempts have focused on the Progress Party, trying to demonstrate that its breakthrough was the result of an "uproar" by a petty bourgeoisie in economic distress and threatened by social deroute.

Glans (1984) - himself normally working from class theoretical assumptions - has subjected these interpretations to a devastating critique. He shows that there is no empirical justification for considering the Progress Party a party of the petty bourgeoisie, no matter how liberal a definition of this "class" is employed. With support from Henriksen (1978) he also draws into doubt the other central premise in the proposed explanations which asserts that the petty bourgeoisie was at the relevant time economically and socially threatened. Glans' conclusion is clear: The outcome of the 1973 and subsequent elections, and especially the breakthrough of the Progress Party, cannot be accounted for in terms of class factors alone.[13]

Instead, Glans points to the role played by economic and other macro-political factors prior to 1973, not the least a number of expectations left unfulfilled by the liberal-conservative government 1968-71.[14] Thus Glans moves close to the (non-deterministic) position of, e.g., Key (1966), who saw the voting decision as "... an appraiser of past events, past performances, and past actions".

Another class theorist, Johs. Andersen (1980; 1981; 1982), seems to agree with Glans as to the lack of explanatory power of the class concept as far as the electoral outcomes in the seventies are concerned. But the reason he gives is a very different one. According to Andersen, electoral campaigns have lost most of their political content and have been turned into hollow shows. Consequently the voters' decisions are increasingly de-termined by such "random" or irrelevant factors as a particular candidate's appearance on TV, rather than by class and ideology. According to Johs. Andersen, "... voters have to make their choice between the parties on a very restricted basis. They may either assess the parties on the basis of their "depoliticized" way of treating problems, or they may be forced to choose a party based on the more entertaining, dramaticized and emotional material on which the parties themselves mostly rely".[15] Empirical findings, i.a.

---

[13] As is also pointed out by Glans, this does not imply that the correlation between class and voting has disappeared or is no longer of interest. Goul Andersen (1979, 1984a, 1984b, 1984c) has analyzed and described the restructuring of the relationship between class and party that took place during the seventies, with special emphasis on the changing class basis of the left wing parties.

[14] In marked contrast to the careful dataanalysis supporting his arguments elsewhere, Glans does not offer any evidence (beyond common sense) for this part of his reasoning.

[15] Andersen (1982, pp. 58-59). My translation, quotation-marks in the original.

some of those to be presented below, clearly contradict his thesis of the "meaninglessness" of the party choice in the Danish setting, however.[16]

It hence appears that the electoral results of the seventies cannot satisfactorily be accounted for on the basis of class theory alone, and that this has come to be acknowledged by at least some class theorists. But the additions to structural theory offered by both Glans and Johs. Andersen are not without problems which go far beyond their lack of empirical evidence already noted. In both cases, they seem to presuppose a large element of non-determinism in voting behavior, which is simply irreconcilable with the basic assumption in structural theory.

From the perspective of the Michigan theory of voting, the key-issue brought up by the electoral volatility from 1973 onwards naturally becomes the strong and persistent deviation from the "normal vote" (i.e. the distribution of the votes that would have been expected from party identification alone), or - to rephrase the problem - why party identification failed to determine the results in the way it was supposed to.

The crux with the above-mentioned explanation offered by the Michigan theory for electoral outcomes which differ from the "normal vote" is that it borders on a tautology (Robertson, 1976; Jensen, 1979). What it is lacking is an independent, operational criterion which would allow us to separate the effects of party identification and of short-term factors, respectively, on the vote. As it stands, "short-term factors" is just a label pinned on the residual - that part of the election results that cannot be accounted for by party identification. To say that the outcome of an election or a series of elections was determined by short-term factors is thus the same as saying that it was not determined by party identification. But that still does not tell us what made things go that way.[17]

As in the U.S., the observable increase in the importance of short-term factors in the Danish elections from the beginning of the 1970's onwards led to a stronger emphasis on issue-voting than may be found in the original

---

[16] The theses of Johs. Andersen have never been given much attention by the political science profession, due largely to their strained relationship with facts. Instead, they have received quite extensive coverage in Danish TV, which repeatedly has had Johs. Andersen comment on political developments, seen from his particular point of view.

[17] In my view, it is not in itself an explanation of the outcome of the 1973-election to state that it "... up to a point follows the mechanism of 'surge' election, as described by Angus Campbell." (Borre, 1974, p.201). That is a classification (or generalized description) at best. In passing, it should also be noted that the resemblance to a 'surge' election may seem somewhat superficial. According to Campbell, 'surge' elections are elections where strong short-term factors bring about high participation. This mobilization will mainly affect non-identifiers, which otherwise would not have participated. Due to the increased participation by non-identifiers, the electoral outcome in a 'surge' election may deviate strongly from what would be predicted from party identification alone. But the increase in voting turn-out between the "maintaining" 1971-election and the election of 1973 was just a meager 2 pct. (from 87 pct. to 89 pct.), which seems somewhat out of proportion with the size of the deviations from the "normal vote" that occurred in 1973.

formulations of the Michigan theory of voting.[18] Borre (1984b), e.g., shows that attitudes on a number of ideological issues correlate with the vote decision (for a socialist or a non-socialist party, respectively), and that the strength of these correlations tends to grow throughout the seventies.

The problem with this kind of results is, however, that they do not tell us how important attitudes on one or several issues really are in determining the vote decision. Strictly speaking, they can not even tell us that attitudes on issues influence the vote decision at all. The reason is, of course, that we cannot know for sure the direction of the causal relationship. It may run from issue position to vote decision, but it may as well run the opposite way.

Thus it appears perfectly reasonable to expect that a voter holding a certain attitude on an issue may vote for a party with a stand on this issue that appears sympathetic to the voters attitude, because the voter knows the party to have adopted that stand. But it is no less reasonable to envisage a respondent in an interview situation to express as his attitude on a certain issue the stand adopted by "his" party. Parties certainly do function as opinion leaders on many occasions.

Most figures reported on the correlation between issue positions and vote decision in Danish elections must be suspected to contain both causal links at the same time. To get rid of this contamination, one would have to demonstrate that a change in issue position is followed by a change in party voted for. So far, this has not be done.

Another problem with the concept of issue-voting appears to be the level of information about issues and parties' stands on issues it presupposes. While it may well be that some studies have tended to exaggerate the degree of desinformation in the electorate, issue-voting studies have been accused of being prone to exaggerate the degree of insight to be attributed to the voters (Margolis, 1977).

In short, then, neither of the two competing "puppet-programs" in Danish electoral research - class theory and social-psychological theory (with or without the addition of issue-voting), respectively - have yet thrown up an exhaustive or compelling interpretation of Danish electoral behavior in the seventies. There is ample room left to try out other, alternative points of view. This, in fact, makes the five Danish elections of the seventies a rewarding and near-ideal testing ground for competing theories of voting.

---

[18] Fiorina (1981) describes this development as kind of a revisionist attack on the Michigan theory. Issue-voting studies can certainly be that, but - as pointed out by Miller (1976) - the phenomenon of issue-voting is not per se irreconcilable with the concept of party identification.

1.3. The present study: Aims and premises

The major aim of the present study will be to take a look at Danish electoral behavior in the seventies from an angle which so far has been almost totally missing in Danish electoral research: The basic view of the voter and the act of voting to be presented in the following will not be the common "puppet"-view of structural or social-psychological theory. Instead, we shall adopt a perspective which will be close to the "liberal constructor"-view (Poulsen, 1979) of classic democratic theory, interpreting voting as an instrumental act by which the voter wants to accomplish something.

The main thesis, on which this study rests and which it sets out to demonstrate empirically, is this: Danish voters of the seventies were neither automatons nor fools. Their behavior in the elections from 1971 to 1979 can be seen as a fairly reasonable reaction, given the alternatives they had to choose from. It would have been more strange had they not reacted to them the way they did.

This thesis may sound reminiscent of the "perverse and unorthodox argument" put forward by V.O. Key (1966, p.7), and that, in certain ways, is what it is intended to. (The wording, however, is a paraphrase of Rasmussen (1987, p.112)). But there are also differences from what Key intended to do in his famous study and how he did it, which shall be made explicit here.

As in Key (1966), voting in this study is considered mainly retrospective or reactive, the electorate being "...an appraiser of past events, past performances, and past actions. It judges retrospectively; it commands prospectively only insofar as it expresses either approval or disapproval of that which has happened before", as Key put it with usual eloquence. On election day the electorate passes a verdict; it does not issue a command. There is good empirical evidence to suggest that such may be the case, cf. the results referred to above of testing the "responsibility hypothesis" in macro-studies.

The psychological backbone in Key's notion of reactive voting appears to be some kind of simple psychological reward-punishment theory of action: The voters will tend to repeat actions which in the past brought them rewards (in terms of situations they agree with) and to avoid actions which in the past have shown themselves to produce disagreeable results (Borre, 1984a, p.81).

But there is another line of reasoning which also leads to viewing the vote decision as mainly reactive. It can be found in Downs (1957), and it starts out from considering the cost to the individual of acquiring the information necessary to vote instrumentally. Knowledge of the past is cheaper to acquire (some of it even comes free, like tax bills) than knowledge about various plans for the future, and, besides, it may even be more reliable knowledge. Hence reactivity comes in as a cost-reducing device in the vote decision.

Given the generally low level of information on particular political issues regularly found in mass surveys of the electorate, as well as the equally low level of consistency and stability in political attitudes towards such issues (and Denmark is no exception in that respect), it appears that most voters are not prepared to invest too heavily in acquiring the information that would be needed for prospective voting. Thus judged from the normally existing level of information in the electorate, it appears plausible that if voting is instrumental at all, it should be mainly reactive.

Following Downs, then, in this study we assume that the voter decides on the basis of two sets of premises. The first one consists of some factual knowledge about what the alternatives at hand represent in terms of broad policy alternatives; this knowledge is primarily founded in experience, viz. comes from observing what the parties actually did do in the past. The other set of premises consists of individual political preferences attached to various policy alternatives.

It is further assumed that the voters have their perception of policy alternatives and of their own policy preferences structured by a political belief system. Such a belief system is supposed to work as a perceptual grid or filter which imposes some order on the complexities of modern politics and cuts down the amount of information received to manageable size.[19] More will be said about the belief system in the following section.

The study's basic assumption about instrumental, reactive voting then becomes that the voter will vote for that particular party the position of which is perceived to be in closest agreement with his or her own political preferences. The voter's perception of the position of the parties will be heavily contingent upon their actual behavior in the past.

The voters' preferences will largely be taken as given in the present context (exogenous variables). Though interesting in their own right, the origins or content of these preferences is not relevant to the argument to be presented. The important thing is the assumption that voters do in fact have political preferences. If we are mistaken in assuming that, then the whole construction will collapse.

On the other hand, information plays a crucial role in the argument. The voting-as-conditioned-choice view of elections implies that the voter can make (and in many cases does make) a choice without really knowing the difference between the alternatives; the voting-as-instrumental-act view does not. Hence the focus of the subsequent analyses must be to demonstrate that the voters do possess the type of knowledge of parties and issues they are assumed to, that it is structured by a belief system, that it is related to party behavior, and that the voters do actually react to it.

In defining the aims of this study, it should be stressed that although it is exclusively concerned with instrumental, reactive voting, this is not meant to imply that other variables, i.a. some of those which commonly appear in "puppet-view" studies of electoral behavior, are unimportant or

---

[19] For a similar view see, e.g., Heath et al. (1985, pp. 107-123).

irrelevant.[20] The justification for neglecting them altogether in this context, however, is an interest in the "explanatory bite" of a rational choice approach to the interpretation of Danish voting behavior in the unruly seventies.

1.4. Propositions, and how to test them

The evidence on which we shall rest our case as presented in the preceding section will necessarily be purely circumstantial or indirect. No direct observation of the processes leading to the individual vote decision is possible.

As is known to connoisseurs of detective novels, it is not so much the piecemeal strength of the evidence as the existence of a logical link between its parts that brings down the villain in the end. To facilitate the comprehension of the empirical analyses to follow, the main links in the chain of evidence shall be presented as propositions in advance. It should be noted that, regardless of the exact wording, the presumed scope of their validity is restricted to the Danish general elections of the seventies, and they refer to trends and tendencies - albeit strong ones.

As noted before, a prerequisite of any kind of instrumental voting must be information. To be able to vote instrumentally the voter needs to know what the parties stand for and how - and in what respects - they differ. This leads to the first proposition:

Proposition 1.1.: The voters have a clear perception of the party system and of the parties' position within that system.

Clearly, this proposition runs counter to the popular notions in social-psychological theories of the unknowledgeable or poorly informed voter. It also flatly contradicts the above-mentioned thesis of Johs. Andersen. Previous studies, e.g. Damgaard and Rusk (1976), Rusk and Borre (1976), Nannestad (1984), and Worre (1987), nevertheless suggest that the proposition might be correct.

Being unobservable in itself, the voters' perception of the party system and of the parties that make up it has to be inferred from observable behavior. In this study we shall use sympathy data as the basis of that inference.

The sympathy data were collected by asking the respondents in the surveys to express their sympathy for each party in turn as a temperature

---

[20] If the voters' preference structure had not been taken for given in this study, structural as well as social-psychological variables would probably have had to be introduced to account for this aspect of voting behavior.

grade on a "sympathy thermometer".[21] Thus, for each respondent we have a measure of how (s)he felt towards each party.

To be able to draw inferences from the voters' feelings towards the parties to their underlying perception of the party system and the parties' position in it, we have to make two crucial assumptions.[22] The first assumption states that the stronger the sympathy, a voter expresses for a particular party, the smaller the psychological distance between this voter and the party. If a voter expresses strong sympathy for two parties, A and B say, then we can infer that his distance to both A and B must be small and hence that the distance between A and B must be small, too: The voter perceives parties A and B as being similar to each other, i.e. close to each other in the party system. On the other hand, if the voter expresses strong dislike of two parties, C and D, then we can infer that they must both be separated from the voter by a large distance. What we cannot infer, however, is that both being far away from the voter, parties C and D must necessarily be close together. They might as well be far away from the voter and at the same time far away from each other.

To be able to decide whether two parties that are both disliked by a voter are close together or far away from each other, we need the judgement of a voter who likes one of these two parties. If he likes one of them, but not the other, then they must indeed be far away from each other. If he likes them both, then they must be close together. For this reason, we can only make inferences in the way described here, if each party is the most preferred one for at least one voter.[23]

To make the argument stick, we have tacitly made a second assumption. It states that basically all respondents in our analysis share a common perception of the party system and of the parties' position in it. This is a rather strong assumption, but the studies cited above and the results to be presented later indicate that it is at least approximately true.

The central conception on which the inference from sympathy data to perceived structure hinges is the concept of (psychological) distance. Distance being a geometrical or spatial concept, the idea comes naturally to describe the voters' perception of the party system by a spatial model. As already noted by Stokes (1966, p.161), "(t)he use of spatial ideas to interpret party competition is a universal phenomenon in modern politics".

The most famous example of the use of spatial models to interpret party competition is undoubtedly to be found in the work of Downs (1957). Drawing on earlier work on spatial economic competition, Downs

---

[21] A further discussion of these data will be given in section 1.6. below.

[22] Actually, we have to make several other assumptions as well, but they are mainly technical in character. They will be more fully discussed in section 1.5. below. Since that section necessarily will be somewhat technical in nature, most readers may not want to read it. Therefore, the most essential information is presented in the present context.

[23] This requirement is often overlooked in practice. In the present context it implies that it will often be impossible to analyze the perception of the party system in homogeneous subgroups only, for example among those who identify with the Socialdemocratic party.

envisages the voters as well as the competing parties to be strung out on the same one-dimensional 'ideological' continuum. Both parties and voters are rational actors: Parties try to maximize their share of the votes, voters try to promote their "utility income". Adding various other assumptions, Downs is able to deduct empirically testable propositions, e.g. as to the way the parties will behave, the position in the space they will strive to obtain and keep, or the number of parties that will exist in the party system.

Applying the assumptions and the logic of inference presented above to the sympathy data (plus a little mathematics and quite a bit of computer power), we can construct a map of the party system as perceived by the voters. To distinguish it from other maps of the party system, it shall normally be referred to as a map of the perceived party space.

Such a map will show us the parties' positions in the party system as perceived by the respondents. Parties which are perceived as similar will be close together on the map; parties which are perceived as very different will be separated by long distances.

We may further enhance this map by adding to it the respondents' positions vis-a-vis the parties. A respondents location or "ideal point" should be close to the location of parties, (s)he has expressed strong sympathy with, and far away from those parties (s)he dislikes. In this way, we also obtain a picture of the respondents' positions in the political spectrum. Moreover, respondents who exhibit the same preference structure towards the parties will cluster together in the same regions of the map.

Using spatial models or analogies is in many respects just a convenient and comprehensible way to talk about data and data structures. For example, it can help us to make operational what is meant by the phrase "clear perception of the party system" used in the formulation of proposition 1.1. above.

In the empirical analyses to follow, we shall consider it evidence of the existence of a clear perception of the party system in the respondents, if this perception can be adequately represented by a well-structured and simple spatial model (or map).

Such a model is well-structured, if the parties form distinct clusters and regions on the map, or, in short, if the distribution of the parties' positions on the map is non-random. Obviously, this is what we must expect, if the respondents do have a clear perception of the party system and of the parties' positions within it as the basis of their sympathy judgements.

We also require the model to be simple. By this we mean that only a small number of dimensions - preferably just two (as in an ordinary road map) or three - is needed to obtain an adequate description. The reason for this is that it does not seem realistic to expect the respondents to harbor exceedingly complex perceptual structures. If it turns out that the respondents' perception of the party system can only be adequately described by very sophisticated models, the validity of such a description appears problematic.

Last, but certainly not least, the model (or map) must fit the data adequately. How well it fits the data can be measured in different ways. In this study, three different ways of expressing the fit will be used.

In the first place, one can compare the distances between a respondent (or, more precisely, a respondents "ideal point") and the parties on the map to the same respondents sympathy grading of the parties. If the model fits the data from this respondent, then there should be a functional relationship between the sympathy scores given by the respondent to the parties and his or her distance to the parties on the map. Again, the degree to which such a relationship exists can be measured in different ways. In this study, we employ the familiar coefficient of determination (R^2). Obtaining a R^2-value for each respondent and averaging over respondents, we obtain a summary measure of the models fit with the sympathy data on which it is based.[24]

Whether to deem a particular numerical fit-value adequate must to some extent be a matter of discretion. The values to be presented in the empirical analyses below are generally high by political science standards (usually above 0.60 for the unweighted R^2). Such values will be considered adequate.

As a second expression of fit, we shall examine how well the model agrees with the distribution of votes reported in the surveys. If we assume that respondents vote for the party closest to them on the map, then we can use the positions of the parties and of the voters on the map to "hindcast" the respondents' votes and compare the "hindcasted" distribution of votes over parties with the reported one in the survey. If the deviations are small, this will strengthen the plausibility of the model. The size of the deviations will be measured using an index of non-similarity (NS-index), which is described below.

Finally, we may move to the individual level and examine, if the "hindcasted" vote of each individual respondent agrees with the reported vote for that individual. A high proportion of agreements will be taken as a further confirmation of the models validity. (Typically, the proportion runs around 70-80 pct.).

Having thus established the criteria needed to decide whether proposition 1.1. is supported by empirical data, we may address another problem. Models and theories which require individuals to possess information are often accused of being founded on unrealistic assumptions with regard to the individuals' capacity for information processing. The amount and complexity of information generated in modern society, so the argument runs, gravely overtaxes the individuals' ability to absorb and use it in a meaningful way.

This objection carries some weight. It requires us to indicate how we think voters mould their perception of the parties out of the mass of information provided to them, how they go about relating parties with issue

---

[24] Since weighting of the data is used to take into account differences in reliability, actually two R^2-values will be reported, one weighted and one unweighted, cf. section 1.6. below.

positions, and how they relate their own policy preferences to party positions. The next proposition is intended to provide a broad answer to these questions.

Proposition 1.2.: The perception of the party system is structured by a small number of 'ideological' dimensions.[25] These dimensions are used to "bundle"[26] parties and issue-positions.

What proposition 1.2. says is basically that the voters do possess some kind of belief system, albeit a rather simplistic one. This belief system they use as a perceptual frame of reference or mental grid which helps to impose some order on the information provided to the voters.

A belief system is defined by the 'ideological' dimensions it contains. By an 'ideological' dimension is here understood an over-arching, general attitude from which attitudes towards more specific objects, like a particular political issue or a political party, may be derived. The best known example of such an 'ideological' dimension is probably the ubiquitous left-right dimension of European political systems.

In a famous article, Converse (1964) has documented the near-total absence of even a rudimentary belief system in the American mass public. According to his results, an ideological belief system could only be found in a comparatively small intellectual elite. A belief system contains stable and consistent attitudes towards a large number of political objects. Drawing on data from a three wave-panel, Converse demonstrated that there was neither stability (over time) nor consistency in the attitudes of the mass public towards a number of political issues.

These findings cannot simply be shrugged off as specific to the American mass public only. Data from France, e.g., collected by Converse and Dupeux, exhibit much the same picture (Converse and Dupeux, 1966). Even in Denmark, correlations between the positions taken by respondents in the first and second wave of the 1971-73 panel on a number of issues are not impressive (Nielsen, 1979). A major study on mass politics in Denmark asserts that "... only very few voters have precise, consistent and stable opinions on what policy should be pursued on the multitude of singular issues which are put up for decision in the government and the Folketing".[27]

---

[25] Here and in the following, the adjective 'ideological' is attached to the term dimension to avoid confusion with the purely geometric concept of dimension. The inverted commas are used to indicate that an 'ideological' dimension need not be part of an ideology proper, like socialism or liberalism.

[26] Cf. the expression used by Downs (1957): According to it, voters vote on "packages of policy proposals".

[27] Kristensen in Damgaard (ed.) (1980, ch.2, pp.33-34), my translation. Interestingly, the empirical foundation for this sweeping assertion remains obscure. The reference given in a note attached to the quoted passage is to an article by Wahlke (1971) which, alas, turns out not to contain a single specific reference to Denmark or the Danish Folketing.

On the other hand, it has also been shown that at least in 1979 Danish voters were able to place themselves consistently on a left right-continuum, and that their self-placement was related to the positions they took on a number of issues concerning both economic and foreign policies (Borre, 1983; Lindrup and Pedersen, 1983). Moreover, the self-professed position on the left right-continuum was also clearly related to party choice. From the outset, these findings seem to support proposition 1.2. above.

To find out whether and how the voters' perception of the parties and the party system is in fact structured by 'ideological' dimensions, and to possibly identify the issue content of such dimensions, we shall revert to the maps of the party system derived from the sympathy data in order to interpret their structure. Up to now, we have intentionally been vague about the exact meaning of the axes or dimensions on these maps. When we derive them from the thermometer data, the axes are undefined. It is the task of the researcher to see if they correspond to meaningful directions or patterns in the spatial location of parties or "ideal points", and what substantial interpretation may be suggested by these patterns.

Thus the patterns in the clustering of parties and/or of the respondents' "ideal points" on the map can be hoped to reveal something about the structuring principles at work. If, e.g., it is found that socialist parties cluster together on one side of the map, with the bourgeois parties located on the opposite side and centrist parties in between them, an interpretation in terms of a left-right dimension suggests itself.

To identify patterns in the distribution of the respondents' "ideal points" which may help us to pin down the structuring principles that produce a particular map, we shall have to examine whether the location of the "ideal points" is systematically related to the respondents' stand on various policy issues. Data on the respondents' position on a number of issues were collected as part of the surveys.

The respondents' issue positions on various issues were typically recorded by presenting the respondents with an item describing a policy stand or opinion like "higher education ought to result in higher earnings" and asking them to indicate if they agreed or disagreed with that stand. The responses were recorded using a five point Likert-type scale with "agree completely", "do agree in part", "do neither agree nor disagree", "do disagree in part" and "do disagree completely" as alternatives.

The resulting scales may be used for structural (or dimensional) interpretation of the perceived party space in various ways. One may run a linear regression analysis with the respondents' scores on a scale as the dependent and the coordinates of their "ideal points" as the independent variables. If there is a relationship between the scores on the scale and the location of the "ideal points" on the map that can be satisfactorily described by a linear model, direction cosines can then be computed which indicate a direction in the space defined by the relationship between positions on the issue (viz. the scores on the scale) and the location of the "ideal points"

(Kruskal and Wish, 1978). Such directions may be useful in interpreting the overall structure of the map.

A related, but somewhat "softer", approach is suggested by Enelow and Hinich (1984). They plot and examine the median "ideal points" of the respondents falling in each of the response categories on the scale belonging to a particular item to see if these median "ideal points" line up in some direction in the space. In the present study their approach has been preferred to the regression approach, mainly in order to avoid the strong assumptions involved in doing a linear regression analysis.

The decision whether a set of median "ideal points" does in fact line up in the perceived party space to a sufficient degree is left to the spectator. In order to reduce the inherent arbitrariness of this decision, the following criteria have been laid down as preconditions for speaking of a set of median "ideal points" exhibiting a pattern.

In the first place, the median "ideal points" for respondents in the two intermediate response categories ("do agree/disagree in part") must be located between the the median "ideal points" for respondents in the extreme categories ("do agree/disagree completely"), and they must appear in the correct order, i.e. the median "ideal point" for respondents in the "do agree in part"-category must be closer to the median "ideal point" for respondents in the "agree completely"-category than is the median "ideal point" for respondents in the "do disagree in part"-category. Correspondingly, the median "ideal point" for respondents in the "do disagree in part"-category must be closer to the median "ideal point" for respondents in the "disagree completely"-category than is the median "ideal point" for respondents in the "do agree in part"-category. If the median "ideal points" for respondents in the two intermediate categories are not located on a straight line connecting the median "ideal points" for respondents in the extreme categories on the scale, this condition applies to their projection onto that line.

In the second place, the median "ideal point" for respondents in the neutral category on the scale ("do neither agree nor disagree") must be located between the median "ideal points" for respondents in the two extreme categories, but it is not required to be located between the median "ideal points" for respondents in the two intermediate categories as well. The reason for making this weaker requirement with respect to the location of the median "ideal point" for respondents in the neutral category is the assumption that in many cases the neutral category will contain two different types of respondents: The genuinely neutrals and a group of respondents who are undecided, uninformed with regard to this particular item, or uninterested in it. The second group can be expected to make for a large amount of randomness in the neutral category.

A third method to detect patterns in the distribution of "ideal points" in a party space is to divide the map into regions and to see if the propensity to take a certain stand on an issue (i.e. to agree or disagree to a particular item) differs systematically between regions. This can easily be done by computing the net majority (in percentages) for each region of those agreeing (totally or in part) to an item among the respondents who have their "ideal point" located in that particular region. While the results of this method may lack some of the intuitive appeal of the two others by not being graphically depictable on the maps themselves, they have the advantage of telling something about the balance of opinion on the issue involved. Therefore this method will also be occasionally employed in the following.

'Ideological' dimensions are sometimes considered the ideological expression of structural cleavages in society.[28] For example, the left-right dimension can be seen as the ideological expression of the labor-capital cleavage. Therefore, we shall also examine whether and to what extend the 'ideological' dimensions we may be able to identify in our maps do correspond to structural cleavages.

Together, proposition 1.1. and 1.2. establish that the voters have relevant information pertaining to the parties they have to pick from. But even if they have such information, this by itself does not necessarily contradict the Michigan theory of voting (nor, supposedly, any structural theory).

The Michigan theory of voting does not imply that the voters do not have or use information. On the contrary, the importance of finding out how the voter sees the world has been repeatedly stressed,[29] and studies of this question have been conducted within the confines of the Michigan theory,[30] employing very much the same methodologies and types of data as the present one.

But the Michigan theory of voting has to assume that the information the voter possesses is conditioned (by party identification). This is a consequence of the position ascribed to party identification in the "funnel of causality" leading to the vote decision. Proposition 2.1. expresses the crucial difference in that respect between a social-psychological theory of voting (or indeed any "puppet-view" theory of voting) and a theory of voting as a voluntaristic, instrumental act.

Proposition 2.1.: The voters' perception of the party system and the parties' position in it is only marginally affected by party preference, party identification, or class.[31]

The obvious way to test this assertion empirically against Danish data would appear to be by analyzing the perception of the party system in the way described above for each relevant group separately and comparing the

---

[28] Cf. Valen (1981, ch. 12).

[29] Cf. Miller (1976).

[30] Cf. for example Weisberg and Rusk (1970); Valen and Converse (1971); Rusk and Weisberg (1972).

[31] A number of recent American studies (Pages and Jones, 1979; Fiorina, 1981, pp.47-49) seem to indicate that such is indeed the case, even in the US.

results. For example, one would analyze the perception of the party system among those who identify with the Socialdemocrats and compare it to the perception among those who identify with, say, the Agrarians. If party identification conditions perceptions the way it is supposed to, then the perception of the party system among Socialdemocratic and Agrarian identifiers should differ systematically.[32]

For the technical reason given above, we are not able to conduct this kind of systematic test for differences between the perception of the party system among those who identify with different parties.[33] We therefore have to settle for other, admittedly weaker, criteria.

In the first place, it must be remembered that the maps of the party system are constructed under the assumption that all respondents share the same perception of the party system and the parties' positions in it. To the extent that by working from this assumption we are able to construct maps which fit the data well, the assumption to the contrary - that groups of respondents perceive the party system in entirely different ways - is rendered less plausible. Of course, this evidence is not conclusive, unless perfect fit is obtained (it never is in this study). On the other hand, given the goodness of fit we are actually able to obtain under the assumption of common perceptions, it seems safe to conclude that whatever group differences there may exist, they must indeed be marginal.

To further strengthen this conclusion we shall examine how well relevant subgroups among the respondents - for example those who identify with a particular party - are represented by the maps obtained. This can be done by applying the fit-criteria discussed above to such subgroups separately. If proposition 2.1. is tenable, then differences with regard to goodness of fit between the relevant subgroups among the respondents should be small.

Since we may assume the mass media to be the voters' main source of information about parties (and politics in general), some corroborating, circumstantial support for the thesis of a common perception of the party system in proposition 2.1. can be found by considering the development and structure of the Danish mass media. Thus, it seems plausible that the spread of TV (with only one channel) to virtually the whole population should be conducive to a rather homogeneous perception of the party system. Moreover, the traditional Danish "four newspaper system", which meant

---

[32] We might even be able to indicate what differences to expect. In keeping with the idea of identification, one would expect party identification to produce a "we against the others"-perception. Thus we would expect Socialdemocratic identifiers to have a rather clear perception of the position of their party vis-a-vis some parties close to it, as the Socialist Peoples' Party and the Radical Liberals, while the rest would be a rather undifferentiated mass of adversaries in considerable distance from the Socialdemocratic party. Correspondingly we would expect identifiers with the Agrarians to have a clear perception of the Agrarians' position vis-a-vis e.g. the Conservatives, while the socialist parties would be seen as a relatively undifferentiated mass of adversaries.

[33] Since classes turn out to be far less homogeneous with respect to party sympathy than groups of party identifiers, in some instances it would be possible to conduct this kind of tests for the influence of class on perception of the party system.

that each of the four major parties (Socialdemocrats, Agrarians, Conservatives, and Radical Liberals) had their own newspaper in a city or region, has gradually dissolved over time and given way to a newspaper system based on a small number of papers with country-wide circulation, supplemented by normally only one local or regional paper. Thus the information provided by the newspapers is no longer specifically targeted at adherents of particular parties either; the mass communications structure appears to be biased in favor of a rather homogeneous perception of the party system.

But if the voters' perception of the party system is not conditioned by party identification or other forces beyond their control, what does determine its content? This question is answered by proposition 2.2.

Proposition 2.2.: The perception of the party system and of the parties' position in it is strongly related to the parties' parliamentary behavior.

Proposition 2.2. is close to the proposition of Downs (1957, ch.7) that since ongoing governmental activities and policy discussions are continually and somewhat automatically monitored, they are "cheap" information. Being "cheap", while other kinds of policy relevant information are costly, information on governmental activities and policy discussions will make up a large part of the information "consumed" by the voters.

Whatever the cost, we do not expect the voters to monitor roll call divisions in the Folketing painstakingly, however. Rather, the relationship between parties as expressed in their roll call behavior is taken here primarily as an observable indicator of the general pattern of political relationships that exists between parties at any particular time.

To demonstrate proposition 2.2. empirically, we shall have to derive still another type of model or map of the party system. This map will be based on the parties' roll call behavior in the Folketing.

Using the recorded roll call divisions on government bills,[34] an "index of distance" can be computed for all pairs of parties.[35] Basically this index expresses how often two parties voted in the same way in the roll calls. Assuming that the smaller the (political) distance between any two parties, the higher the proportion of identical roll call voting, we can locate the parties on the map in such a way that the distances between the parties' position on the map optimally reflect the distance index values between them.

If we derive such a map from the roll calls in the legislative term leading up to the election, we may examine the relationship between the party system as it is mirrored in the parliamentary behavior of the parties and the

---

[34] A fuller discussion will be given in section 1.6. below.
[35] Cf. Pedersen (1967).

perception of the party system in the voters at election time by comparing the two types of maps. After removing "irrelevant" differences between them - for example differences due to different units of measurement or different orientations - by a transformation known under the sinister name of "Prokrustes rotation",[36] we can obtain a measure of agreement between the two maps (M). In many respects, M can be interpreted in the same way as the well-known coefficient of determination (R^2): The closer M is to 1, the closer is the agreement between the two maps.

Once more, the values of M to be reported later are high by usual political science standards, exceeding (with one explainable exception) 0.70. Thus proposition 2.2. above enjoys rather strong empirical support.

There are, of course, parties the perception of which cannot possibly have been derived from monitoring parliamentary behavior, namely parties running in the election without having been represented in the preceding Folketing. The voters' assessment of where such parties fit into the picture has to be made on a different basis. But it is interesting to notice that - when judged from the proportion of "don't knows" and neutral responses - the voters are generally less secure of how they feel towards such parties than how they feel towards parties which can be judged by their parliamentary performance in the past. This fact strengthens the assertion of proposition 2.2. above that the parties' parliamentary record is an indicator of party relationships and an important source of information as to their perceived position in the party system.

The propositions stated so far establish that the voters do possess the information necessary to make a deliberate choice (as defined above) between the parties: They have a clear picture of the parties' positions vis-a-vis each other in the party system. They also have a picture of how the parties relate to a number of 'ideological' dimensions and - through these - to a number of issue positions. Moreover, this perception is mainly unconditioned; rather it quite accurately reflects the parties' parliamentary behavior in the past parliamentary term.

Even so, the voters might still make their decision by flipping a coin or so as to please their spouses - at least in principle. What remains to be established is a connection between the information and the actual vote.

Just to establish empirically that voters do in general vote for the party they perceive to be the closest one to their own position ("ideal point") will not suffice. It might be that they actually voted for the party they express the highest degree of sympathy with, because they liked that party best. But it might equally well be that they just expressed the highest degree of sympathy for the party they voted for in order to appear consistent in the interview situation.[37] Thus the real problem becomes to find out what is the dog and what is the tail here.

---

36 Cf. Schönemann and Carroll (1969). The actual computations were done using the rotation procedure in GENSTAT (NAG, 1980).

37 In that respect the situation is the same as with the relationship between issue-positions and vote decision.

The best way to do this is probably to look at the reactions to changes in the party system. If voters in general vote for the party they perceive to be closest to their own position, and if a party is perceived to have moved to a new position between two elections, then it should lose voters in the region it moved away from to parties staying put in that region (since they now become the closest ones to the "deserted" voters), and it should pick up voters in the region it has moved into.[38] By that logic, proposition 3 below establishes the necessary link between information and vote.

Proposition 3.: Voter movements follow party movements

What proposition 3 implies is that voting is mainly reactive or retrospective. If proposition 2.2. on the relationship between parliamentary behavior and the perception of the party system is recalled, the joint implication of the two propositions becomes that the vote decision is mainly a reaction to party behavior as reflected in legislative behavior. The voters do not primarily vote on programs, nor on the promises, gags and gimmicks of the campaign, nor even on personality[39] - they mainly vote on past behavior, seen in the broad framework of a small number of 'ideological' dimensions.[40]

Before turning to how this proposition might be tested empirically, there is one objection we shall have to deal with. Page and Jones (1979) among others[41] regard thermometer data as a surrogate for voting intentions rather than as a causal influence on the vote decision. If this view is sustained, proposition 3 may seem to degenerate into a simple tautology.

For this reason it is important to keep in mind the exact position of proposition 3 in the "causal link" we have struggled to establish. Proposition 3 does not imply that whatever is expressed by the thermometer data is the causal reason for the vote. If seen in connection with proposition 2.2., it becomes clear that "perception of the party system" (or, if Page and Jones are right, "voting intention") is positioned as an intermediate variable between what goes on in the parliamentary arena (as an observable indicator of what goes on in the political arena) and the voters' vote decision. While the link from vote intention to vote decision may be close to a tautology, the link from party behavior via vote intention to vote decision is certainly not.

---

[38] A number of studies indicate that this mechanism works in practice, showing that the frequency (or probability) of voter shifts between parties is somehow related to party distances, cf. Bjorulf (1970), Worre (1975; 1987).

[39] Empirical evidence to support that - somewhat surprising - assertion will be presented in ch.2 and ch.3 below.

[40] This agrees well with the above-mentioned findings in i.a. Paldam and Schneider (1980) .

[41] Borre (1984a, p.80) points in the same direction; Fiorina (1981, p.187) quotes Page and Jones with approval.

In order to be able to test proposition 3 against data we shall have to specify how party movements are supposed to be related to voter movements. Once more the most convenient way of doing this is by way of spatial concepts and measurements.

In formulating a model on the basis of proposition 3, we shall have to make one crucial assumption. It states that the respondents' "ideal points" do not change position from one election to the next. In substantive terms this assumption implies that voters do not shift position with respect to the 'ideological' dimensions. For example, if there is a left-right dimension, the voters do not move to the left or to the right, but remain where they are. Only parties may move.[42]

Now consider first a situation where a party (i) moves from its position in the party space at time (t-1) to a new position at time (t), and that the new position taken up by party (i) is in the vicinity of the position occupied by party (j) at time (t-1). If anything else remains constant, party (i) should pick up voters close to its new location in the party space at time (t). These voters will have been voters for party (j) at time (t-1). Thus we shall expect party (i) to pick up voters who voted for party (j) at time (t-1). Moreover we shall expect the probability of a voter deserting party (j) and changing to party (i) to increase as the distance between the location of party (i) at time (t) and the location of party (j) at time (t-1) decreases. We can measure this distance by superimposing the map of the perceived party system at time (t) on the map of the perceived party system at time (t-1) and computing the distance.

Of course, the degree to which party (i) will be able to pick up voters from party (j) will also depend on the movements of party (j). If party (j) itself has moved away from its location in the party space at time (t-1), leaving its voters behind, then we shall expect a greater shift of voters from party (j) to party (i) than if party (j) stays put. Once more we can measure the extent of party (j)'s movement by superimposing the two maps and computing the distance.

But the chances for party (i) to lay its hands on voters who voted for party (j) at time (t-1) also depends on what the other parties in the system do. If many parties rush into the vicinity of party (j)'s position at time (t-1), then they will compete for party (j)'s voters, and each must be expected to receive a smaller proportion than it could have obtained if it had been the sole bidder.

Thus we also have to measure the "competitiveness" in the region, party (i) has moved into. Here we can use two crude measures. In the first place, we can use the number of parties that are closer to the position of party (j) at time (t-1) than is party (i). In the second place, we can use the mean distance between the location of party (j) at time (t-1) and the three parties being closest to that position at time (t).

---

[42] This assumption is also made by Downs (1957).

Finally it seems reasonable to expect that the number of voters party (j) had at time (t-1) may influence the probability of a shift: Given a certain distance between party (i) at time (t) and the location of party (j) at time (t-1), the probability for party (i) of "hitting" a voter for party (j) (i.e. of being the new closest party to a voter for party (j)) is greater when there are many voters than if there are few. This factor we may measure as the proportion of votes received by party (j) at time (t-1).

The model proposed bears some resemblance to gravitational models known from physics and geography. In keeping with this analogy, it may be reasonable to expect the relationship between the variables in the model to be multiplicative rather than additive.[43]

Thus we arrive at the following formulation of a model of reactive voting, based on (perceived) party movements:

$$Y_{ij} = b_{i0} - b_{i1}\log(DIST_{ij}) + b_{i2}\log(DIST_{jj}) - b_{i3}\log(NCLOSE_j)$$
$$+ b_{i4}\log(DIST3_j) + b_{i5}\log(VPROP_j) + u_i$$

where

$Y_{ij} =$ Proportion of voters for party (j) at time (t-1) who switch to party (i) at time (t);

$DIST_{ij} =$ Distance between location of party (i) at time (t) and party (j) at time (t-1);

$DIST_{jj} =$ Distance between location of party (j) at time (t) and time (t-1);

$NCLOSE_j =$ Number of parties that at time (t) are closer to the location of party (j) at time (t-1) than party (i);

$DIST3_j =$ Mean distance between the location of the three parties that at time (t) are closest to the location of party (j) at time (t-1);

$VPROP_j =$ Proportion of voters obtained by party (j) at time (t-1);

$u_i =$ Errorterm

---

[43] This assumption is supported by the data, which shows the relationships to be highly nonlinear.

Thus the probability of switching from party (j) to party (i) between two elections is expressed as a function of party movements, accentuated (or attenuated) primarily by factors expressing the competitiveness of the region in the party space involved.

From the outset there seems little reason to expect the various exogenous variables in the model to carry the same weight with all parties. For example, a party located in an isolated region in the perceived party space - i.e. far away from other parties - will be able to change its location by a greater distance without losing voters than a party located close to other parties. Similarly, an isolated party will have to move a greater distance in order to make inraids into the constituencies of other parties than a party which is located close to other parties. By the same logic it may even be that not all exogenous variables in the model are relevant or necessary to account for the gains and losses of a particular party.

For these reasons the model will be fitted for each party separately under the constraints[44]

$$b_{i1}, b_{i3} \leq 0$$
$$b_{i2}, b_{i4}, b_{i5} \geq 0$$
$$\Sigma_j Y_{ij} = 1$$

To apply the model empirically, data on voter movements are needed. For the elections of 1971 and 1973 panel data exist which are, of course, ideally suited. For the rest of the elections, we have to make do with recall data, i.e. the party vote at time (t-1) reported by the respondents at time (t) alongside with their vote at time (t). The reliability and validity of recall data is normally assumed to leave something to be desired, but in the context of the present study they have the distinct advantage of being collected from the same respondents as the thermometer data on which the map of the perceived party system is based.

Although the model looks somewhat like a familiar regression model, one important difference should be noted: The dependent variable (Y_{ij}) is restricted to vary between 0 and 1. For this reason, the model cannot be fitted to data by ordinary regression procedures. Logistic regression has to be used instead.[45]

---

[44] It might be objected that by imposing these constraints the model is in effect made immune against being falsified by "wrong" signs of the coefficients. However, as will be seen later, the variables actually included (i.e. those with the "correct"signs) allow us to account for the observed voter movements to a very high degree of precision. From this it follows that the importance of the variables excluded (i.e. those which might have "wrong" signs) is quite insignificant.

[45] Thus the regression coefficients to be reported in later chapters do not refer to the formulation of the model of reactive voting given above, but to a transformed version of it. In the first place, the proportions (the dependent variable) are transformed to logits. Logits (and intercept) are divided by 2 to approximate probits, and 5 is added to make the logits non zero.

As one consequence of using logistic regression, the normal measure of goodness of fit in regression (R^2) is no longer valid. To give some impression of how well the model fits our data, we shall rely on a comparison between the table of voter movements between parties that can be computed from the survey data, and the corresponding table of voter movements that can be computed from the model above.

Still some kind of summary measure would be useful in order to give a quick and concise expression of the degree of similarity between the two tables. Chi-square is not well suited here, since the tables will contain many zeros, and since the numerical value of this statistic has no intuitively appealing interpretation. Thomsen (1987, pp. 85-86) has proposed a measure of non-similarity (NS-index) between two tables which is computed as "half the cumulated absolute differences between equally positioned proportions in the two tables". The index has a minimum value of 0 (if the two tables are equal) and a maximum value of 1. Intuitively, the value of the index can be interpreted as indicating the amount of proportions which would have to be moved in one table in order to construct the other one.[46] In the following this index shall be used to indicate the goodness of fit of our model of reactive voting.[47]

If we are able to account well enough for the observed voter movements by the model formulated above, then we shall consider this success empirical evidence supporting proposition 3. This conclusion might be contended, however, by pointing out that it rests on an unreasonable assumption, viz. the assumption that voters do not change their positions relative to the 'ideological' dimensions between two elections.

But to the degree this assumption is in fact violated in practice - as we must expect it to be to some degree - this will obviously lead to a poorer fit for our model than what would have been obtained, if the assumption was met. Thus, if the model fits, it does so despite and not because of the assumption not being met in practice. Hence, as the Chinese proverb has it: "The color of the cat does not matter, as long as it catches the mice".

The preceding discussions may now be drawn together and summarized in the following way: It is asserted that in general the voters make their decision on the basis of two types of premises, namely factual, largely

---

[46] One shortcoming of the NS-index is that it does not distinguish between the occurrence of numerous, small and the occurrence of few, large deviations, viz. between imprecision and bias. It would be possible to correct for this by dividing the NS-value by the number of deviating cell values found. The definition of the NS-index would then become "the average amount of proportions which would have to be moved between cells in one table in order to construct the other one".

[47] This also allows us to relate and compare the values of the NS-index found in this study with values of this index obtained in other situations. For example, the value of the NS-index for the tables on voter movements constructed from two different surveys of the 1973-election is 0.135, while the amount of non-similarity between Thomsen's ecological estimates of voter movements and the two surveys is 0.162 and 0.177, respectively, which is considered a validation of the ecological estimates (Thomsen, 1987, p.86). The values of the NS-index to be reported in the following chapters are below these figures.

unconditioned, retrospective knowledge about the alternatives at hand, plus a set of individual political preferences (which we take as given in the present context). To prove this assertion, it shall be demonstrated empirically that with respect to the Danish general elections in the seventies

- the voters did indeed have a clear perception of the party system and the parties' position within it;

- this perception of the party system was structured by a belief system which "bundles" party perception and policy issue-positions;

- the perception of the party system was only marginally affected by party preference, party identification, or class;

- the perception of the party system primarily reflected the parties' past parliamentary record;

- the voters in general voted for the party they - by the information they did have - perceived to be closest to their own "ideal points". If parties behaved in a way that was perceived as a change of position in the party system, the voters tended to switch from the party which had moved away to the party which by that move had become the closest one to their "ideal points".

1.5. Models and methods

In the following section, we shall take a closer look at some methodological and technical issues involved in the empirical analysis. Thus we shall make explicit some assumptions and limitations that are so to speak "built into" the models of the perceived party system we are going to use. We shall also discuss some problems in fitting these models to data and a problem in treating the results. Finally, we shall shortly dwell upon the question of significance testing and defend the decision not to report any significance tests at all in this study.

Although nothing close to a full account of the models and assumptions of multidimensional scaling is intended - a treatment of these topics may be found elsewhere[48] - the present section will of necessity be somewhat more technical than both the preceding and the following ones. Readers not interested in technical matters should be able to skip it without loss of continuity.

---

[48] Nannestad (1985).

As has been mentioned before, the main assumption on which the construction of maps of the perceived party system from sympathy data depends is that the sympathy grades given by a respondent to the parties are functionally related to the psychological distances between the voters and the parties. But up to now, the concept of (psychological) distance has been treated as if it was unambiguous.

The concept usually associated with the term distance is presumably that of an Euclidean distance between points in space ("as the crow flies"). Most people will probably tend to employ this notion of distance habitually when asked to interpret a map, even in cases where the Euclidean distance may be different from the relevant distance, as may sometimes be the case on road maps.

The number of mathematical functions which fulfill the metric axioms, and hence define distances, is legio, and the Euclidean distance is just a very special case of a much larger class of distances (Shepard, 1974). Although it is the "natural" one for us to deal with in the physical space we sense, it is by no means evident that it also must be a valid one when we are dealing with psychological spaces and psychological distances.

The widespread and largely unreflected use of Euclidean spaces as models of psychological spaces has been repeatedly criticized, e.g. by Coombs (1964, p.206) and Boyd (1972). Their objections have mainly been based on general psychological arguments. Converse (1966) has contributed with a critique which bears directly on the use of Euclidean spaces as models (or maps) of perceived party spaces and of Euclidean distances as representations of psychological distances between voters and parties.

With support from data obtained in France and Finland, Converse argues for the need to allow for individual differences in the perception of distances between voters and parties when modelling perceived party space. The kind of space he has in mind is a space with axes the length of which can vary according to the way a particular voter perceives the party system. According to Converse (1966, p.193; p.197) "... the absolute length of the axes or coordinates of the perceived party spaces vary inversely as a function of political involvement and/or information ... for voters intensely involved in the system, the axes of the party space appear very long, and the distance between parties forbidding." Besides that, the perceived length of the axes also varies with the centrality of that dimension to the voter (Converse 1966, p.198): "... party differences along dimensions which are unimportant or not of central concern to a given voter would not generate as great a psychological distance as those which are highly central for him".

What this amounts to is a map (with the perceived party locations on it) which may be individually and differentially shrunk or extended in the direction of its axes by each voter. The function defining the distance between voter (i) and party (j) in a r-dimensional space would hence become:[49]

$$d_{ij} = [\Sigma_a \, w_{ia}(x_{ia} - x_{ja})^2]^{1/2}$$

which differs from the ordinary Euclidean distance function only in the presence of the weights w_{ia} which are specific to voter (i) and dimension (a). These weights represent the centrality or saliency of each dimension to the voter.

A model like this could indeed be fitted using the techniques of multidimensional scaling[50] (Carroll, 1972). So could other models which allow for other relevant types of individual differences.[51]

Although the arguments put forward by Converse are difficult to contend, simple Euclidean models will be used exclusively to represent the perceived party space in the context of this study. The reasons for this choice are both technical and substantive.

Euclidean models have the great advantage of being mathematically tractable and numerically robust. They entail a far smaller risk of degenerate or suboptimal solutions than do other, non-Euclidean models. Thus they are in general more reliable.

Moreover, the information they contain is far easier to comprehend than the information in non-Euclidean models. After all, one of the salient justifications for using spatial models at all is their illustrative capacity as expressed in the saying that "a plot is worth a thousand numbers". Normally this advantage should not lightheartedly be sacrificed for a model which will be at least as intuitively uninterpretable to most people as would the original array of numbers it is derived from.

Finally, experience has shown the differences between Euclidean and non-Euclidean models to be slight in most cases as far as the location of objects (parties) is concerned. If these locations are the main focus of analysis, as they are in the present study,[52] then non-Euclidean models may simply not be worth the while. The substantive interpretation as to the perceived structure of the party system will not differ much, regardless of the type of model used.

---

[49] There are, actually, two possible mathematical formulations of the same basic idea. Although they have somewhat different mathematical implications, which makes for differences with regard to their falsifiability, their substantive interpretation is identical, cf. Nannestad (1985, pp. 96-97).

[50] It is one of the distinct advantages of multidimensional scaling, compared to other methods, that it is an "open" method, allowing a wide range of different models to be fitted within its general framework.

[51] For example a "mixed metrics"-model as suggested in Nannestad (1981; 1985).

[52] If what we were interested in happened to be the psychic processes by which the voters arrive at the perception of the distances between themselves and the parties, the situation would be very different. and non-Euclidean models might be called for, cf. the discussion in Taylor (1971, pp. 350-351).

Another important question as to what spatial models of party competition do depict and what they do leave out is brought forward by Stokes (1966). He suggests that issues fall into two categories, labelled 'valence issues' and 'position issues', respectively. 'Position issues' he defines as "... those that involve advocacy of government actions from a set of alternatives over which a distribution of voter preferences is defined", as opposed to 'valence issues' which are "... those that merely involve the linking of the parties with some condition that is positively or negatively valued by the electorate" (Stokes, 1966, pp.170-171). If the distances between parties and voters are determined by their relative positions on 'ideological' dimensions (as perceived by the voters), as indeed they are in a distance model, then the 'ideological' dimensions must correspond to 'position issues'. There is no way to represent 'valence issues' (or non-policy issues) in a spatial model.[53]

Barry (1970, pp. 144-146) has attacked Stokes' distinction between 'position' and 'valence' issues. According to his view all that is involved here is a continuum "... from issues on which the electorate is evenly divided to issues on which hardly anyone is in the minority". In the present context, this does not solve the problem, however. Since there is no variation in the way, the voters feel towards a valence issue, a valence dimension cannot be constructed in the spatial model in the same way as a policy-related dimension.

The threat posed by this problem to the validity of spatial models depends on whether or not to expect 'valence issues' to influence the voters' perception of the parties. One of the most likely candidates for such a 'valence issue' in the context of the present study appears to be 'competence in handling the country's affairs'. For example, the upsurge of the Agrarians in the 1975-election under the leadership of Poul Hartling (cf. chapter 4) would from the outset appear to be most easily explained by recourse to a 'valence issue' of competence.

Judging from the fit obtained with our spatial models, it seems that the omission of 'valence dimensions' has not had any damaging effect. Why this should be so, we can only guess at. One possible reason could be that the 'valence issue' suggested above was only relevant for a small number of parties, maybe just two of them - the incumbent party and its major challenger. Another possible explanation could be that all parties were judged about equally low on competence or related valence issues, as might indeed be inferred from the widespread distrust in politicians invariably expressed in the surveys.

Before being able to fit a spatial model to the data, one further question (again with possible bearings on the validity of the resulting map) has to be decided upon. Up to now, we have been speaking somewhat vaguely of assuming a functional relationship between (psychological) distances and

---

[53] Enelow and Hinich (1984) propose a model that allows for a valence dimension to be present in the mathematical formulation of the model and in the data. By their method it is filtered out before the spatial model is constructed, cf. pp. 174-175.

sympathy scores. To be able to fit a model, we need to specify the nature of this functional relationship.

Although it is possibly not warranted by the level of measurement in the sympathy scores used,[54] we shall force this relationship to be linear.[55] This assumption is of course more restrictive than the alternative assumption of just a monotone relationship between psychological distances and sympathy scores, but it makes it more easy to avoid certain types of undesirable (partially or totally degenerate) solutions.[56]

The second assumption about the relationship between psychological distances and sympathy scores we shall make states that the postulated (linear) relationship may differ between respondents. This implies that even if two respondents have used exactly the same thermometer grades to express their sympathy for the various parties, their ideal points need not (but certainly may) coincide on the map. Thus we realize that the respondents may have used the sympathy thermometer in different ways.

Most previous studies of the voters' perception of the party system[57] have been based on correlations (over respondents) between the parties' sympathy scores as input data instead of using the respondents' sympathy grades directly. This strategy has the main advantage of reducing the amount of data to be handled.[58] Moreover, it reduces the amount of random error in the data by aggregating over individuals.

Unfortunately, it also carries the risk of arriving at invalid solutions. The reason for this is that we cannot tell if two parties are close to each other or far from each other, when both receive low sympathy grades from a respondent. But if a respondent administers low sympathy grades to two parties, he contributes to the covariation between the two parties' sympathy scores. Hence two parties which are almost equally disliked by a big part of

---

[54] Cf. section 1.6. below.

[55] To correct for possible nonlinearities in the data, at least to some extend, rank numbers are used as input instead of the raw scores. See Nannestad (1985, p.342) for a discussion of the effect of such a transformation.

[56] Cf. Heiser (1981) and Nannestad (1985, pp.257-272). Incidentally, this may give rise to another problem. When trying to find the respondents' "ideal points" on the map, we have to start from a trial configuration of these points. If the trial position for a respondents "ideal point" happens to be badly misplaced so as to make its distances to the parties an increasing function of the sympathy scores (instead of a decreasing function, as it should be), then in the final map this respondent will end up being represented by his "anti ideal point". To circumvent this problem, a mixed metric/nonmetric strategy is employed as proposed in Kruskal, Young and Seery (1977, pp.42-45), although it is implemented in a different way.

[57] Except for Nannestad (1984) where a reduced sample is used.

[58] With the 1971-survey, for example, the difference is 55 data values (when correlations are used) as against 14322 data values (when the sympathy scores are used directly). Given the limitations on the computer resources readily available to social scientists, numerical problems of such size remained virtually intractable until a few years ago. Thus there was no real choice: One had either to reduce the amount of data one way or the other, or give up the analysis. Today, there is no longer any reason (or excuse) for continuing with this practice, as e.g. in Worre (1987).

41

the respondents will end up with a rather strong correlation, indicating that they must be close together. But they may equally well be far from each other as well as far from the bulk of the respondents. To avoid this trap, the models in the present study are fitted to the sympathy data directly.[59]

Turning to the information contained in the maps, it can be expressed numerically as coordinate values for the party positions and the "ideal points" and as distances. Sometimes we may want to report and analyze summary measures for coordinates or distances, for example their central tendency or dispersion. In those cases, ordinal measures, especially the median, will be preferred.

The main reason for this choice is robustness. While the positions of the parties on the map are ordinarily very stable, the location of the "ideal points", being based on relatively few observations only, may occasionally be "noisy". Therefore, robust measures are called for, despite the fact that the level of measurement for coordinates is clearly interval.

The final methodological choice to comment on is the choice not to conduct or report significance tests of the results, despite the fact that we are working with data from samples. There are both technical and substantive reasons behind that decision.

In the first place, significance tests are simply not available for the goodness of fit of our models. Further, since the models' overall fit cannot be assessed, it appears to make little sense to apply the heavy machinery of inferential statistics to measurements derived from these models.

In the second place, our data come from samples, but due to both dropouts and weighting, these samples are not simple random samples. One might, of course, just treat them as if they were, but there seems not much of a point in evoking an impression of great numerical precision in the estimation of possible errors, when this precision can only be - at best - approximate!

Finally, the main objective of this study is to show certain relationships to exist, and not to determine the exact value and distribution for certain variables throughout the Danish population.[60] Therefore, the interesting question is whether what we find agrees with the patterns to be expected on theoretical reasons. Since what the theory predicts are primarily patterns in the data, not singular data values, the risk of obtaining confirming results by pure chance need not be among the most pressing concerns.

---

[59] In the terminology of multidimensional scaling, multidimensional unfolding of the thermometer data is used. METFOLD (a FORTRAN program designed for use with large datasets) has been used to perform the actual computations. To forestall a certain kind of "misunderstandings", it shall be stressed that the program was written by the present author. Graphical postprocessing of the results was done using the graphical dataanalysis package MacSpin™.

[60] The same argument is put forward in Borre and Katz (1973).

1.6. Data

The major part of the data used in this study comes from a series of surveys conducted in connection with the general elections of 1971, 1973, 1975, 1977 and 1979 by a group of researchers from the universities of Copenhagen and Aarhus.[61] In the first two surveys the staff of the Danish Institute for Social Research (SFI) was used for interviewing. The others were part of the regular Gallup-omnibuses.[62] Table 1.2. contains some information about the samples.

Table 1.2.: National election surveys 1971 - 1979

Year	Staff	Target n	Sample n unweighted	weighted
1971 pre	SFI	2114	1499	1499
1971 post	SFI	1499	1302	1302
1973	SFI	1302	533	533
1975	Gallup	1600	1148	1600
1977	Gallup	1600	991	1607
1979	Gallup*	?	1989	1989

*Two omnibuses combined

The surveys of 1971 and 1973 were planned as a panel. Of the 2114 respondents in the sample, 1499 were interviewed prior to the election in 1971. Of these 1499 respondents, 1302 were interviewed again after the election. The datafile for 1971 consists of these 1302 cases.

Of the 1302 respondents left after the post election-interview in 1971, 533 could be interviewed again after the election in 1973. Thus the panel consists of 533 cases. In the present study, only the cases in the panel - i.e. the 533 respondents interviewed all three times - are used. Although there is a couple of months separating the first from the second wave of the panel, we shall ordinarily treat data from the first two waves as if they came from the same survey.

For the purpose of this study, the thermometer grades given to the parties[63] are among the most important variables. While the way of posing the question remained basically unchanged from the first to the last survey

---

[61] The principal members of this group were Ole Borre (Århus), Hans Jørgen Nielsen, Steen Sauerberg, and Torben Worre (Copenhagen).

[62] The data are deposited in the Danish Data Archives. Ole Borre kindly allowed me access to his versions of the datafiles.

[63] In 1971, thermometer grades for party leaders as well as for several social groups (e.g. students), professions (e.g. police) and organizations (e.g. trade unions) were obtained too. In 1973, thermometer grades were obtained for political leaders.

in the series,[64] the way of recording the answers did change somewhat. In 1971 the thermometer ran from -100 to +100 degrees. The respondents could name any integer value on this thermometer. In the coding process, the responses were truncated by removing the least significant digit and replacing it with zero. In 1973, the thermometer was shortened to the range from -50 to +50 degrees. The responses were neither rounded nor truncated. From 1975 onwards, the thermometer was back in the range -100 to +100 degrees, but the responses were coded in steps of 20. For this reason, comparisons between the results from the 1971- and 1973-surveys and the rest (as well as between the 1971- and the 1973-survey) are bound to be problematic. Moreover, the measurement level one may safely attribute to the thermometer scores cannot possibly be higher than ordinal.

The way of coding the responses to the thermometer question implies that a recorded score on the sympathy thermometer must be taken to refer to an interval on the thermometer rather than to a particular value. For that reason median thermometer scores will be computed under the assumption that respondents with the same recorded score are distributed evenly throughout the interval.

We may assume the reliability of the responses to be satisfactory as far as the most and the least preferred parties are concerned. Some kind of check is possible by comparing the reported party vote to the sympathy grades given to the parties. The proportion of cases where the most preferred party is not the party voted for is low.

The grading of the parties "in between" the most and the least preferred ones may be suspected to be somewhat less reliable. Typically they must be assumed to be parties of rather low saliency to the respondent. Thus it might well be that the grades administered to the "in between"-parties and the rank order among them are more or less random.

In the analysis of the thermometer scores this problem could be dealt with in two ways. One could weight the thermometer grades, giving most weight to the supposedly most reliable ones, i.e. the grades given to the most preferred parties (and conceivably also to the least preferred). One could also tie the grades of the "in between"-parties and treat these ties as indeterminate relations.

As far as the location of parties is concerned, the supposedly lower reliability of the scoring of "in between"-parties probably does not matter much. If "in between"-parties are scored more or less at random by the individual respondents, then these random errors can be expected to cancel out. Consequently, the position of the parties on the map will primarily

---

[64] The question was administered in the following way. The respondent was shown a card and asked: "We would like to know how you feel about the various parties. Here is a card. It shows some kind of thermometer, which we call a sympathy thermometer. We shall ask you to give temperature grades to the parties, depending on how well you like them. To all parties you do like, you shall give plusgrades, and the better you like a party the higher temperature grades shall you assign to it. To parties, you feel unfavorably towards, you shall give minusgrades. If you feel neither favorably nor unfavorably towards a party, you shall assign a temperature of zero degrees to it."

depend on the grades given to them by those respondents for whom the parties are not "in between", but are among the most or the least preferred ones.

Unfortunately the same does not hold true with respect to the location of the respondents' "ideal points", however. Since "ideal points" are important in this study, it has been decided to weight the thermometer scores in order to give greater weight to the supposedly most valid ones, viz. the scoring of the most and the second most preferred party.

In the absence of externally given weight factors, this decision raises a new problem: In theory it would be possible to weight the first two choices (i.e. the most and second most preferred parties) so heavily as to force the solution to truthfully represent them, possibly at the expense of the rest of the scores. This would amount to utilizing only the information contained in the two highest thermometer grades administered by each respondent, throwing away the rest. Clearly such a procedure would be a waste of information.

What is needed is to strike a balance between forcing the solutions to truthfully represent the perceived distances between each respondent and his most and second most preferred party and simultaneously forcing the solution to still represent the perceived distances between the respondent and the rest of the parties acceptably well. In practice this balance can be monitored by comparing the values of the weighted and the unweighted R^2: Basically what is wanted is to increase the value of the weighted R^2, without lowering the value of the unweighted R^2 too much. Thus there is a trade-off between the increase in weighted R^2-value that results from giving more weight to the thermometer scores administered to the most and second most preferred parties, and the decrease in the unweighted R^2-value that may become the consequence of such weighting. In practice, then, the weights used were chosen such as to approximately balance the increase in the weighted and the decrease in the unweighted R^2-values.[65]

Another problem arises from the way, the zero point on the thermometer is interpreted and used by the respondents. There is evidence to suggest that the respondents have used the zero point, even when they had no feeling or attitude at all towards the party in question, especially in the case of small, new and relatively unknown parties. In other cases the zero indicates a "genuine" neutral attitude.

The relatively high proportion of zero grades given to small and unknown parties will exert a pull on them towards the center of the map. But since many of these zeroes will not be expressions of genuine neutrality, the validity of the positions assigned to this type of parties in our models has to be looked at with considerable suspicion. But since there is no way of

---

[65] With the 1979-data no weighting was done, since weighting turned out to lead to an unacceptable drop in the unweighted R^2-value, compared to an only modest improvement in the weighted R^2 value.

deciding which zeros reflect genuine neutrality and which reflect a non-attitude, nothing can be done about it.

Besides data from the surveys, data on roll call divisions on government bills are used. These data were compiled from the Folketing's official publication, Folketingsårbogen,[66] and are used to compute distance index-values for the parties.

In general the reliability of the recordings in the Folketingsårbog is satisfactory. In the recordings from 1970 and 1971, however, there is a problem with the vote cast by the single member representing the Communists, which is not always reported. In many cases it is impossible to establish whether she participated in the roll call at all.[67]

The validity of scoring abstention as a position in between "aye" and "nay" in the computation of the distance index may be dubious on some occasions. Abstention has in some situations been used to express a refusal to participate in a decision at all, rather than to express a neutral stand on the bill. Such situations have occurred infrequently, however, and hence do not affect the overall picture much.

The validity of roll call analysis of the type used in this study has sometimes been drawn in doubt as not being able "to tell the whole story".[68] By virtue of the data used, so the argument runs, this kind of analysis only deals with one aspect of parliamentary behavior, and it only covers the final step in the legislative process, neglecting all the preceding phases.

The relevance of this type of criticism depends on what it is one wants to demonstrate and how results from the analysis are interpreted. In the present study the interest is concentrated upon how the party system was perceived by the electorate and how this perception relates to the parties' behavior, of which parliamentary behavior is taken to be an important indicator. In that respect, roll call behavior probably constitutes the most visible - and most highly publicized - source of information on the relationship between the parties available to the voters. We do not pretend to show what the relationship between the parties "really was" (whatever that may mean), but what the electorate was able to see. In that respect, roll call divisions constitute data of satisfactory validity.

---

[66] The data for the period 1971 - 1979 were collected and kindly made available to me by one of my colleagues, Palle Svensson.

[67] As a rule, divisions in the Folketing are anonymous. What is recorded is the parties' stands.

[68] E.g. by Nilson (1977). For a rebuke see Pedersen (1977).

2. Prelude: The general election of September 1971

2.1. Background, campaign, and outcome[1]

On the 31st of August 1971, Prime Minister Hilmar Baunsgaard (RV) announced elections to the Folketing to be held on the 21st of September. The term of the Folketing elected in 1968 was drawing to its end. It would have expired by January 1972. By calling elections about four months ahead of this date, it was hoped to avoid interrupting the parliamentary session bound to start in the beginning of October. The early date would also give the new government time to sort out the numerous problems related to Denmark's entry into the EEC, which was envisaged to take place by the 1st of January 1973.

The election of 1971 was thus not triggered off by a parliamentary crisis, as should subsequently become the rule in the seventies. The parliamentary situation had been stable since 1968. The coalition government formed by the Radical Liberals, the Conservatives and the Agrarians and headed by the leader of the Radical Liberals, Hilmar Baunsgaard, was backed by a comfortable majority in the Folketing. Despite traditionally strong political differences between especially the Conservatives and the Radical Liberals, the three parties had managed to get along quite well. Some questions which could have endangered the cohesion of the coalition had been effectively shelved. On others, acceptable compromises had been worked out.

The opposition was dominated by the Socialdemocrats who had been ousted from government in 1968 for the first time in 15 years, but nevertheless had remained the largest party in the Folketing. Despite its opposition role the party had cooperated with the government and the parties behind it on a number of issues, most notably the EEC-issue. In contrast, the Socialist Peoples' Party had led a much more pronounced opposition policy. The same had been true for the Left Socialists, a group that had broken away from the Socialist Peoples' Party in 1968, hereby causing the downfall of the Socialdemocratic government. It had obtained four seats in 1968, but shortly afterwards two members had broken away, forming the Socialist Working Group (Socialistisk arbejdsgruppe). One of the members of this group had finally ended up proclaiming herself a representative of the Communists, which had not been able to make it to the Folketing on their own since 1960.

Besides the seven parties thus represented in the Folketing in 1971 - SD, RV, KF, SF, DKP, V, and VS - three other parties entered the electoral contest. Of these, the Justice Party (DR) was the oldest, having lost its representation in the Folketing in 1960. In its platform it combined Georgeism and commitment to economic liberalism and free trade and it

---

[1]The main sources of the historical accounts are Wendt (1978), Andersen (1982), and Avisårbogen.

was vigorously opposed to Danish membership of the EEC. The Christian Peoples' Party (Krf) had been founded in 1970, mainly as a reaction against the freeing of pornography and introduction of sex education in schools. The Schlesvigian Party (Slp) was the party of the German minority in Southern Jutland and did run candidates in this region only.[2] Altogether then, there were 10 parties to choose among.

The dominating issues the parties focused their campaign on were taxes, the labor marked and the economy.[3] The EEC-question, on the other hand, was kept somewhat in the background, since it had been decided to have a referendum on that question in 1972.[4] The voters, however, were quite uninterested in the labor marked issue. To them, the economy and the EEC seemed the most important problems. Taxes were ranked fifth in importance (Siune, 1982, p.177).

On the issues of taxes and the economy, the government and its parties found themselves on the defensive. Taxes had been rising dramatically since 1968, probably much to the chagrin of non-socialist voters who remembered the Conservatives' prior proclamations that "money is best kept in the citizens' pockets". The government had also repeatedly been forced to put brakes on the economy to prevent it from getting too heated. Nevertheless, inflation had been running at about 8 pct. a year, and the balance of payments was constantly in the red (about ÷3 billion dkr. a year). Unemployment, on the other hand, was below 2 pct.

Opinion polls up to the election had the Socialdemocrats and - to a somewhat lesser extend - the Socialist Peoples' Party to gain seats, while the Conservatives and the Agrarians were facing losses. The final electoral results came very close to these predictions, cf. Table 2.1. below.

Thus only five parties gained seats in the new Folketing, although the Christian Peoples' Party with 1.999 pct. came extremely close to passing the threshold of 2 pct. of the valid votes cast. The parties in government lost 10 seats, but while the Conservatives suffered badly, losing six, the Radical Liberals showed surprising strength, being able to hold on to the 27 seats they had obtained in 1968, when they had more than doubled their parliamentary representation. (Ordinarily such gains used to be rather short-lived).

Though none of them gained seats, the small parties managed to almost double their electoral support from 3.7 pct. of the votes cast in 1968 to 6.7 pct. in 1971. Only the Left Socialists suffered a predictable loss.

---

[2] For this reason, the party will not be included in the analysis.

[3] Cf. Siune (1982, ch.8).

[4] This procedure had originally been proposed by the Socialdemocrats with the obvious intention of keeping the EEC-issue, on which its followers were deeply divided, out of the pending electoral campaign. The Radical Liberals, finding themselves in very much the same predicament as the Socialdemocrats, had supported the idea. Conservatives and the Agrarians, on the other hand, both being strongly pro-EEC, tried to make EEC-membership a campaign issue. An account of the party maneuvers up to the referendum can be found in Petersen and Elklit (1973).

Table 2.1.: Electoral results 1971 (with 1968 for comparison)

Party	23.1. 1968		21.9. 1971	
	votes (pct.)	seats	votes (pct.)	seats
SD	34.2	62	37.3	70
RV	15.0	27	14.4	27
KF	20.4	37	16.7	31
DR	0.7	0	1.7	0
SF	6.1	11	9.1	17
DKP	1.0	0	1.4	0
Krf	-	-	2.0	0
V	18.6	34	15.6	30
VS	2.0	4	1.6	0

While the government parties still held a precarious majority of 88 seats against 87 seats to the Socialdemocrats and the Socialist Peoples' Party after the election, the situation was reversed when the results from Greenland and the Faeroe Islands came in. With the support from two of these four "north-atlantic seats", a 89:88 majority backing the formation of a Social-democratic minority government headed by J.O. Krag could be established. On October 11, 1971, Hilmar Baunsgaard left the reins to J.O. Krag.

2.2. Perception of the party system in 1971

How did the electorate perceive of the parties running in the 1971-election? Table 2.2. below may provide a first impression. It shows the median sympathy grade given to each party, depending on the respondents' re-ported vote.

The first noteworthy thing in Table 2.2. appears in the bottom line. It shows that, on average, the five "old" parties - SD, RV, KF, SF and V - were perceived favorably by the electorate, while the feelings towards the small parties were just below zero for the three of them. The sole party eliciting massive negative response were the Communists. They were probably still hurt by being associated with the Soviet invasion of Czechoslovakia in 1968.

This predominantly positive attitude towards the political parties stands in a marked contrast to the apparent lack of trust in politicians which emerges from the responses on a number of "distrust"-items in the 1971-survey: Here more than 80 pct. of the respondents agreed completely or in part to the statement that "politicians spend the tax-payers' money too lavishly". More than 70 pct. agreed (completely or in part) that "politicians usually do care too little about what the voters think". And more than a half of the respondents agreed completely or in part to the statement that "people who want to get to the top in politics are forced to give up most of their ideals".[5]

The bottom line in Table 2.2. - and a roughly parallel one on party leaders to be reported below - seems to call for a somewhat cautious interpretation of these measures of political distrust. For the moment, however, we shall not pursue this topic any further.

Table 2.2.: Sympathy scores by reported vote (medians), 1971
(bold: most preferred party; italic: next most preferred party)

Voted for	SD	RV	KF	DR	SF	DKP	Krf	V	VS
SD	**81.5**	21.7	-0.1	-0.6	*37.5*	-19.3	-2.2	-0.2	-1.4
RV	18.9	**78.5**	*40.8*	0.3	-0.3	-78.5	-0.6	39.9	-10.0
KF	0.8	*44.6*	**80.2**	-0.9	-28.6	-97.9	0	42.8	-60.0
DR	5.0	*10.0*	0	**60.0**	-40.0	-47.5	0	0	-20.0
SF	*40.0*	18.9	-1.8	3.3	**81.7**	1.8	-20.0	-2.9	1.5
DKP	20.0	-5.0	-55.0	-15.0	40.0	**90.0**	-95.0	-80.0	*80.0*
Krf	-1.7	30.0	35.0	5.0	-50.0	-90.0	**90.0**	*55.0*	-30.0
V	0.1	*40.7*	40.2	-0.7	-30.7	-98.2	-0.3	**81.7**	-57.5
VS	-20.0	0	0	20.0	*50.0*	30.0	-80.0	0	**60.0**
All	40.1	40.1	19.9	-0.1	0.7	-48.5	-0.2	21.1	-0.5

The second thing about Table 2.2. to notice is that visual inspection at once reveals the existence of two clusters of parties. The parties in government (RV, KF and V) make up one tightly knit cluster. The other, somewhat looser one, consists of the Socialdemocrats and The Socialist Peoples' Party. This structure we may expect to find in the model as well. Figure 2.1. below presents a map of the perceived party space as derived from the thermo-meter data.[6]

The structure of the parties' positions on the map - and hence in the voters' perception of the party space and the parties in it - appears quite clear and definitely non-random. As expected, the three parties behind the government form one cluster. Obviously, they were seen as rather close to each other. Another, less tightly knit, cluster consists of the socialist parties (Socialist Peoples' Party, Communists, and Left Socialists). The Social-democrats are positioned between these two clusters, but closer to the socialist one.

---

[5] On the other hand, close to 60 pct. of the respondents endorsed totally or in part the view that "In general one can trust our political leaders to make the right decision for the country".

[6] The map is based on the thermometer grades from 515 out of 533 respondents in the panel who were interviewed in all three waves. For technical reasons, respondents who have not given valid thermometer grades to at least two parties have to be excluded.

Fig. 2.1.: The perceived party system 1971

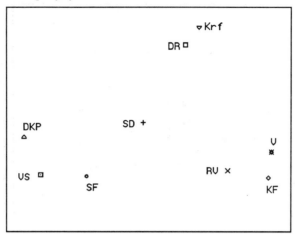

The two small non-socialist parties, running in the election without having been represented in the Folketing 1968-71, are inhabitants of a region of their own, which offsets them clearly from the rest of the parties. Their location suggests that they were about equally disliked by respondents associated with the bourgeois and by respondents associated with the socialist parties. In fact, this may be all they had in common.

In Figure 2.2. the respondents "ideal points" have been added to the map of the parties. The distribution of these "ideal points" does not appear to be random either. As can be seen, the mass of the respondents is positioned somewhere near the center of the space, but there are discernible "stretches" in the distribution, roughly running from the lower right to the upper left corner as well as from the center towards the upper right corner, giving the distribution of "ideal points" a somewhat heart-shaped appearance.

The map fits the data well (unweighted $R^2 = 0.76$; weighted $R^2 = 0.88$). Moreover, if we use it to "hindcast" the votes, assuming that the respondents vote for the party closest to their "ideal point", a rather close agreement (NS = 0.05) between the "hindcasted" distribution of votes and the distribution of the reported votes in the sample is found, cf. Table 2.3. below. The greatest "miss" is the "hindcast" of the vote for the Agrarians, which turns out to be 2.8 pct. off the mark. Finally, in 84.7 pct. of all cases, the vote "hindcasted" for a respondent from the map agrees with the reported vote from the respondent.[7]

---

[7] In comparison, Enelow and Hinich (1984, p.182; p.198), using a different type of model in the analysis of the presidential elections of 1976 and 1980, report correctly "hindcasted" votes in the range between 82.5 pct. and 92.0 pct. It should be noted, however, that their task was somewhat easier, since they had to "hindcast" the result of the choice between two candidates only.

Fig. 2.2.: Parties and "ideal points" in perceived party space 1971*

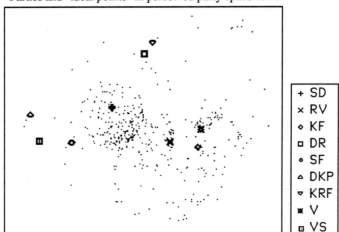

+ SD
× RV
◇ KF
□ DR
• SF
▵ DKP
▿ KRF
✻ V
▫ VS

* 10 outliers removed.

Given the goodness of fit of the model and the clearly non-random pattern in the distribution of parties and "ideal points" on the map, it seems safe to conclude that the thermometer data provide evidence to the fact that the respondents in 1971 did have a clear perception of the party system and the parties in it. So far then, proposition 1.1. is sustained by the data.

Table 2.3.: Reported and "hindcasted" distribution of votes 1971

| | Distribution of votes | |
| | reported | "hindcast" |
Party	(n = 476)	(n = 515)
SD	41.4	43.3
RV	17.0	16.1
KF	10.7	11.8
DR	1.5	1.8
SF	7.4	6.6
DKP	0.6	1.2
Krf	1.7	2.3
V	19.3	16.5
VS	0.4	0.4

Our next question is how to interpret the structure of the space defined by the distribution the parties and "ideal points". Quite evidently, the arrangement of the parties in the horizontal direction corresponds well to the coventional left-right ordering of the parties in the Danish party system. Thus it seems that one important 'ideological' dimension used by the respondents to structure their perception of the party system might be the familiar left-right dimension.

We may try to substantiate this (not very surprising) conjecture by using the thermometer grades given by our respondents in the 1971-survey to "leftists" or "rightists", respectively. In the present case, we shall be using the grades for the "rightists".[8]

These grades are first converted to a five point-scale. Grades in the range -100 to -51 are scored '1', grades in the range -50 to -1 are scored '2', et cetera. The neutral grading of zero is scored '5'.

Using the converted scores and the respondents "ideal points", the median position (or median "ideal point") for the respondents in each of the categories on the five point-scale is computed. Thus we find the median position for respondents feeling extremely cold (-100 to -51) towards "rightists", for respondents feeling somewhat less cold (-51 to -1), and so on.

Fig. 2.3.: Perceived party space and attitude positions towards "rightists" in 1971

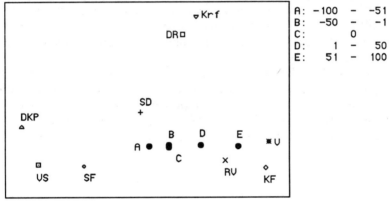

A:	-100	-	-51
B:	-50	-	-1
C:		0	
D:	1	-	50
E:	51	-	100

If the horizontal direction on our map does indeed correspond to an 'ideological' left-right dimension in the perceived party system, then we should expect the respondents to become more and more sympathetic towards "rightists" as we travel horizontally from the left to the right across the map. As can be seen from Figure 2.3. above, this is exactly what happens. At the same time, there is almost no variation in the vertical position of the median "ideal points".

Thus a rather clear relationship exists between how the respondents feel towards "rightists" - and hence what we may assume is their own position on

---

[8] In effect, we are using these gradings as a surrogate for data on the respondents' self-placement on a left right-continuum. Unfortunately (from the perspective of this study), thermometer scores on "rightists" and/or "leftists" were obtained in the 1971-survey only, and the respondents' self-placement on a left right-continuum was first elicited in the 1979 survey.

the left right-continuum - and how they feel towards the various parties.[9] Respondents who like "rightists" normally don't see themselves close to socialist parties, and respondents located close to socialist parties normally dislike "rightists". There is little doubt, then, that a left-right dimension does structure the respondents' perception of the party system and the parties in it.[10]

But the left-right dimension does not only structure the respondents' perception of the parties' position in the party system. It is part of the underlying structure in their positions on a number of policy issues as well. This is what we are going to show next.

Economic policy issues are the most likely candidates for issues the position on which can be expected to exhibit a left right-ordering. In the 1971-survey, the respondents' positions were recorded on 12 economic items in the pre-election wave, and on three economic items in the post-election wave. Basically, the economic items presented belong to three issue-categories. Five items in the pre-election and one in the post-election wave have a direct bearing on the role of the state in the economy.[11] Five items, all of them in the pre-election wave, deal with economic equality.[12] Two items in the pre-election and two items in the post-election wave deal with taxes.[13]

To illustrate the relationship between the respondents' issue positions and their spatial positions on the map, we use the same technique as with the attitudes towards "rightists": We compute and display the median "ideal point" for the respondents falling in the various categories on the five point-scale used to record their attitude towards the issue.

---

[9] As indicated by the nearly coinciding positions of the median "ideal points" in categories B and C, those who are neutral and those who are mildly negative towards rightists are not clearly distinct with respect to their position on the left right-dimension, however.

[10] For a similar result, based on a different analysis, see Elklit et al. (1972).

[11] Pre-election wave: VAR191 ("The state should own all enterprises"), VAR195 ("The railroads should be made a private enterprise"), VAR199 ("There is too much public interference with the right of private property"), VAR203 ("It is important to keep a system of free competition"), and VAR210 ("There is too little state control with private investments").
Post-election wave: VAR349 ("A public board should oversee all credit giving to private business").

[12] VAR192 ("High education ought to result in high earnings"), VAR196 ("All people should earn the same"), VAR204 ("In politics one should strive to make economic conditions equal for all, regardless of education and job"), VAR206 ("The public should guarantee a job with decent pay to all"), and VAR212 ("People should be prevented from getting rich just by inheritance').

[13] Pre-election wave: VAR200 ("High incomes should be taxed more heavily") and VAR207 ("Those who save should not be punished for it by property taxes").
Post-election wave: VAR347 ("The tax advantages of house owners should be abolished") and VAR348 ("Taxes on income should be cut by raising the VAT instead").

Fig. 2.4.: Perceived party space and issue positions on the role of the state in the economy 1971

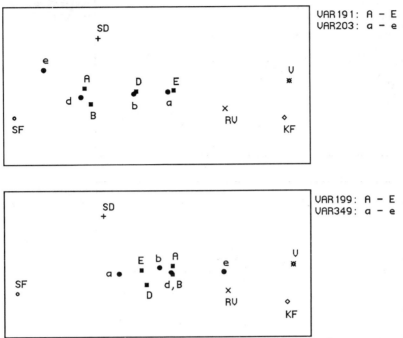

A, a: Agree completely; B, b: Do agree in part; D, d: Do disagree in part; E, e: Disagree completely

The role of the state in the economy, naturally, is an almost classical left-right issue. Thus we should expect agreement to positions demanding state interference with the economy to diminish as we move horizontally from the left to the right across the map in Figure 2.4. above. (To improve readability, the median "ideal points" for the issue positions appear on two separate maps instead of just one, and only a "zoom picture" of the relevant part of the map is shown).

The responses to two items (VAR195 on turning the railways into a private enterprise and VAR210 on state control with private investments) do not conform to the expected left right-pattern.[14] The others do so quite well. Issue positions on VAR191 and VAR203 are almost mirror images of each other, as indeed they should be since the wording of the two items is complementary.

---

[14] VAR195 seems to concern a pseudo-issue: De-nationalization of the railroads was not on the political agenda, and it did not appear in the platform of any party in the contest. Thus the question can safely be assumed to have had low centrality to the respondents, making for largely random reactions.

Fig. 2.5.: Perceived party space and issue positions on economic equality 1971

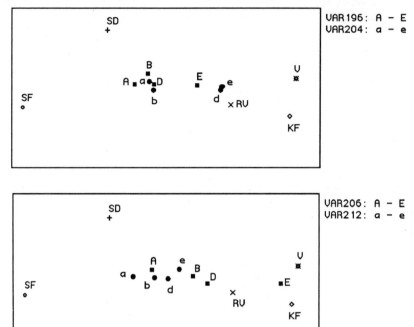

A, a: Agree completely; B, b: Do agree in part; D, d: Do disagree in part; E, e: Disagree completely

Turning to the items which bear on economic equality, the same tendency should be expected to be found: As one moves horizontally from the left to the right across the map, agreement with positions favoring economic equality should be expected to diminish. Figure 2.5. above, which closely parallels Figure 2.4., shows that this is indeed the case, except for one item (VAR192 on people with high education being entitled to high income).

As may be seen from Figures 2.4. and 2.5., attitudes favoring state intervention in the economy as well as economic equality were not an isolated left-wing phenomenon in 1971. They enjoyed support - or at least lip service - even from respondents fairly close to the center. If one compares the attitudes towards this two sets of economic issues, it turns out that economic egalitarianism had the broadest appeal, cf. Figure 2.6.

Of the four tax-items[15] presented, three items produce issue positions that are ordered along the horizontal direction on the map. Only the item

[15] VAR200 ("High incomes should be taxed more heavily"), VAR207 ("Those who save should not be punished for it by property taxes"), VAR347 ("The tax advantages of house owners should be abolished"), and VAR348 ("Taxes on income should be cut by raising the VAT instead").

concerning the tax advantages of house owners (VAR347) does not entirely conform to this pattern.[16] Otherwise - as should be expected - leftists tend to support heavier taxation of high incomes and to oppose the view that those who save should not be punished for it by property taxes or that taxes on income should be cut by raising the VAT instead, while rightists take the opposite position.

Fig. 2.6.: Perceived party space and median position of respondents favoring state intervention in the economy and economic equality 1971

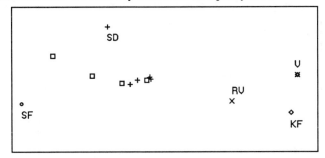

+ Agree completely to position favoring economic equality
    (VAR196, VAR204, VAR206, VAR212)

▫ Agree completely to position favoring state intervention in the economy
    (VAR191, VAR203, VAR199, VAR349)

Besides economy, foreign policy is a policy area in Danish politics where some issue positions might be expected to follow a left-right dimension. Especially Danish membership of NATO has traditionally been an issue separating the right and the left. In the 1971-survey, the respondents were confronted with five foreign policy-items.[17]

Figure 2.7. shows that for one NATO-item (VAR216 on leaving NATO as soon as possible) the median "ideal points" for the respondents in each of the five categories on the scale do exhibit a left right-pattern. As one moves

---

[16] It turns out that those who disagree strongly to abolishing the tax advantages of house owners are located "too close" to the center of the map, and to the left of those only disagreeing in part. Thus the strongest defense of the tax privileges of homeowners did not come from the right but rather from right of center. This is interesting to notice in view of later developments: In 1973, the Center-Democrats picked up the bulk of their voters just right of the center after having campaigned strongly in defense of the interests of homeowners.

[17] VAR190 ("The nordic countries ought to have a common defense"), VAR194 ("Denmark ought to increase her contribution to NATO"), VAR198 ("The nordic countries ought to establish a common government"), VAR216 ("We should leave NATO as soon as possible") and VAR219 ("Western cooperation should be strengthened considerably").

horizontally from the left to the right on the map, support for NATO-membership tends to increase. Issue positions on the other two items dealing with NATO and Western cooperation (VAR194 on increased contributions to NATO and VAR219 on strengthening Western cooperation) do not exhibit any clear pattern. Figure 2.7. also shows that anti-NATO attitudes reached well into the Socialdemocratic constituency in 1971.

Fig. 2.7.:   Perceived party space and issue positions on foreign policy issue 1971

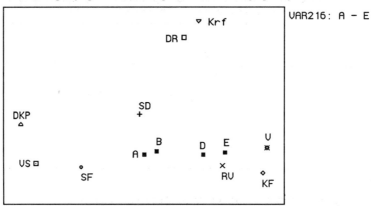

A: Agree completely;   B : Do agree in part;   D: Do disagree in part;   E: Disagree completely

Issue positions on nordic cooperation, on the other hand, are not structured by the left-right dimension. In fact, they do not exhibit any clear pattern at all. The reason might be that this issue had low saliency: An attempt to create a framework for nordic economic cooperation (NORDEC) had failed just a few years earlier and had left "nordism" as an idea everybody would pay lip service to and very few would see as a realistic policy option.

So far then, an 'ideological' left-right dimension has been shown to be one of the dimensions underlying the respondents' perception of the party system in 1971. This dimension had both a socio-economic and a foreign policy content. Thus the interpretation of the horizontal direction in the map of the perceived party system in 1971 has been established.

While the perceived party space of 1971 is well structured in the horizontal direction by the left-right dimension, its structuring in the vertical direction appears less clear, as may be seen from the more "amorphous" distribution of the locations of "ideal points" in that direction. Nevertheless a pattern can be identified. Table 2.4. shows the net majority of the percentage of respondents agreeing (completely or in part) to three different items in each quartile of the vertical distribution of their "ideal points" in Figure 2.2. . Row 1, for example, gives the difference between the percentage of respondents agreeing and disagreeing to the three items among the 25 pct. of the respondents who have "ideal points" with the highest values on the y-coordinate, i.e. are placed closest to the top of the map in Figure 2.2.

Table 2.4.: Net majorities agreeing to three distrust-items 1971[18] within each quartile of the distribution of "ideal points" in the vertical direction

	VAR351	VAR352	VAR354
1. quartile	63.6	75.9	46.5
2. quartile	57.9	67.2	39.8
3. quartile	54.8	61.1	19.2
4. quartile	36.8	45.6	14.5

The common denominator of these three items is clearly distrust in or dissatisfaction with the authorities in the sense of Easton.[19] (VAR351 on the politicians not paying enough attention to the viewpoints of the voters, VAR352 on the politicians spending the taxpayers' money too lavishly, and VAR354 on giving up principles to make it to the top in politics). Table 2.4. demonstrates that there is a tendency for the strength of this attitude to increase as one moves vertically from the bottom towards the top of the map of the perceived party space in 1971.

As can be seen from the table, the "surplus" of respondents agreeing to each of the three items diminishes as one moves from the top of the map towards the bottom. But there definitely is a net majority of distrustful respondents in all four quartiles on all three items.

Thus some kind of political distrust or dissatisfaction was seemingly already beginning to creep up in the respondents' perception of the political parties in 1971. Its importance as an structuring factor in the perception of the party system may still have been rather low, however. The dominating 'ideological' dimension was - as has been shown - the traditional left-right dimension. On the other hand, a new attitude towards the parties was obviously developing, just needing a catalyst or two to gain strength.

Taking into consideration the high proportion of respondents expressing total or partial agreement to the distrust-items it may seem strange that this attitude did not have a more marked influence on the perception of the parties than what has been found. We shall revert to this question below (section 2.2.).

It has been repeatedly proposed that the EEC-issue (which was beginning to become salient in 1971) belongs among the issues that by "cutting across" the left right-cleavage in the Danish party system has contributed to a

---

[18] VAR351 ("Politicians usually do care too little about what the voters think"), VAR352 ("The politicians spend the taxpayers' money too lavishly"), and VAR354 ("Those who want to make it to the top in politics have to give up most of their principles").

[19] Cf. Easton (1965).

loosening of the traditional ties between class and party.[20] Hence it may be interesting to examine whether the stand on the question of Danish EEC-membership produced a separate pattern in the distribution of "ideal points" on the map of the party system in 1971.

In the 1971-survey the respondents were confronted with ten items concerning various aspects of and attitudes towards EEC-membership.[21] Figure 2.8. shows the median "ideal points" for the respondents falling in each of the five categories on the scales belonging to the eight pre-election EEC-items. A line has been fitted to the point scatter by least squares. The issue positions cluster quite closely around the line, and the categories invariably appear in the correct order. As one moves along the line from the right to the left, attitudes towards the EEC and towards Danish membership tend to get increasingly negative.

Fig. 2.8.:: Perceived party space and issue positions on EEC-membership 1971

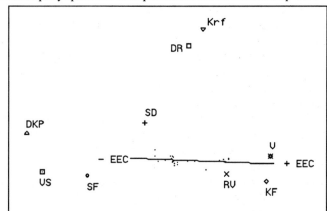

Attitudes towards the EEC and towards Danish membership of the EEC can be seen to correlate very strongly with the left-right dimension in 1971.[22] The notions of socialist internationalism and rightist nationalism notwith-

[20] Cf. Borre (1981; 1982).

[21] Pre-election wave: VAR202 ("Denmark should join the EEC together with England"), VAR221 ("If we become a member of the EEC, we shall loose any possibility to conduct our own foreign policy"), VAR222 ("The EEC is governed in a way which is incompatible with danish democratic traditions"), VAR223 ("EEC-membership means giving up our national independence"), VAR224 ("Relationship with the EEC will be a great economic advantage to Denmark"), VAR225 ("Foreign capital will gain too much influence in Danish industry if we become a member of the EEC"), VAR226 ("We shall not join the EEC under any circumstances") and VAR227 ("Membership of the EEC will be a threat to our Danish culture").
Post-election wave: VAR362 (same as VAR226), VAR363 (same as VAR202).

[22] Cf. Elklit et al. (1972).

standing, anti-EEC attitudes were highly correlated with a leftist position on the left-right dimension. Liberal or conservative EEC-opponents could be found, of course, as well as left-wing EEC-supporters, but they obviously numbered sufficiently few in 1971 as to leave the general picture undisturbed.

There is a very slight deflection of the regression line towards the northwestern corner of the map. This finding indicates that EEC-opponents tended to be slightly more distrustful towards politicians than EEC-supporters. Given the stand taken by the major parties, which all recommended Danish membership of the EEC more or less wholeheartedly, one might hypothesize that EEC-opponents may have been somewhat more distrustful of the wisdom of politicians than other respondents.

From the preceding analyses it can be concluded that in 1971 the respondents' perception of the party system and of the parties in it was predominantly structured by an 'ideological' left-right dimension. The issue content of this dimension has been shown to encompass, i.a., economics (state intervention in the economy; economic equality), foreign policy (NATO), and also the EEC-issue. But on closer inspection an emerging distrust- or dissatisfaction-dimension could be identified as well.

Finally we shall see if the 'ideological' left-right dimension in the respondents' perception of the party system in 1971 corresponds to a structural cleavage in society. Clearly this is what one would expect, given the origins of the left-right dimension in European politics.

In Figure 2.9. the median "ideal points" of the respondents belonging to different social classes or groupings are shown.[23] With an eye to later developments, the classification has been broken down according to employment in the private and the public sector of the economy, respectively. For the same reason, respondents out of work (unemployed, old age-pensioners etc.) have not been assigned to class according to previous occupation.

Figure 2.9. shows that in 1971 the 'ideological' left-right dimension did closely correspond to the existing class cleavage. As would have been expected, workers tend to position themselves to the left, self-employed to the right, with white collar workers in the middle. It should be noticed that - despite the student and youth unrest which occurred in Denmark as well as in other Western countries - students, apprentices and the like were seemingly not very leftist yet.[24] It should also be noted that mode of employment (public or private) did not make for systematic differences in 1971. Nor did other forms of economic dependency on the public.

---

[23] Housewives not in the work force have been assigned to husband's class. Married wives in the work force have been assigned to class in accordance with their own occupational status.

[24] Since the number of respondents under education in the survey is small, this result should be approached with some caution.

Fig. 2.9.: Perceived party space and class 1971

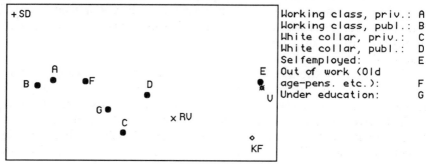

Working class, priv.:	A
Working class, publ.:	B
White collar, priv.:	C
White collar, publ.:	D
Selfemployed:	E
Out of work (Old age-pens. etc.):	F
Under education:	G

So far then, our first two propositions concerning the informational aspect of the vote decision are supported by the 1971-data: The respondents did have a clear perception of the party space and the parties to chose from, and this perception was structured by two 'ideological' dimensions, with the left-right dimension in a dominating role.

2.3. Digression: Perception of party leaders 1971

Before moving on to confront the second set of propositions - viz. propositions 2.1. and 2.2. - with data from 1971, we shall take a short detour to look at the respondents' perception of party leaders in 1971 as revealed by the grades given to them on the sympathy thermometer.[25] The reason for this is threefold.

In the first place we shall try to see if - and to what extent - the perception of party leaders is structured in the same way as the perception of the parties. It is not at all clear that this need to be the case. Quite to the contrary, it would be easily conceivable that the perception of party leaders was influenced by a number of valence dimension which were not relevant to the evaluation of the parties.

If, on the other hand, the perception of party leaders can be shown to be structured in basically the same way as the perception of the party system, this will not only strengthen our trust in the empirical validity of the results on the perception of the party system. It will also demonstrate how "ingrained" the perceptual structure (the respondents' belief system) really was that surfaced in the perception of the party system.

---

[25] Sympathy grades are available for the leaders of seven of the nine parties only. For economic reasons, respondents were not asked to grade the leaders of the Justice Party (DR) and the Communists (DKP).

In the second place, by comparing the party leaders' sympathy scores to the sympathy scores of the parties as well as to the attitudes towards politicians measured by the "distrust"-items in the survey, we shall try to shed some further light on the question of distrust in politicians. As was shown in the preceding section, political distrust and dissatisfaction appear to have had only a limited influence on the perception of the parties and the party system, despite the frequent occurrence of such sentiments when measured by the distrust-items in the survey. Clearly some explanation is needed here.

Finally, we shall try to use the data on the voters' perception of party leaders to get some hints as to the role of personality factors in the vote decision. The view can often be met - both in the press, among politicians and even in the profession - that voters tend increasingly to vote on personality instead of parties, not to mention policies. Sometimes the performance of a political leader on television is made responsible for the fate of his party on election day.[26] We shall use this opportunity to compare the voters' sympathy for parties and for party leaders in various ways to gain an impression whether it is the eyecatcher or the merchandise that sells.[27]

Table 2.5.: Sympathy scores for party leaders by reported vote 1971.(medians).
(Bold: most preferred leader; italic: next most preferred.leader)

Voted for	Sympathy scores for						
	Krag	Bauns-gaard	Ninn-Hansen	Larsen	Christen-sen	Hartling	Sigs-gaard
	(SD)	(RV)	(KF)	(SF)	(Krf)	(V)	(VS)
SD	**60.5**	38.2	1.9	*58.6*	0.2	1.0	0.4
RV	-0.1	**81.1**	*41.7*	40.8	0.4	40.3	-0.7
KF	-7.5	**76.5**	*61.7*	21.1	0.8	44.1	-15.0
DR	0	*25.0*	5.0	**40.0**	0	0	-10.0
SF	*21.3*	19.6	-0.5	**80.5**	-1.4	-2.3	19.7
DKP	30.0	32.5	10.0	**80.0**	-75.0	0	*55.0*
Krf	-20.0	*63.3*	45.0	15.0	**70.0**	65.0	-50.0
V	-0.2	78.6	50.4	20.0	0.1	*72.0*	-18.7
VS	0	30.0	-10.0	*60.0*	-20.0	20.0	**60.0**
All	19.6	57.8	20.3	40.7	0.1	20.2	0

[26] Thus Hilmar Baunsgaard was almost universally credited with the strong success of the Radical Liberals in the 1968-election. Likewise Aksel Larsen's appearance on TV prior to the 1960-election is often mentioned as an important contribution to the parliamentary breakthrough of his newly founded Socialist Peoples' Party.

[27] The finding that party leaders play a role in the vote decision need not be incompatible with considering the vote decision a deliberate choice. If the function of the party leader is to make the voter vote for his party just because (s)he likes the appearance of the party leader, i.e. if the merchandise is bought because of the eye-catcher, then we are outside the realms of deliberate choice. If, on the other hand, the function of the party leader is to alert the voter's attention to the existence and the policy position of his party, i.e. if the eye-catcher makes the customer notice the merchandise and its qualities, compare it to competing brands, etc., then we are inside deliberate choice.

Table 2.5. gives the median sympathy grade for each party leader, broken down according to reported vote. Visual inspection at once reveals the existence of a familiar-looking clustering: Voters of the government parties (RV, KF and V) express high esteem for the leaders of these three parties. Socialdemocratic voters hold the leader of the Socialist Peoples' party in next highest esteem, while voters of the Socialist Peoples' party give the next highest median score to the leader of the Socialdemocrats. In general, those who vote for non-socialist parties tend to administer low sympathy grades to the leaders of socialist parties (with the notable exception of the leader of the Socialist Peoples' Party, Aksel Larsen), while those who vote for socialist parties tend to react in the same way to the leaders of non-socialist parties (with the notable exception of the leader of the Radical Liberals, Hilmar Baunsgaard).

The structural features mentioned above must also be expected to become visible in the spatial model of the "party leader space" which is presented in Figure 2.10. below. The map brings out the existence of a tightly knit cluster of non-socialist party leaders, clearly offset from a much more loosely knit cluster of socialist party leaders. The leader of the Christian Peoples' Party does not belong to any of these clusters.

The ordering of the party leader-positions with respect to the horizontal direction corresponds acceptably well to the customary arrangement of their parties on a left right-continuum, and also acceptably well to the horizontal order of the party positions in Figure 2.1. There is little doubt then, that basically the perception of party leaders is structured by the same 'ideological' left-right dimension as the perception of their parties.

Fig. 2.10.: Perception of party leaders 1971

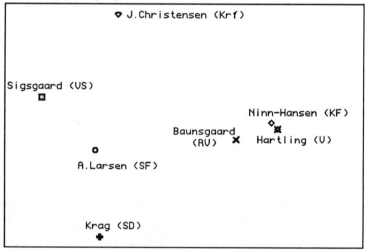

On the other hand, discrepancies between the orderings of parties and party leaders in the vertical direction in Figure 2.1. and Figure 2.10., respectively, are visible. They presumably reflect the influence of one or several valence dimensions on the perception of party leaders. The fit of the map with data (Unweighted $R^2 = 0.70$), which is lower (although still satisfactory by usual standards) than the fit obtained for the map of party perceptions, despite the smaller number of objects to be fitted in the case of party leaders, points in the same direction. For the same reason, the measure of correspondence between the maps in Figure 2.1. and Figure 2.10. remains relatively low (M = 0.48).

We may hence conclude that in 1971 there was a common denominator in the voters' perception of parties and party leaders. This common denominator was the 'ideological' left-right dimension. No matter how trustworthy they looked from the posters or how skillfully they tried to communicate through the media, the basic factor in the perception of the party leaders remained their position on the left right-continuum, and in that respect they remained quite closely tied to the positions of their parties.

Turning to the problem of distrust in politicians, a glance at the bottom line in Table 2.5. shows that the median sympathy score is non-negative for all party leaders, although barely so for the leaders of the two small parties, Krf and VS. The two most popular party leaders (Baunsgaard (RV) and A. Larsen (SF)) even managed to receive positive median scores from voters supporting parties which strongly oppose their owns. Their median sympathy scores highly exceed their parties' median sympathy scores and mark them as the most popular among the party leaders in that election.

This generally high sympathy for party leaders does not agree too well with the low esteem of politicians which is expressed in the respondents' reactions to the "distrust"-items in the same survey. So, on the one hand, the respondents appear deeply suspicious of politicians in general; this attitude was even beginning to creep up in their perception of the parties and the party system. On the other hand, they have been found to exhibit generally favorable attitudes towards party leaders.

This type of discrepancy is not an all that uncommon finding in attitude measurement, however.[28] In studies of tolerance and prejudice, for example, it has been found that the same respondents could express one set of attitudes towards abstract principles or towards issues only remotely relevant to themselves, and a totally different set of attitudes towards concrete issues or in "real" situations calling for the application of just those principles they would endorse in abstract terms.[29]

---

[28] A somewhat sinister indication of how pervading it is can be found in a speech by the notorious chief of the SS, Heinrich Himmler, in which he ridiculed the attitudes of his fellow Germans towards the Nazi-measures against the jews: "... (t)hen they all come, all these 80 million good Germans, and each of them has his decent jew. Sure, all the others are bastards, but this jew is a real fine jew". (The quotation is in Arendt (1964, p.171)).

[29] Cf. Hansen and Nannestad (1975).

Such an apparent inconsistency calls for an explanation.[30] Hypocrisy could be part of it, the interview situation, the leading effect of the items etc. could be another. But it could also be that the respondents were in fact answering two different questions when asked about their attitudes in an abstract and in a more concrete way. When the question is posed abstractly, without any specific references, the answers may well tend to reflect what the respondent thinks is the general norm or the prevailing mood on the issue. When the question is made specific, we may expect to get closer to the respondents' own innermost attitudes - and to how (s)he will act in practice.[31]

If this line of reasoning is applied to the contradictory findings on distrust in politicians in the 1971-survey, one may conclude that the responses to the "distrust"-items demonstrate how the respondents perceived the "general mood" towards politicians (and this "general mood" was obviously rather distrustful and negative). On the other hand, the generally favorable attitudes towards party leaders (and parties as well) seem to indicate that the respondents had not yet internalized this general distrust to a degree where it would be allowed to determine their actual behavior or their feelings towards specific politicians or political parties. This would also explain why the "distrust"-dimension is only just discernible in the perception of the party system in 1971, despite its apparent strength when measured by the "distrust"-items.

So, if the "landslide" in the 1973-election is to be explained by reference to i.a. distrust in politicians, it will not be sufficient to look at the positions taken on the "distrust"-items alone: One shall also have to look for other signs of possible dissatisfaction with and diminishing trust in party leaders and parties.

Finally we shall present some data relevant to the discussion of the importance of sympathy for party leaders in the vote decision. Comparing the median sympathy scores for parties in Table 2.2. to the median sympathy scores for party leaders in Table 2.5. it can be seen that in all but one case those who voted for a particular party gave a higher median score to that party than to its leader. The only exception in that respect is Baunsgaard (RV) who received a slightly higher median thermometer grade by radical liberal voters than did his party. In general then, those who vote for a particular party tend to be more sympathetic towards the party as such than towards its leader.

---

[30] Rasmussen (1987, pp.35-37) suggests an interpretation in terms of the concept of complementarity. Since it is a minor point in the present context, we shall not enter into a discussion of the tenability of this point of view.

[31] This is at least what can be learned from the results of the study mentioned above. As long as the questions were cast in general terms, making no reference to specific minorities at all, the respondents showed high tolerance. As soon as the same questions were made to refer to specific groups, tolerance showed a tendency to dwindle. Reactions to the sudden influx of a substantive number of refugees from Iran and the Middle East showed that the high level of (abstract) tolerance was not in general a good predictor of actual behavior.

Basically the same picture emerges when we look at the proportion of voters for a party that gave a higher thermometer grade to the party leader than to the party itself. These percentages, as shown in Table 2.6., range from about 40 pct. to 0 pct.

Table 2.6.: Percentage of voters giving higher thermometer grade to party leader than to party 1971

	Party						
	SD	RV	KF	SF	Krf	V	VS
Pct. of voters	7.7	39.5	12.5	17.1	0	11.2	0

Once more the popularity of Hilmar Baunsgaard stands out clearly, but in general it seems that a majority of voters tend to vote for a party not because of their feelings towards the party leader, but because of their feelings for the party.

The question as to the relative importance of sympathy for the party and sympathy for the party leader in the vote decision may be approached from still another angle: For the voter of each party one can count the number of times (s)he has given a higher sympathy grade to the leader of a party different from the one (s)he voted for, while at the same time giving a lower sympathy grade to this other party than to the party (s)he voted for, i.e. the number of times party sympathy "overruled" party leader sympathy. Since we have thermometer data for seven party leaders, the maximum number of times party sympathy can "overrule" party leader sympathy in this way is six per voter. In the same way one can count the number of times party leader sympathy "overruled" party sympathy.

Table 2.7.: Party and party leaders in the vote decision 1971

	Party						
Party overrules* party leader	SD	RV	KF	SF	Krf	V	VS
Pct.	13.0	6.0	11.3	3.3	0	9.4	0
(N)	158	29	36	7	0	53	0
Party leader over-rules* party							
Pct.	0.7	1.4	0.3	1.4	0	1.4	0
(N)	8	7	1	3	0	8	0

*see text for explanation

Table 2.7. gives the result. Percentages are computed relative to the theoretical maximum number of "overrulings" among those who voted for a particular party (= number of voters * 6). As can be seen from these figures, the number of times party leader sympathy is allowed to "overrule" party sympathy in the vote decision is small, both absolutely and relatively. It is also considerable smaller than the number of times, party sympathy "overrules" party leader sympathy. Thus, when there is a conflict between sympathy for parties and sympathy for party leaders, party sympathy usually wins.

We may hence conclude that at least in 1971 there is little evidence to suggest that the respondents voted on leader personality rather than on parties or policies. Although findings to the contrary would not necessarily have been damaging to the idea of interpreting voting as an instrumental act, cf. note 27, the present findings are encouraging from the general view of voting on which this study is based.

2.4. The impact of party identification, party vote, class, and party behavior on the perception of the party system 1971

Returning to our main line of argument, we shall examine if there is evidence to suggest that the respondents' perception of the party system and of the parties in it might have been conditioned by their party identification, party preference, or class. As has been mentioned above, identification theory requires us to expect the perception of the party system to be conditioned by party identification, and it was assumed that the same must be true for any class theory of voting. Proposition 2.1. contends this view by asserting that the influence of party identification or class on the perception of the party system will be marginal, if it exists at all.

The goodness of fit (unweighted $R^2 = 0.76$) obtained with a model assuming that all respondents perceive the party system in basically the same way may be taken as a first, crude indication of the validity of proposition 2.1., as far as the election of 1971 is concerned. In Table 2.8. below, this overall measure of fit has been broken down according to party identification[32] and the party voted for (party preference).

From the marginals in Table 2.8. it would appear that the difference with regard to fit of the model between party identifiers and non-identifiers is

---

[32] Respondents are classified as party identifiers, if they gave an affirmative answer when asked the following question: "Many people consider themselves adherents of a particular party. There are also many who do not consider themselves adherents of a party. Do you think of yourself as, e.g., a Socialdemocrat, a Radical Liberal, a Conservative, an Agrarian, a Peoples' Socialist, or something else, or do you not consider yourself an adherent of any of the parties?"

negligible. Taken as a whole, the model fits both groups about equally well. The columns, however, reveal some more pronounced differences to which we shall presently return.

The differences between voters from the various parties with regard to the fit of the model are much more visible. Moreover, they exhibit a rather clear pattern: The communist voters aside, it appears that the model represents the perception of the party space by the voters of the four "old" parties (SD, RV, KF and V) somewhat better than its perception by voters of the small parties. The perception of the party space by voters of the Justice Party and the Christian Peoples' Party seems to be especially "poorly"[33] captured by the model.

The explanation for this finding is probably that voters of these two parties tended to "march to their own tune" and to evaluate the parties in a somewhat different light from the rest of the electorate. The Christian Peoples' Party emphasized moral issues under the heading of "idea politics"; voters attracted by it can hence be imagined to have been people de-emphasizing the left-right dimension in their way of looking at parties, which will make for a relatively poor fit of a model based mainly on this dimension, as is the model shown in Figure 2.1. above.

Table 2.8.: R^2 for perceived party space 1971, broken down by party identification and party voted for

Voted for	R2		
	Party identifiers	Non-identifiers	All
SD	0.74	0.78	0.76
RV	0.83	0.78	0.80
KF	0.85	0.80	0.82
DR	-	0.47	0.47
SF	0.69	0.68	0.68
DKP	0.85	0.88	0.86
Krf	0.53	0.67	0.58
V	0.79	0.76	0.78
VS	-	0.67	0.67
All	0.77	0.74	0.76

Of the Justice Party it has been said that it "... was circling around in the party space throughout its post-war existence. There was neither con-sistency from period to period nor from arena to arena. This party has sometimes been described in Danish political debate as a right-wing party, and sometimes as a party in the middle of the spectrum. Sometimes the party saw itself as truly progressive." (Pedersen et al., 1971, p.100). It seems

---

[33] Still, it should be kept in mind that the R^2-values reported here are high by usual political science standards, even for these two parties.

plausible that voters for a party so flatly defying the left right-continuum in its behavior will tend not to employ an 'ideological' left-right dimension as the main structuring device in their perception of the party system either.

By the same logic it seems explainable why our model should represent the perception of the party system by voters of the orthodox socialist party (DKP) better than its perception by voters of newer, non-orthodox socialist parties (SF and VS). Likewise, keeping in mind the origins and the history of the Danish party system, it seems sensible to expect a model strongly based on a left-right dimension to be able to represent the perception of the party space by adherents of the "old" parties.

Turning to the differences between party identifiers and non-identifiers, in all but three cases party identifiers can be seen to be slightly better represented by our model than are non-identifiers. This finding agrees well with other findings (e.g. Borre and Katz, 1973) showing party identifiers to be more interested in and knowledgeable about politics than non-identifiers. Hence we should expect data on perception of the party system from party identifiers to be less "noisy" than data from non-identifiers, which naturally makes for differences with regard to goodness of fit obtainable.

The fact that respondents identifying with the Christian Peoples' Party are represented poorer by the model than are non-identifiers seems to agree with the explanation suggested above for the generally poorer fit obtained for the voters for this party: If the reason is that they did "march to their own tune", then one should expect those who identify with the party to be even more out of tune with the rest of the respondents. But the result is based on a very small number of observations, so probably not too much should be made of it. The same is true of the difference with regard to fit between identifiers and non-identifiers with the Communists. Here the number of observations is even smaller.

On the other hand, the difference observed with Socialdemocratic identifiers and non-identifiers, respectively, cannot be neglected in the same way. It indicates that the perception of the party system in 1971 by Social-democratic party identifiers did deviate slightly, but systematically, from other respondents' perception.

We may conclude that the differences with regard to the goodness of fit of our model between voters of the various parties and between party identifiers and non-identifiers appear non-random, but exhibit a pattern. Hence party identification and party vote did both have some influence on how the respondents perceived the party system in 1971. But this influence is very limited: A multiple classification analysis (MCA) with the individual respondents' R^2-values as the dependent variable and party identification and party vote as the independent variables shows that the two independent variables jointly account for about 10 pct. of the variance in the R^2-values.[34] It hence seems justified to assert that the influence of party identification and party vote on the perception of the party system was indeed

---

[34] The exact value is $R^2 = 0.09$.

marginal in 1971, as required by proposition 2.1.

In Table 2.9. the overall measure of fit for our model has been broken down by the respondents' class. Housewives and wives assisting their husbands have been assigned to their husbands' class, while married women in the labor force have been assigned to class without regard to the class of their husbands. Respondents not in the labor force (and not under education) are kept as a separate group. Since party identification has been shown to (marginally) influence goodness of fit, the relationship between class and goodness of fit is controlled for party identification.

As can be seen from Table 2.9., there is some variation in goodness of fit according to class, and this variation is not changed when party identification is controlled for.[35] The perception of the party system by people in the middle class and by the self-employed is obviously somewhat better represented by our model than is the perception by working class respondents and by respondents outside the labor force - not to mention respondents under education.

The differences with regard to fit between the first four groups in Table 2.9. do not exceed what might be attributed to different levels of "noise" in the data, however. This also agrees with the pattern exhibited by these differences: We find fit below average in groups which are relatively low in political resources and fit above average in groups that are relatively high in political resources. It appears reasonable to expect people endowed with few political resources to have less interest in and information about politics and hence also a less clear perception of politics in general and of the party system in particular than people commanding a wealth of political resources.

Table 2.9.: R^2 for perceived party space 1971, broken down by class and party identification

	Working class	Middle class	Self-employed	Out of labor force	Under education	All
Party identifiers	0.74	0.83	0.83	0.74	0.76	0.76
Non-identifiers	0.71	0.80	0.77	0.73	0.66	0.74
All	0.73	0.81	0.79	0.74	0.68	0.76

The "noise" interpretation of the differences is supported, when a solution based solely on working class-respondents is obtained. In this group all parties, except for the Left Socialists, are the most preferred party for at least one respondent, and a separate solution - although omitting the Left

---

[35] The same is true when party vote is introduced as controlling variable.

Socialists - can hence be found for this group. The result is shown in Figure 2.11. below, superimposed upon the solution obtained by using the data from all respondents. The bold symbols belong to the working class-solution.

The separate solution fits the working class-respondents somewhat better than does the solution based on data from all respondents (unweighted $R^2 = 0.75$), but the improvement is not exactly dramatic. Moreover, as can be seen at once, the two solutions are very like each other, and the M-value is high (M = 0.89). We may conclude that the model in Figure 2.1. does not misrepresent the perception of working class-respondents in any systematic way.

The goodness of fit obtained for respondents under education, however, suggests that somewhat more than just "noise" may be involved here. Although the number of cases in this group is small and hence susceptible to the influence of a few "misfits", it appears that the perception of the party system in this group might not be as clearly structured by a left-right dimension as it is with other respondents. One might be tempted to hypothesize that the respondents belonging to this group have just not internalized the "usual" way of looking at the party system yet. But it should also be kept in mind that even with this group, we are dealing with R^2-values well above 0.60.

Fig. 2.11.: Perceived party space 1971 with separate solution for working class respondents (bold symbols)

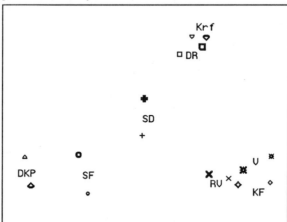

On the basis of the findings reported so far it seems justified to conclude that party vote, party identification and class had only marginal influence on the perception of the party system in 1971. A multiple classification analysis (MCA) with R^2-values as the dependent and party preference, party identification, and class as independent variables accounts for 13.2 pct. of the variance in the respondents' goodness of fit with the model. Clearly, the perception of the party system was only mildly influenced by these factors. Proposition 2.1. is thus supported by the data.

Turning to proposition 2.2., we shall finally show the strong resemblance between the perception of the party system by the respondents in 1971 and the patterns in the parties' legislative behavior that emerges from an analysis of roll call-data from the legislative period 1968-71. Figure 2.12. below shows the map of the party system, derived from the parties' be-havior in roll calls at the final reading of government bills 1968-71 (the "legislative party space"). For easy reference, this map has been superim-posed on the map of the perceived party space from Figure 2.1.

The map of the legislative party space fits the roll call-data well ($R^2 = 0.92$). Moreover, it can be seen to be structured in very much the same way as the perception of the party system by the respondents. The measure of agreement between the two maps is satisfactory ($M = 0.64$). One of the most marked deviations in the position of the parties on the two maps occurs for the Communists, which may be attributable to the rather low reliability of the voting records for the DKP in the 1968-71 legislature (cf. section 1.6. above).

Fig. 2.12.: Legislative party space 1968-71 (bold symbols) superimposed on perceived party space 1971

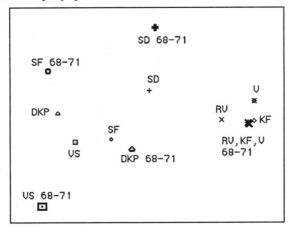

As far as the seven parties represented in the Folketing prior to the election in 1971 are concerned, there is a rather close correspondence between their position in the "legislative party space" and their position in the party space as perceived by the respondents. But if this relationship is to be interpreted as indicating that the parties' legislative behavior determines how they are perceived by the electorate we must also account for how the respondents assess the positions of parties not represented in the Folketing.

The most likely alternative source of information for the respondents to base this assessment on would appear to be party communications during the electoral campaign. An analysis of party communications in radio and television during the electoral campaign in 1971 (Siune, 1982) shows that - as measured by the frequency of positive or neutral references to each other among the parties running in the election - the Justice Party and the Christian Peoples' Party were extremely isolated in the party system. This seems to agree well with their perceived position, cf. Figure 2.1. above.

Thus proposition 2.2. can be considered sustained by the analysis of the 1971-data, as was proposition 2.1. Of course the relationship between the legislative party space 1968-71 and the perceived party space in 1971 does not proof a causal relation to exist. But there is certainly nothing in the data so far to contradict the assumption of a causal link connecting party behavior to the perception of the party system and the perception of the party system to the vote decision that lies at the heart of the concept of voting as deliberate choice.

2.5. Signs of the gathering storm?

The 1971-election has been characterized as a "maintaining" or "normal" election (Borre and Katz, 1973), and as a "low-interest" election (Worre, 1987, pp.53-55). These assessments are based on, i.a., a number of indicators for interest in the campaign, importance of short time-factors, and voter volatility. On these indicators, the 1971-election did indeed differ markedly from the three following elections. On the other hand, voting turn-out was high in 1971 (87 pct.), only 2 pct. below participation in the 1973-election and only about 3 pct. lower than participation in the EEC-referendum in 1972, which both were high interest events. Thus the suspicion remains that beneath the relatively calm surface in 1971 developments might already have been on their way that found their well known expression in the election of 1973.

Looking at our data from that perspective - and, of course, aided by the wisdom of hindsight - the emergence of the second dimension in the respondents' perception of the party system in 1971 may indeed seem to foreshadow the things that were to come: It turns out that the location of the respondents' "ideal points" relative to the second dimension in the maps in Figure 2.1. and 2.2. is related to their probability to switch to the two new parties in 1973, the Center-Democrats and the Progress Party. This can be seen from Table 2.10., which gives the percentage of respondents with their "ideal points" in each of the four quartiles of the vertical distribution of "ideal points" in Figure 2.2., who reported a vote for either the Center-Democrats or the Progress Party in 1973.

As can be seen, the percentage of respondents reporting a vote for the CenterDemocrats in 1973 increases as one moves from the bottom of the

1971-maps towards the top. This agrees well with the proposed interpretation of the vertical direction as being related to dissatisfaction or distrust.

Table 2.10.: Percentage of respondents reporting a vote for CD or Frp in 1973 in each quartile of the vertical distribution of "ideal points" in 1971

	CD	Frp
1. quartile	10.0	12.9
2. quartile	8.5	12.7
3. quartile	5.8	9.1
4. quartile	5.3	19.3

With respondents reporting a vote for the Progress Party in 1973 things look somewhat different. Although the percentage goes down as one moves from the top of the map towards the bottom, it suddenly leaps to its highest in the fourth quartile: The Progress Party in 1973 obviously recruited most successfully among respondents who had their "ideal points" located close to the bottom of the map in 1971, i.e. were in general low in distrust.

This finding does not necessarily contradict the relationship between the vertical direction on the 1971-maps and the tendency to switch to the Progress Party in 1973, however. In the case of the Progress Party, this dimension interacts with the left-right dimension, as can be seen in Table 2.11. Here we give the percentages of respondents with "ideal points" in each of the quartiles of the horizontal distribution of "ideal points" and above and below, respectively, the median of the vertical distribution of "ideal points" who reported a Frp-vote in 1973.

Table 2.11.: Percentage of respondents reporting a vote for the Progress Party in 1973 in each quartile of the horizontal and above/below the median of the vertical distribution of "ideal points" in 1971

Vertical distribution	Horizontal distribution			
	(leftmost) 1. quartile	2. quartile	3. quartile	(rightmost) 4. quartile
above median	10.3	9.4	19.1	14.9
below median	5.0	10.9	15.5	20.3

Table 2.11. indicates that as one moves from right to left across the map, the location of the respondents' "ideal points" relative to the vertical direction tends to get increasingly important for the probability of the respondents switching to the Progress Party in 1973. This means that the Progress Party had a double recruitment basis in 1973: It recruited from people to the right in the political spectrum in 1971, and among these the position of the "ideal points" relative to the vertical direction did not enhance the Progress

Party's chances - rather to the contrary. But it did also recruit from respondents who were in 1971 center-right, center-left, and even left in the political spectrum, and in this group the Progress Party did generally better with respondents who in 1971 had their "ideal points" closer to the top of the map than with those who had their "ideal points" closer to its bottom. Simplifying a good deal one might say that the Progress Party in 1973 recruited from among the rightists, regardless of their level of dissatisfaction in 1971, and among the non-rightists depending on their level of dissatisfaction in 1971.

Turning to one of the big losers in 1973, the Conservatives, the data show that this party was in a precarious situation in 1971 already: Table 2.12. below gives the median distance between each of the four "old" parties and its voters in 1971. As can be seen at once, the median distance between conservative voters and their party clearly exceeds the median distance between the rest of the "old" parties and their voters. Thus we have in 1971 a group of voters to the right in the party space the "ideal points" of which are at an unusual distance from the position taken up by their party.[36]

Table 2.12.: Median distances between the four "old" parties and their voters in 1971

	SD	RV	KF	V
Median distance	0.38	0.29	0.51	0.21

Obviously, these voters were "captive" in the sense of Downs (1957) in 1971. They did not like the position of the Conservatives particularly well, but they apparently had no alternatives (except for the "exit"-option, i.e. non-participation). In 1973, there was an alternative: Not surprisingly, those who voted for the Conservatives 1971, but switched to the Progress Party in 1973, turn out to be voters who did indeed have a larger median distance to their party in 1971 (median distance = 0.54) than did those who stayed with it (median distance = 0.43).

Thus the data suggest that there were in 1971 already voters who were not properly "looked after" by the parties running in the election. There was a vacuum to be filled in the party system, and that is exactly what the two "upshot" parties of 1973 did: As shall be shown in the next chapter, they moved in where the existing parties had left them fertile soil to cultivate.

---

[36] It is tempting to hypothesize - though it cannot be proved by data - that this "estrangement" was brought about by the participation of the Conservatives in a government, which occasionally was ridiculed as "the best Socialdemocratic government ever". At least to some conservative voters, this must have appeared as a desertion to the left by the party.

3. Peripathy: The general election of December 1973

3.1. Background, campaign, and outcome

The events that triggered off the general election of December 1973 have been described in the introductory section above (section 1.1.). In the present section we shall try to convey some further background information relevant to the situation in which the campaign and the election took place.

The parties that participated in the election were mainly the same that had run in the 1971-election. Only the Schlesvigian Party (Slp) stayed out.[1] In addition, two new parties entered the electoral contest, viz. Mogens Glistrup's Progress Party and Erhard Jakobsen's Center-Democrats. Thus in 1973 there were 11 parties to choose among, five of which (SD, RV, KF, SF, and V) were currently holding seats in the Folketing.

Of the five parties represented in the Folketing of 1971, three entered the electoral contest in various states of disarray. These were the Social-democrats, the Conservatives and the Socialist Peoples' Party. These three parties had all experienced a relative recent shift in leadership, accompanied by discussions of and disagreement as to the future direction of the party's policies.

The Socialdemocrats had gone through a period of severe stress in connection with the debate on the EEC-issue. While the party leadership was pro-EEC, the left wing in the parliamentary group, a considerable part of the organization, and roughly half of the constituency was against membership. The trade union movement, with its extremely close ties to the Social-democrats, was divided on the issue too, the split running in some cases between unions and in some cases right through them.

In this situation the party had allowed those opposing the official party line to work actively and openly against it - which they had done vigorously. A committee of "Socialdemocrats against the EEC" (Socialdemokrater mod EF) had been formed to orchestrate a Socialdemocratic campaign against membership - and against the official policy of the party - prior to the referendum on October 2nd, 1972.[2] Thus the usually so highly disciplined party had offered a rare demonstration of open factionalism threatening to tear it apart.

With the EEC-issue tucked away after the referendum, there were wounds to heal and gaps to bridge in the party. The stepping down of the

---

[1] By arrangement with the Center-Democrats, the Schlesvigian Party had a candidate elected on the Center-Democrats' ticket.

[2] The leading figure in the Socialdemocratic EEC-opposition at that time was a young political scientist, Svend Auken. Ambitious, intelligent, and with a keen sense of tactics he seized the opportunity to make himself known as one of the party's rising stars. But at the same time he was wise enough to leave the formal leadership of the committee in the hands of another young Socialdemocratic politician, Karl Hjortnæs, his equal in ambitions.

Socialdemocrats' leader through more than a decade, J.O. Krag, and the appointment (on J.O. Krag's initiative) of Anker Jørgensen as his successor as party leader and prime minister - despite the very limited parliamentary and the non-existent governmental experience of the latter - was intended to facilitate the process of rebuilding unity.

To judge from what was done, it appears that erosion on the left wing was seen as the most imminent danger, and hence the Socialdemocrats under Anker Jørgensen's leadership began courting the left. In the Folketing, co-operation with the Socialist Peoples' Party was intensified on a number of issues, culminating in the "deal" on housing policy in 1973. In programmatic terms, the position of the Socialdemocrats was redefined to be "left of the center". In his very personal and emotional stand on the Vietnam war, Anker Jørgensen adopted and espoused "leftist", anti-American positions. And finally a number of left-wingers and former prominent opponents to EEC-membership were raised to the rank of cabinet ministers in a major cabinet re-shuffle during the summer of 1973.[3]

But the attempts to mend the fences on the left kindled opposition from the opposite side within the party. The appointment of Anker Jørgensen, who was generally considered to be a left-winger, had met with internal dissent in the parliamentary group, though the dissenters had quickly bowed to the pressures applied from the party leadership.[4] As time went by, Erhard Jakobsen emerged as the most prominent critic of the new line, and his criticism gained momentum during the summer of 1973. This finally led to his exodus in November that caused the downfall of the government, when he did not turn up in the Folketing for a roll call division. In struggling to avoid a breach on their left wing, the Socialdemocrats had managed to incur it on the right instead.

The big losers of 1971, the Conservatives, had other reasons for worrying. Their long-time leader, Poul Møller, had resigned from his cabinet post and the party leadership in 1971 due to poor health.[5] He had been replaced in both functions by Erik Ninn-Hansen. The Conservatives had long been split into a number of quarreling factions that disagreed as to the proper role and position of a conservative party in modern society.

---

[3] The above-mentioned Karl Hjortnæs was made minister of justice. Another former committee-member, Ritt Bjerregaard, was made minister of education.

[4] The number of members of the Socialdemocratic parliamentary group who were opposed to the appointment of Anker Jørgensen and preferred the leader of the parliamentary group and centrist socialdemocrat, Orla Møller, for the post instead is not known officially. It has been maintained - especially in the press - that on a paper napkin Orla Møller did have the signatures of a majority of group members who favored him for their new leader and prime minister.

[5] Poul Møller had been minister of finance in the coalition government. Rumors had it that his health problems were caused or at least aggravated by the appearance of Mogens Glistrup in a TV-program in 1971. In this program Glistrup had proved that he - despite high earnings from his tax lawyer business - managed to pay no income taxes at all. This program marked the start of Glistrup's career in politics.

While the new leader represented a rather conventional approach to conservatism, other groups nourished visions of a centrist mass party.

An attempt in 1972 to bring about a settlement between Ninn-Hansen and his strongest rival, Erik Haunstrup-Clemmensen, by appointing the latter chairman of the party organization, while the former retained the parliamentary leadership, had utterly failed. Under the impression of the success of the newly founded Progress Party in the opinion polls,[6] the strife continued and intensified. The Conservatives were thus seriously weakened on the eve of the 1973-election.

So was the Socialist Peoples' Party which had lost its founder and leader in 1972, when Aksel Larsen died. He had become an immensely popular figure, even among the party's strongest adversaries (cf. section 2.3. above). Inside the party he had, i.a., played the role of an integrative symbol, managing to keep together (in most situations[7]) the various currents of socialism that had found shelter in the party. Under the new two-person leadership, the members of which had somewhat different political outlooks, tensions in the party had started to become more visible.

The dominating issues the parties focused on during the campaign were taxes, the labor marked, and housing (in that order).[8] Although taxes were not exactly a new subject in Danish electoral campaigns, their prominence as the prime campaign issue of 1973 was brought about by the Progress Party and the Center-Democrats which campaigned heavily on that issue and hereby forced the other parties to defend themselves or to clarify their positions.[9] The sudden interest for housing as a campaign issue stemmed from the SD-SF "deal" on housing policy concluded in 1973 under exclusion of other parties (cf. section 1.1.) as well as from the Center-Democrats' defense of the interests of house owners.

Having no parliamentary record or historical liabilities to defend, the Progress Party and the Center-Democrats were able to campaign aggressively. Especially the Progress Party relentlessly attacked the "old" parties, viz. the four hitherto dominating parties (SD, RV, KF, and V), invariably referred to as the "veteran parties" by Glistrup.

The Progress Party, of course, campaigned mainly on the tax-issue, demanding tax cuts through budget cuts. Civil servants were attacked as inefficient paper shufflers to be laid off in numbers as quickly as possible. On the other hand, the party demanded improvements in the conditions of old

---

[6] Before founding his own party, Mogens Glistrup had tried to be accepted as a candidate for the Conservatives, but had been turned down.

[7] Defections from the party had occurred, though. The most important took place in 1967 when a left-wing group broke away to form the Left Socialists, hereby causing the downfall of the Socialdemocratic government that was depending on support from the SF.

[8] Cf. Siune (1982, ch.8).

[9] In the broadcasted campaign programs, about 41 pct. of the Center-Democrats' and 39 pct. of the Progress Party's statements contained references to the tax-issue, cf. Siune (1982, pp. 284-289).

age-pensioners. The Center-Democrats concentrated upon taxes with special attention to the tax burdens on house and car owners.

To the voters, taxes appeared the most central political issue, too. On the other hand, they did not consider housing or the labor marked especially pressing problems. Instead, the economy and social problems were ranked second and third in importance.[10]

The results of a number of opinion polls had shown ups and downs for various parties during the campaign. The trend, however, was very clear: The parties represented in the Folketing elected in 1971 (SD, RV, KF, SF, and V) were going to lose votes and seats, and the two new parties stood to profit from it. But only few politicians or observers seem to have envisaged the order of magnitude of the changes the actual election brought about. Table 3.1. below summarizes the outcome of the 1973-election.

Table 3.1.:   Electoral results 1973 (with 1971 for comparison)

Party	21.9.1971		4.12.1973	
	votes (pct.)	seats	votes (pct.)	seats
SD	37.3	70	25.6	46
RV	14.4	27	11.2	20
KF	16.7	31	9.2	16
DR	1.7	0	2.9	5
SF	9.1	17	6.0	11
DKP	1.4	0	3.6	6
CD	-	-	7.8	14
Krf	2.0	0	4.0	7
V	15.6	30	12.3	22
VS	1.6	0	1.5	0
Frp	-	-	15.9	28

Of the five parties represented in the Folketing elected in 1971, Conservatives, Socialdemocrats and the Socialist Peoples' Party were the biggest losers. The Conservatives lost about 50 pct. of their seats (15); from having been the second largest party in the Folketing, they were reduced to the fifth rank. The loss incurred by the Socialdemocrats - they lost 24 seats - was still bigger in absolute numbers, but they retained about 2/3 of their previous strength. The Socialist Peoples' Party also lost one third of its seats (6). The other two parties in the 1971-Folketing - those not burdened with internal strive on the same scale as the three above-mentioned parties - fared slightly better: Both the Agrarians and the Radical Liberals managed to hold on to about 3/4 of their previous strength. Nevertheless, between them the five "old" parties lost about 30 pct. of the vote between 1971 and 1973.

The big winners were the Progress Party - with its 28 seats the second largest party in the new Folketing - and the Center-Democrats. But also the "traditional" small parties in the Danish party system profited: Once more,

---

[10] Siune (1982, p.177).

they succeeded in almost doubling their share of the votes (3.7 pct. in 1968, 6.7 pct. in 1971 and 12.0 pct. in 1973) and, with the sole exception of the Left Socialists, all gained representation.

Forming a government not opposed by a majority from the start was no easy task, given the distribution of seats in the new Folketing. In the vacuum following the resignation of the Socialdemocratic government the day after the election, the leader of the Agrarians, former foreign minister Poul Hartling, seized the opportunity and - bypassing and outmaneuvering his former partners in government, the Radical Liberals and the Conservatives[11] - formed a government, headed by himself as Prime Minister and based solely on the Agrarians' 22 out of the Folketing's 179 seats. It has been guessed that he had come to some kind of understanding with the Center-Democrats and the Christian Peoples' Party beforehand, allowing him to count on their votes. Besides, he probably reckoned that neither the Radical Liberals, the Conservatives, or the Progress Party would dare to join forces with the socialist parties in overthrowing a non-socialist government. On December 19th, 1973, the "narrow" Agrarian government, as it came to be called, took over.

3.2. Perception of the party system 1973

The aim of this section will be to confront propositions 1.1. and 1.2. with data pertaining to the 1973-election. We shall thus be dealing with the informational aspects of the vote decision in 1973.

What did the party system look like to the voters in December 1973? If they were confused, they could hardly be blamed. As has been mentioned already, three of the "old" parties were undergoing a painful process of leadership change, accompanied by the usual diadochian strife about the proper position of the party in the political spectrum. Two new parties had presented themselves within a short span of time, both approaching complex problems which were annoying many people with catchy slogans and offers for handy solutions. Their messages were often unconventional in form as well as in content.

Nevertheless it appears that the voters managed to retain a surprisingly well-structured perception of the party system in connection with the election in 1973. Table 3.2., giving the median sympathy scores by reported vote, conveys a first impression.

Starting in the bottom line, it can be seen that the pattern in the attitudes towards the parties in 1973 resembles the pattern found in the 1971-data. Four of the five "old" parties - SD, RV, KF, and V - were perceived

---

[11] "The Conservatives are in no position to make claims" Hartling retorted when conservative leaders demanded the resurrection of the coalition government based on the Radical Liberals, the Conservatives, and the Agrarians (Avisårbogen, 1973, 13.dec.).

favorably by the voters, obtaining median thermometer grades well above zero. The Socialist Peoples' Party's score had dropped to a little below zero, but since it was only just above that mark in 1971, this constitutes a very modest change. As in 1971, the median scores of Socialdemocrats and Radical Liberals were practically equal, but it can be seen that the Agrarians had managed to catch up, bypassing the Conservatives, which were about equal with the Agrarians in median sympathy in 1971.

Table 3.2.: Sympathy scores by reported vote 1973 (medians).(Bold: most preferred party; italic: next most preferred party)

Voted for	Sympathy scores for										
	SD	RV	KF	DR	SF	DKP	CD	Krf	V	VS	Frp
SD	**49.2**	*22.8*	-0.4	1.0	13.0	-0.2	1.6	1.6	6.3	-0.9	-26.1
RV	9.5	**48.5**	23.2	0.5	-2.4	-25.6	10.0	15.0	*25.0*	-23.7	-2.0
KF	1.0	24.7	**47.5**	1.4	-22.5	-47.5	12.5	18.8	*26.5*	-25.0	0.6
DR	2.5	*18.5*	7.5	**48.3**	-7.5	-24.7	-7.5	7.5	12.5	-1.3	-5.0
SF	*25.0*	0.4	-15.0	9.0	**48.2**	22.7	-0.7	-1.1	-1.4	1.7	-47.7
DKP	24.0	1.1	-0.9	2.5	*28.8*	**40.0**	-4.2	-0.3	0.4	10.0	-46.9
CD	*24.4*	23.7	1.0	-0.1	-2.3	-23.4	**48.5**	16.7	23.0	-2.9	0.3
Krf	0.5	*24.3*	23.1	2.5	-25.0	-49.0	23.4	**47.5**	26.4	-12.5	-0.5
V	9.8	*24.6*	24.3	-0.4	-21.3	-48.2	12.3	22.9	**49.4**	-28.9	0.2
VS	18.8	-10.0	-25.0	10.0	*25.0*	7.5	-10.0	-12.5	-10.0	**50.0**	-45.0
Frp	1.9	*15.5*	7.5	0.9	-23.8	-47.8	14.0	15.5	*24.5*	-24.0	**47.8**
All	24.9	24.7	9.7	0.4	-0.3	-24.2	9.3	10.4	24.4	-0.5	-0.1

Three small parties which had also been running in the 1971-election - DR, DKP, and VS - also exhibit the same pattern in their median sympathy scores as in 1971. The Justice Party and the Left Socialists received median scores just below zero, while the Communists retained their position as the on average most disliked Danish party. The Christian Peoples' Party, on the other hand, had managed to improve its standing with the voters remarkably, obtaining a median score well above zero in 1973, even surpassing the Conservatives in popularity.

The two new parties - CD and Frp - were perceived differently by the respondents. While the Center-Democrats got a median thermometer grade above zero and equalled the Conservatives and the Christian Peoples' Party in sympathy, the Progress Party was rated just a little below zero on average.

On the face of it, the median thermometer grades in the bottom line in Table 3.2. contain little evidence to support the assertion that general distrust in parties and politicians was the distinguishing feature of the 1973-election. The stability found in the patterns seems to suggest that the general attitudes towards the parties had not changed dramatically between 1971 and 1973.

There might,of course, have occurred an "across the board" drop in the level of sympathy towards the parties in the party system, paralleling the rise in the proportion of respondents that agreed to distrust positions on the distrust items in the survey.[12] Since the thermometer grades were measured using different calibrations of the thermometer in 1971 and 1973, the numbers in Table 2.2. and Table 3.2. cannot be compared in a straightforward manner.[13] Thus we cannot tell if sympathy for the various parties has dropped between 1971 and 1973. We shall revert to this question below.

Turning to the rows in the table, it can be seen that in 1973 the Radical Liberals, the Conservatives, and the Agrarians were still perceived as being rather close to each other by their voters. The Agrarians were the second most preferred party for voters for both the Conservatives and the Radical Liberals, while the Radical Liberals were the second most preferred party for Agrarian voters. The Christian Peoples' Party was also perceived rather positively by the voters for these three parties, and voters for the Christian Peoples' party had the Agrarians as their second most preferred party. Thus in 1973 the Christian Peoples' Party was perceived as quite close to these three parties, and the former three-party cluster of liberal-conservative parties had been changed into a four-party cluster by 1973.

On the other side of the political spectrum, ties between Socialdemocrats and the Socialist Peoples' Party seem to have loosened between 1971 and 1973, which may appear surprising keeping in mind the overtures towards the left made by the Socialdemocrats after the EEC-referendum. But it can be seen that in 1973 Socialdemocratic voters did have the Radical Liberals as their second most preferred party, as against the Socialist Peoples' party in 1971, while the Socialdemocrats were still the second most preferred party for voters for the Socialist Peoples' Party in 1973. Both groups still did not care much for the Conservatives or the Agrarians.

The "sympathy profiles" of the voters for the two new parties - CD and Frp - exhibit some interesting similarities as well as differences. CD-voters did have the Socialdemocrats as their second most preferred party. They also liked the Radical Liberals, the Agrarians, and - to a somewhat lesser degree - the Christian Peoples' Party. But they did definitely not care much for the Conservatives or for the Progress Party! Frp-voters, on the other hand, also liked the Agrarians (actually their second most preferred party), the Radical Liberals, and the Christian Peoples' Party quite well, and they were positive towards the Center-Democrats. But they also showed a some-

---

[12] Between 1971 and 1973, the proportion of respondents agreeing that "the politicians spend the taxpayers' money too lavishly" went up by 11 pct. The rise in the percentage agreeing that "politicians generally care too little about what the voters think" was 6 pct., the rise in the percentage agreeing that "people who want to get to the top in politics have to give up most of their principles" was 10 pct., while the percentage disagreing that "in general one can trust our political leaders to make the right decisions for the country" went up by 12 pct.

[13] In 1971, the thermometer ran from -100 to +100. In 1973, it ran from -50 to +50. Since the thermometer grades are probably not exactly linear in "sympathy", just doubling the 1973-scores will not yield valid results.

what surprising chilly attitude towards the Conservatives (as did CD-voters), while it can hardly be surprising that as a whole Frp-voters did not hold the Socialdemocrats in high esteem.

If we look at the perception of the Progress Party by voters from the other parties, it can be seen to have been extremely negative. Only voters from three parties - KF, CD, and V - gave it a positive median score, which in all cases was barely above zero, however. Thus the Progress Party evoked mainly negative responses, except from its own voters. In that respect it was very different from the Center-Democrats which got negative median grades from socialist voters and voters from the Justice Party only while being quite positively perceived by the rest of the electorate.

Figure 3.1. shows the map of the perceived party space in 1973, derived from the respondents' thermometer grading of the parties.[14] The structure of this map is clearly non-random. It exhibits a number of clusters of parties that are perceived as being close to each other by the respondents.

Fig. 3.1.:   Perceived party system 1973

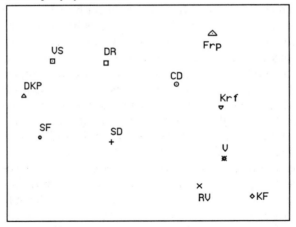

In the lower right corner appears the four party-cluster of RV, KF, Krf and V that also could be identified by visual inspection of Table 3.2. In this region we have the liberal-conservative parties in the party system. As can be seen at once, the distances between RV, KF, and V are somewhat bigger in 1973 than they were in 1971. This is not very surprising, taking into account the change in the parliamentary situation between 1971 and 1973: In 1971, the three parties had been in the government together for three years and had hence been forced to exhibit a higher degree of unity than in their opposition period from 1971 to 1973. It seems only natural that the

---

[14] The map is based on data from 510 respondents returning at least two valid thermometer gradings of the parties.

voters' perception of the parties' positions should reflect these changes.

On the opposite side one finds the socialist parties SD, SF, DKP and VS. These parties are clearly set off from the liberal-conservative parties, but the distances between themselves are also quite substantial. Though the respondents perceived a socialist bloc to exist in the Danish party system in 1973, they also perceived it as rather heterogeneous. Not surprisingly the Socialdemocrats were seen as the socialist party closest to the non-socialist bloc. In fact, they were perceived as being just "left of the center".

The position of the Justice Party relatively close to the socialist bloc, and not the least to the Left Socialists, may surprise, since this party in a number of respects must be considered an extremely liberal party. Its position in the perceived party system of 1973 was possibly brought about by its marked anti-EEC stand which put it into close contact with a number of socialist parties. As the only non-socialist party, it cooperated with a number of them in the Popular Movement Against the EEC ("Folkebevægelsen mod EF") which may have tinted the perception of its general position in the party space.

The two new parties, CD and Frp, are offset from both the liberal-conservative and the socialist cluster. If seen with respect to the horizontal direction, the Center-Democrats occupy the middle ground between the socialist and the liberal-conservative bloc, i.e. roughly the "vacuum" that could be identified in the perceived party space of 1971. The position of the Progress Party, on the other hand, coincides with the horizontal position of the liberal-conservative cluster of parties. If the horizontal direction on the map in Figure 3.1. can be interpreted as the left-right dimension, as it could on the 1971-map and as is strongly suggested for the 1973-map as well by the positions of the socialist and the liberal-conservative parties, then one may conclude that obviously the Progress Party in 1973 was not perceived as being markedly rightist in orientation.[15]

In Figure 3.2. the respondents' "ideal points" have been added to the map. The distribution of these "ideal points" on the map also shows a clearly non-random pattern. As can be seen, the distribution of the "ideal points" is oriented in a north-eastern direction. This is different from the situation in 1971, where the main direction in the distribution of "ideal points" was horizontal, despite "stretches" running towards the north-eastern and the north-western corners of the map, respectively.

The interpretation of this difference is straightforward: While the position of the "ideal points" in 1971 was mainly determined by the horizontal direction which subsequently could be identified as the left-right dimension the position of the "ideal points" in 1973 is jointly determined by both the

---

[15] In the literature the Progress Party is often described as a rightist, and sometimes even as a radical rightist, party, e.g. in Elder et al. (1988, pp.89-90), but this was obviously not how the voters saw it in 1973. This finding agrees well with findings reported in Nielsen (1979) and Glans (1984), demonstrating that the attitudes of Progress Party voters towards a number of issues were not markedly rightist.

horizontal and the vertical directions. We shall revert to the substantive interpretation of these directions below.

Fig. 3.2.: Parties and "ideal points" in perceived party space 1973*

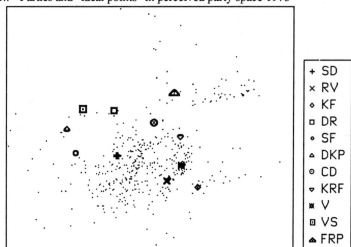

+	SD
×	RV
◇	KF
□	DR
○	SF
△	DKP
⊙	CD
▽	KRF
✳	V
▫	VS
▲	FRP

* 5 outliers removed.

The fit between map and data is quite good (unweighted $R^2 = 0.65$; weighted $R^2 = 0.82$), although it is lower than for the 1971-map. In part this is attributable to the increased number of parties to be fitted in 1973, but it may also partly be an expression of a less clearly structured perception of the party system in 1973.

Table 3.3.: Reported and "hindcasted" distribution of votes 1973

	Distribution of votes	
	reported	"hindcasted"
Party	(n = 493)	(n = 510)
SD	30.0	31.7
RV	12.6	16.1
KF	5.3	6.3
DR	2.2	1.4
SF	5.9	5.5
DKP	2.6	1.8
CD	7.5	6.1
Krf	3.7	4.9
V	16.2	13.3
VS	0.6	0.8
Frp	13.4	12.2

If we look at the "hindcasted" distribution of party votes which can be obtained from the map under the assumption that respondents vote for the party closest to their "ideal point", it appears that the deviations from the reported party vote are greater than in 1971 (NS = 0.08), although the resemblance between the two distributions remains quite close, cf. Table 3.3. As with the 1971-data, the Agrarian proportion of the vote is seriously underestimated in the "hindcast". The Radical Liberals, on the other hand, fare too well this time. These deviations also seem to suggest a slightly less clear perception of the party system in 1973, compared to 1971.

Finally, the proportion of correctly "hindcasted" party votes at the individual level in 1973 is also a bit below the corresponding figure from 1971. Still, in 83.3 pct. of all cases the party a respondent reported to have voted for in 1973 is the party the respondent "should" have voted for according to the position of his or her "ideal point" on the map in Figure 3.2.

Although the goodness of fit of the model is slightly poorer with the 1973-data than it was with the 1971-data on all three criteria, it is still good enough to allow us to conclude that the data provide evidence to the fact that the respondents in 1973 did possess a clear perception of the party space and of the parties in it. Given the highly unusual and unstable situation created by the appearance on the stage of two new parties as well as the disarray in three of the "old" parties, the data show surprisingly little sign of voter confusion: Apparently, the voters knew quite well what they were choosing among. Thus proposition 1.1. shall once more be considered sustained by these findings.

Having obtained a map of the perceived party space in 1973, we may revert to the problem of how to compare the level of sympathy for the parties (as an expression of trust or distrust) in 1971 and 1973 to see if any dramatic changes had taken place between the two elections that may help to explain the "landslide". As was mentioned above, we cannot hope to obtain a valid comparison by looking at the thermometer scores directly, since these scores were obtained using two different thermometers. What we can compare, however, are the distances between "ideal points" and parties on the two maps derived from the thermometer scores.[16]

---

[16] Here we are capitalizing on the fact that using multidimensional scaling models one may derive interval-level measurements from ordinal observations (cf. Nannestad, 1985, pp.21-25). Naturally, reliability and validity of these derived measurements will depend on the validity of the model and the reliability of the solution obtained. Since our models do not fit the observations perfectly, the validity of the distances between "ideal points" and parties as interval-level measurements of the respondents' sympathy towards the parties is less than perfect. It should not be overlooked, however, (as it normally is) that whenever numbers are attached to observations, there is some kind of measurement model involved, and hence the problems of reliability and validity arise in all cases. The main difference seems to be that normally the measurement models applied in political science measurement are not made explicit and that there hence is no way of evaluating their appropriateness numerically. To put things squarely, despite the less than perfect fit of the models there is no a priori reason to expect the derived measurements to be used in this context to be any less reliable and valid than what is normal with most conventional measurements in political science. After all, simply assigning numbers from 1 to n to the categories on a Likert-type scale and using these numbers as interval-level measurements -

After suitable normalization[17] of the configurations in Figure 2.2. and Figure 3.2. (as to make sure they are on the same scale), we can compare the median distances between respondents and parties in 1971 and in 1973. Table 3.4. below shows the changes, expressed as percentages relative to the 1971-medians.

Table 3.4.: Change in median distances between respondents' "ideal points" and parties between 1971 and 1973

	Party								
	SD	RV	KF	DR	SF	DKP	Krf	V	VS
Change in pct. of 1971-median	31.7	16.2	25.4	-16.0	34.7	8.1	-29.3	-7.0	15.1

Table 3.4. suggests that there was no "across the board"-drop in party sympathy between 1971 and 1973. For six parties an increase in the median distances to the respondents' "ideal points" is found. These parties - SD, RV, KF, SF, DKP, and VS - lost sympathy between 1971 and 1973. The most dramatic change occurred for the Socialdemocrats and the Socialist Peoples' Party, but it should be noticed that taken together the three parties mentioned above as "parties in disarray" suffered the heaviest loss of sympathy. On the other hand, three of the parties that ran both in 1971 and 1973 were able to increase their popularity between 1971 and 1973, the Christian Peoples' Party faring best in this respect.

Although it appears that there is not much of a basis for talking of a general loss of trust in political parties between 1971 and 1973 in these numbers, Table 3.4. reveals that four of the five "old" parties had in fact lost sympathy by 1973, while two parties outside this group had gained. Thus the "distrust" seems to have been selective rather than general: A certain estrangement had obviously taken place between voters and four of the five parties making up the core of the Danish party system prior to the 1973-election. But it must be kept in mind that the four of them still obtained median sympathy scores well above zero.

Turning now to our proposition 1.2., the next task becomes to possibly identify the basic dimensional structuring of the distribution of parties and "ideal points" in Figures 3.1. and 3.2. to see if it can be identified as reflecting an 'ideological' structure in the respondents' belief system. The very fact that the respondents proved themselves able to retain a clear picture of the party system and the whereabouts of the parties in it - despite the turmoil leading up to the election of 1973 - suggest some structuring

---

possibly even across scales to form additive indices and the like - is still a widespread practice in the field!

[17] The coordinates of the parties were normalized to 11 (= the number of parties in the 1973-map). The coordinates of the "ideal points" were adjusted correspondingly.

frame of reference to have been at work.

The distribution of parties along the horizontal direction in Figure 3.1. can be seen to be roughly the same as in Figure 2.1. This suggests that the horizontal direction in the party space of 1973 may once more represent an 'ideological' left-right dimension in the respondents' perception of the party system. The main difference between Figure 2.1. and Figure 3.1. lies in the vertical arrangement of the parties.

The vertical direction on the map in Figure 3.1. separates the "core" of the Danish party system - i.e. the five "old" parties (SD, RV, KF, SF, and V) - from its periphery, consisting of the two new and the various small parties. Thus the respondents obviously perceived some kind of "likeness" between the "old" parties on the one hand and between the new and the small ones on the other, a likeness that transcended their different positions with respect to the left-right dimension. We shall revert to the question of what possibly made them perceive the parties in this way after examining the role of the left-right dimension in the perception of the party system in 1973.

In the 1973-wave of the panel, no independent direct or indirect measurements of the respondents' own position with respect to the left-right dimension were obtained. Thus the interpretation of the horizontal direction in Figure 3.1. as the expression of a left-right dimension in the re-spondents' perception of the party system in 1973 cannot be validated using the same procedure as in section 2.2. above.[18] It may be validated, however, by examining the respondents' issue-positions on a number of economic items.

In 1973, the respondents' positions were recorded on four economic items. Two items dealt with taxes,[19] one item with economic equality,[20] and one item with the role of the state in the economy.[21] Three of these items (VAR122, VAR124 and VAR127) were also used in 1971, and the pattern in the responses to them in 1971 has been shown to be structured by the left-right dimension.

Figure 3.3. shows the distribution of the respondents' median "ideal points" in each category on the scales belonging to the four economic items in 1973. For ease of reference the median "ideal points" in the neutral category have been left out, and only a "zoom"-view of the relevant part of the map in Figure 3.1. is shown.

As can be seen from Figure 3.3., agreement to positions favoring eco-nomic equality and state intervention in the economy (state control with in-

---

[18] Contrary to Worre (1987) we do not feel free to combine observations separated by several years in time and relating to rather different situations. Therefore, the attitudes expressed by the respondents toward rightists in 1971 will not be used here.

[19] VAR120 ("Wage-earners should accept to have some of the pending CoL-regulations frozen, if taxes are lowered instead") and VAR122 ("High incomes should be taxed harder than today").

[20] VAR127 ("In politics one should strive to make economic conditions equal for all, regardless of education and job").

[21] VAR124 ("There is too little state control with private investments").

vestments) tends to decrease as one moves from the left to the right across the map in Figure 3.1, and hence from positions close to the socialist parties (with respect to the horizontal direction) towards positions close to the liberal-conservative parties (once more with respect to the horizontal direction) in the party system. So does agreement to positions favoring higher taxes on high income, while support for the idea of "freezing" a number of pending CoL-regulations of wages in return for tax cuts increases as one moves towards the right.

Fig. 3.3.: Perceived party space and issue positions on economic issues 1973

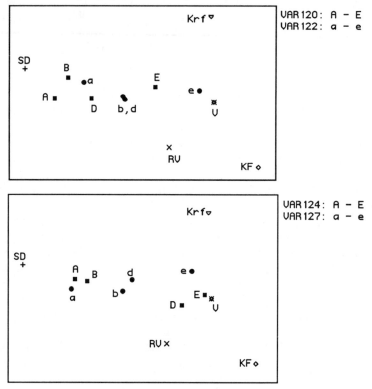

A, a: Agree completely; B, b : Do agree in part; D, d: Do disagree in part; E, e: Disagree completely

The horizontal direction on the map thus clearly has an economic left-right content. Once more it can be seen that agreement to positions in favor of economic equality, state intervention in the economy, and higher taxes on high income extends to near the center of the party space, and hence was not an isolated left-wing attitude in 1973.

Besides economic issues, foreign policy issues could be shown in 1971 to have evoked reactions, the pattern of which was obviously structured by the left-right dimension. In the 1973-wave of the panel, apart from a number of EEC-items, only one foreign policy-item was presented.[22] Figure 3.4. above shows the position of the median "ideal points" corresponding to each of the five categories on the scale.

As can be seen from Figure 3.4., attitudes towards NATO-membership do indeed have a tendency to grow more positive as one moves horizontally from the left to the right across the map of the perceived party system in 1973. But in contrast to 1971, the issue positions appear slightly deflected in the north-western direction.

Part of the explanation of this change is probably the ambivalent attitude towards NATO in the Progress Party. Mogens Glistrup did not consider NATO-membership (or military defense at all) worthwhile for Denmark.[23] In fact, the proportion of Progress Party-voters agreeing (completely or in part) to leaving NATO as soon as possible is far higher than it "should" be if one only looks at the party's position relative to the left-right dimension: Not less than 27.7 pct. of its voters in the 1973-wave of the panel agreed (completely or in part) to the item. In comparison, 3.8 pct. of the voters for the Conservatives, 11.8 pct. of the voters for the Christian Peoples' Party, and 7.8 pct. of the voters for the Agrarians took this stand.[24]

Fig. 3.4.: Perceived party space and issue positions on foreign policy issue 1973

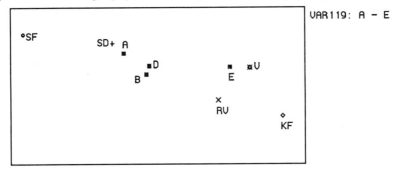

A: Agree completely; B: Do agree in part; D: Do disagree in part; E: Disagree completely

In 1971, the issue positions brought out by various EEC-items had been closely related to position on the left-right dimension, although they had not coincided completely with that dimension: Anti-EEC attitudes had been correlated with leftist positions while supporters of EEC-membership were

---

22 VAR119 ("We should leave NATO as soon as possible").

23 Hence his proposal to have an automatic phone answering service saying (in Russian) "We surrender" take over the functions of the Danish army.

24 Still more surprising, respondents reporting a vote for the Center-Democrats turn out to be even more anti-NATO in 1973, 28.6 pct. agreeing totally or in part to the item. As a party, the Center-Democrats were strongly and outspokenly pro-NATO and pro-EEC.

to be found predominantly to the right in the political spectrum.

The 1973-wave of the panel contained six items on the EEC-issue.[25] Four of these (VAR140, VAR141, VAR143, and VAR144) had also been used in 1971. Issue positions on the two new EEC-items (on establishing an European army and an European government) do not exhibit any clear pattern at all. The reason for this is possibly their hypothetical nature: Neither an European army nor an European government were part of the treaty, Denmark had decided to join. While EEC-opponents could thus be expected to be against an European army and an European government as part of their general anti-EEC attitude, it would be perfectly consistent with a favorable attitude towards Danish membership of the EEC to be against the idea of an European army and an European government. Moreover, as has been seen on several previous occasions, hypothetical or pseudo-issues tend to induce high amounts of randomness in the answers.

Fig. 3.5.:   Perceived party space and issue positions on four EEC-items 1973

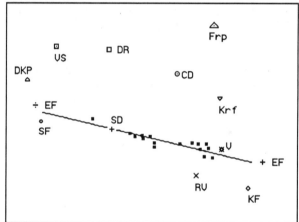

Figure 3.5. shows the median "ideal points" for the respondents belonging in each of the four non-neutral categories on the scales defined by the four EEC-items that produce a pattern. Once more, a line has been fitted to the point scatter by least squares to indicate the overall direction.

As can be seen at once, the picture that emerges is remarkably like the picture in Figure 2.8. Issue positions on the EEC-issue were still strongly

---

[25] VAR139 ("An European army should be established in the course of the next few years"), VAR140 ("The EEC is governed in a way which is incompatible with Danish democratic traditions"), VAR141 ("As a consequence of our membership of the EEC, foreign capital will gain too much influence on Danish industry"), VAR142 ("At some time in the future, the countries in the EEC should establish a common government"), VAR143 ("Membership of the EEC will be a great economic advantage to Denmark"), and VAR144 ("EEC-membership means giving up our national independence").

related to positions on the left-right dimension in 1973, but on the other hand not totally determined by it. The fact that in the meantime the issue had been decided upon does not seem to have had much effect, if any at all.[26]

So far then, the analysis has established the existence of a 'ideological' left-right dimension in the voters' perception of the party system in 1973, corresponding to the horizontal direction in the maps in Figures 3.1. and 3.2. This dimension has been shown to be the ordering principle behind the positions taken on a number of economic issues, while a foreign policy-issue and issue positions on the EEC are partially dependent on it. This leaves the vertical direction in the maps to be accounted for.

With the 1971-data a second dimension, being related to attitudes of political distrust or dissatisfaction, was found in the respondents' perception of the party system. A look at the maps of the perceived party system in Figures 3.1. and 3.2. shows that in 1973 there is a clear vertical separation between the positions of the "old" parties (SD, RV, KF, SF, and V) and the "new" or peripheral ones (DR, DKP, CD, VS, and Frp). This arrangement at once suggests of some kind of distrust- or dissatisfaction-dimension having been at work in the respondents' perception of the parties in 1973. Hence we shall primarily be looking for this feature in an attempt to interpret the vertical direction on the maps.

Table 3.5.: Net majorities (percentages) agreeing to three "distrust"-items in each quartile of the vertical distribution of the "ideal points" in 1973

	VAR128*	VAR131	VAR133
1. quartile	6.1	40.4	76.8
2. quartile	3.4	33.9	58.7
3. quartile	2.5	24.8	56.1
4. quartile	1.2	22.2	56.0

* Polarity of item reversed

In the 1973 panel wave six items pertaining to the "distrust in politicians"-issue were presented, four of which had been used in the 1971-wave as well[27] (where two of them had failed to yield a clear pattern of issue

---

[26] Thus it seems that the conclusion in Petersen and Elklit (1973, p.212), saying that "(F)ears that the emotions evoked during the campaign would die out only slowly and that the conflict over the EEC would remain a salient issue in Danish politics for a long time, in the end proved premature" might itself have been a bit premature.

[27] VAR128 ("In their policies, the various governments take into account the way people like me vote"), VAR131 ("The political parties are only interested in getting my vote, not in what I think"), VAR133 ("Politicians usually do care too little about what the voters think"), VAR134 ("The politicians spend the taxpayers' money too lavishly"), VAR135 ("In general one can trust our political leaders to make the right decisions for the country"), and VAR136 ("People wanting to make it to the top in politics are forced to give up most of their principles").The four items re-used in 1971 as well were VAR133, VAR134, VAR135, and VAR136.

positions). Three of the six items used in 1973 deal with an "estrangement"-aspect of the distrust-attitude (VAR128, VAR131 and VAR133): In one way or another, they deal with the problem of politicians not being responsive to the voters' opinions.

As can be seen from Table 3.5. above, the probability of an affirmative response to these items turns out to be related to the vertical location of the respondents' "ideal points" on the 1973-map: As one moves from the top of the map towards the bottom, the tendency to express attitudes of distrust in and dissatisfaction with the politicians' way of handling their role as representatives tends to get weaker.

Thus respondents with "ideal points" close to the top of the map tend to be the most estranged ones towards politicians. At the same time, they are closer to the "peripheral" parties in the party system than to the "core" parties. This finding then agrees well with the observation of "selective distrust" above, where it was found that sympathy for the "old" parties (minus the Agrarians) had dwindled between 1971 and 1973, while sympathy for some of the small and new parties had increased.

Fig. 3.6.: Perceived party space and issue positions on distrust- and social benefit-item 1973

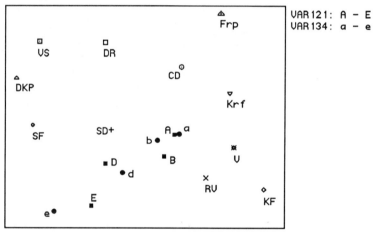

A, a: Agree completely; B, b : Do agree in part; D, d: Do disagree in part; E, e: Disagree completely

Figure 3.6. shows the median "ideal points" of the respondents in each of the four non-neutral categories on the scale belonging to VAR134 (on the politicians spending the taxpayers' money too lavishly). Here the issue positions are strung out in a north-eastern direction, which suggests that the responses to this item are simultaneously determined by both the left-right dimension and the distrust- or dissatisfaction-dimension: In general, people to the right are more prone to agree that the politicians spend the taxpayers' money too lavishly than are leftists, but there is also a clear tendency for respondents endorsing that view to have their "ideal points" located closer to the top of the map than have respondents who disagree.

Moreover Figure 3.6. shows a relationship between the position taken on VAR134 and the position taken on an item dealing with the Danish welfare system.[28] Thus the respondents' dissatisfaction with the politicians' way of handling money appears to have had a concrete policy-content as well.

Figure 3.7. shows the median "ideal points" in each of the non-neutral categories on the scale belonging to VAR136 (On politicians having to give up most of their ideals in order to make it to the top). As can be seen, the median "ideal points" are strung out in the north-western direction in this case.[29] Obviously leftists are more prone to agree to this item than are rightists, but once more there is also a clear tendency for respondents endorsing that view to have their "ideal points" located closer to the top of the map than have respondents who disagree.

Fig. 3.7.: Perceived party space and issue positions on distrust item 1973

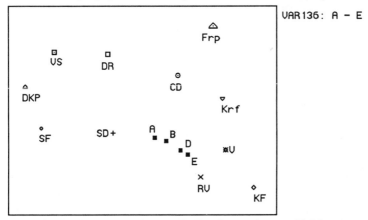

A: Agree completely; B : Do agree in part; D: Do disagree in part; E: Disagree completely

It then appears that in 1973 there was a "right" distrust as well as a "left" one: Rightists tended to distrust the politicians to safekeep money, while leftists tended to distrust them to safekeep ideals.

---

[28] VAR121 ("Too many people get social benefits without really needing them").

[29] In fact, the direction defined by the issue positions on this item are highly parallel to the direction defined by the issue positions on the EEC-issue. Thus we have a connection between being against the EEC and thinking that to get to the top, politicians have to give up most of their principles.

Two other items may help to further clarify the meaning of the vertical direction on the maps in Figures 3.1. and 3.2. The first one can be interpreted as measuring trust in the regime (in the sense of Easton (1965)) rather than in the authorities[30] (as do the above-mentioned items). The second item has bearings on a tolerance-issue, viz. tolerance towards deviant points of view and lifestyles, or towards marginal groups in society.[31] Table 3.6. shows the net majorities in each of the four quartiles of the vertical distribution of "ideal points" in the 1973-maps agreeing to VAR118 and VAR123.

Once more a clear picture emerges: Not only distrust in the authorities, but also distrust in the regime tends to increase as one moves towards the top of the map. Moreover, this distrust or dissatisfaction seems to be accompanied by lack of tolerance towards "outgroups".

Table 3.6.: Net majorities (percentages) agreeing to VAR118 and VAR123 in each quartile of the vertical distribution of the "ideal points" in 1973

	VAR118	VAR123
1. quartile	68.0	44.0
2. quartile	62.7	25.6
3. quartile	52.1	13.8
4. quartile	21.5	10.9

It seems evident, then, that the respondents' perception of the party system in 1973 was structured by a perceptual framework (or belief system) containing two over-arching, general attitudes or dimensions which determined how they perceived the relationship between the parties and how they related themselves to the parties.

The first of these was the traditional left-right dimension of Danish politics. This dimension imposed an ordering of the parties from socialist to conservative and bundled the perceived positions of the parties with issue positions regarding i.a. the role of the state in the economy, economic equality and (in part) membership of NATO.

The other one, cutting across the left-right dimension, may be labelled a "backlash"-dimension. This dimension imposed an ordering of the parties from the "old" and hitherto dominating parties to the new and small (and hitherto peripheral) ones and bundled the perceived positions of the parties with respect to this dimension with positions primarily on the issue of

---

[30] VAR123 ("It might be sensible to have a strong man take power in an economic crisis").

[31] VAR118 ("Christiania should be shut down immediately"). Christiania was a complex of barracks in Copenhagen, which had illegally been taken over by a group of hippies, slum-stormers a.s.o. in 1971. They had made it a center of alternative lifestyles which, however, had shown a tendency to clash with various laws and regulations, for example concerning the possession and use of drugs.

trust/distrust in the "old" parties, their politicians, and some of their policy contents.

As has been shown above, the issue positions on several issues are jointly determined by the left right- and the backlash-dimension, as witnessed by a roughly diagonal arrangement of the median "ideal points" in each of the scales' categories. Reverting to Figure 3.2., it can be seen that the same must be true for the positions of the "ideal points" of the bulk of respondents, since the main direction in the distribution of these "ideal points" on the map runs diagonally towards the upper-right corner. Thus for most respondents, their perceived relationship to the parties was jointly determined by both dimensions.

Finally we shall examine the relationship between the 'ideological' dimensions in the respondents' perception of the party system in 1973 and structural cleavages in society. As in 1971 one should expect the left-right dimension to be related to the labor-capital cleavage of capitalist society. Figure 3.8. shows the position of the median "ideal points" for respondents belonging to different social classes and groups.[32]

Fig. 3.8.:   Perceived party space and class 1973

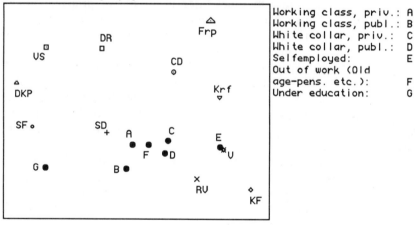

Working class, priv.:	A
Working class, publ.:	B
White collar, priv.:	C
White collar, publ.:	D
Selfemployed:	E
Out of work (Old age-pens. etc.):	F
Under education:	G

As can be seen at once, the horizontal direction in the map does indeed correspond to a labor-capital cleavage: Workers tend to place themselves to the left, self-employed to the right, with white collar occupations between

---

[32] As far as possible, respondents have been classified in the same way as in 1971. Thus married wives in the labor force have been assigned to class according to their own occupational status. Since data on husbands' class are not available in the 1973-wave of the panel, housewives could not be assigned to their husbands' class as they were in 1971. They have been left out of the analysis. Neither has it been possible to identify respondents who were unemployed. They are classified according to their most recent occupational status. Since unemployment was still low in 1973, this probably does not matter much

them. Compared to the situation in 1971 (cf. Figure 2.11.), young people under education seem to have moved to the left: On the 1973-map they appear as the leftmost group, being located just a bit to the left of workers. The most likely explanation is, of course, the "youth rebellion" of the late sixties and early seventies. Since the group numbers very few respondents in 1971, and still fewer in 1973, the result should be approached with some caution, however.

Figure 3.8. reveals another interesting pattern, which was not found in 1971: As can be seen, those being employed in the private sector of the economy or being self-employed are on average located somewhat nearer to the top of the map than those employed in the public sector or being otherwise depending on support from the public. Thus the vertical direction on the map - or the 'ideological' "backlash"-dimension - seems to be related to a certain degree of polarization between occupational groups in the private sector on one side and groups which in one way or the other depend on the public for their income on the other.

Considering the historical records of the various parties as well as the positions announced prior to the election, this finding makes good sense. The hostile attitude of the Progress Party towards civil servants - "the new overlords", as they were sometimes titled in the party's propaganda - has already been mentioned. The party often extolled the virtue of "productive labor" as opposed to academic or paper work. The attitude of the Center-Democrats was not in general quite as negative. They concentrated on criticizing the left-wing propagandist activities allegedly indulged in by employees of the Danish Radio and Television Services and by people in educational institutions. But both parties were strongly opposed to raising taxes, advocating budget cuts to rectify some of the country's economic troubles, a policy that in general could hardly be felt to be in the interest of public employees.

The "old" parties, on the other hand, shared responsibility for building a welfare state based on a large and seemingly ever-growing public sector. The experience of a liberal-conservative government 1968-71 had shown that, regardless of occasional rhetorical bows to ideas of stopping the growth of the public sector and cutting taxes, the bourgeois parties did not pose a threat to the public sector, not even to its continuing growth. From economic self-interest, the choice whether to place one's sympathy with the "old" or the peripheral parties can hardly have been a difficult one for those economically dependent on the public.

Figure 3.8. then seems to witness that an additional structural cleavage in Danish society had become politically relevant and salient in 1973, cutting across the time-honored labor-capital cleavage and arraying those depending on the public for their means of livelihood against those deriving their income from working in the private sector of the economy.

The thesis that the class struggle based on the antagonism of labor and capital is going to be either replaced or supplemented by other forms of "class struggle" has repeatedly been put forward in the literature.[33] It is probably no coincidence, but rather an expression of the prevailing mood (or "Zeitgeist") of the time, that two books dealing with the emergence of a new "ruling class" of civil servants and public employees exploiting those producing goods in the private sector did appear in Denmark in 1973 and 1974, titled "The Ruling Class" (Dich, 1973) and "The Tyranny of Institutions" (Haarder, 1974), respectively.

Usually theses of this type try to establish the existence of "objective" clashes of interest between those allegedly exploiting - be it managers, "Sinnproduzenten",[34] or civil servants - and those allegedly "exploited" by them. But most often they fail to supply empirical evidence that these alledged clashes of interest do indeed translate into political behavior of those affected, as does the labor-capital cleavage. The result presented above may appear to provide a first trace of empirical evidence in that direction.

In conclusion it appears that our propositions 1.1. and 1.2., concerning the informational aspect of the vote decision, have been confirmed. Despite the turmoil leading up to and accompanying the election of 1973, the respondents did retain a clear perception of the party system and of the parties to chose among. This perception was structured by a belief system consisting of two 'ideological' dimensions, viz. the traditional left-right dimension of Danish politics which remains related to the labor-capital cleavage in society, and a new "backlash"-dimension related to a polarization between those having their occupation in the private sector of the economy and those depending on the public for their income.[35]

3.3. Another digression: Perception of party leaders 1973

Once more, we shall embark on a short detour to look at the respondents' perception of party leaders in 1973 before moving on to test our propositions 2.1. and 2.2. As in section 2.2. above, we shall be interested to see if the perception of party leaders in 1973 appears to have been structured by the same belief system as the perception of the parties. We shall also try to produce further evidence as to the development of political distrust between

---

[33] Quite often, such theses are ultimately rooted in the class theory of Veblen (1899). One of the classic examples is Burnham's "The Managerial Revolution" from 1941.

[34] "Sinnproduzenten" (Producers of meaning, e.g. sociologists, psychologists, journalists, academic teachers, and the like) are the exploiting class in modern western societies according to Schelsky (1975).

[35] Therefore, to speak of the "decrease in class polarization" on the basis of decreasing polarization along the left right-dimension alone, as in Thomsen (1987, pp.101-105), is to convey an incomplete impression of how the cleavage structure in Danish society has developed, especially during the later years.

the elections and to its extent in 1973. Finally, we shall once more probe into the role of party leader personality in the vote decision of 1973. In this election, the two victorious parties - the Center-Democrats and the Progress Party - were quite often identified with their leaders, Erhard Jakobsen and Mogens Glistrup, respectively. Thus we shall see if the conclusion arrived at in section 2.2. on the rather limited importance of party leaders (vis-a-vis the party) for the vote decision will stand up.

Table 3.7. gives the median sympathy grades for party leaders, broken down according to reported party vote. As can be seen, sympathy scores were obtained for three Socialdemocratic leaders: Anker Jørgensen (the actual leader of the Socialdemocratic Party), Orla Møller who had been Anker Jørgensen's closest rival to the succession of Krag in 1972 (cf. section 3.1.), and Per Hækkerup who had been a central figure in the party for many years. Likewise, sympathy scores were obtained for the two rival conservative leaders, Ninn-Hansen (the leader of the parliamentary group) and Haunstrup-Clemmensen (the leader of the party organization) who was normally considered the exponent of a "centrist" wing within the party. On the other hand, there are no data for the leaders of the small parties.

Table 3.7.: Sympathy grades for party leaders by reported vote 1973 (medians). (Bold: most preferred leader; italic: next most preferred leader)

Voted for	Sympathy grades for									
	Jørgen-sen (SD)	Hække-rup (SD)	Møller (SD)	Bauns-gaard (RV)	Ninn-Hansen (KF)	Haun-strup (KF)	Lange (SF)	Jakob-sen (CD)	Hart-ling (V)	Gli-strup (Frp)
SD	**47.5**	*27.0*	25.5	22.5	-0.2	1.1	10.6	10.0	8.8	-26.4
RV	1.4	14.8	18.8	**47.9**	24.2	23.5	-1.0	15.5	*26.6*	-5.0
KF	0	6.3	15.4	24.0	25.2	**32.5**	-1.5	16.3	*26.7*	0.8
DR	2.5	-0.5	3.8	*10.0*	1.7	7.5	0.3	-1.0	**12.5**	-1.3
SF	*24.5*	24.0	10.0	1.7	-20.0	-1.0	**25.9**	-0.8	-0.3	-25.0
DKP	22.9	10.0	0.9	2.0	-4.3	0	**23.1**	-2.1	2.0	-40.0
CD	18.3	23.1	*24.7*	23.5	1.5	5.0	-1.9	**49.1**	23.7	-0.3
Krf	-1.3	16.3	22.9	*25.0*	23.8	18.1	-25.0	12.5	**26.9**	-20.0
V	1.2	10.2	20.3	26.3	20.5	24.3	-9.4	20.1	**49.2**	0.2
VS	10.0	-10.0	**25.0**	0	-37.5	-37.5	*20.0*	0	-10.0	-45.0
Frp	-1.3	13.5	8.2	23.2	3.3	13.1	-23.3	22.5	*24.5*	**27.1**
All	14.4	24.5	19.8	23.9	4.6	10.1	0	14.7	24.6	-0.3

The bottom line of Table 3.7. reveals much the same pattern as the bottom line in Table 3.2. Only one party leader - the Progress Party's Mogens Glistrup - got a median score below zero, while the Socialist Peoples' Party's Morten Lange got a zero score. All other party leaders are clearly above that mark. The leaders of the Radical Liberals and of the Agrarians and the most popular leader of the Socialdemocrats (Per Hækkerup) are almost equal in median sympathy, as are their parties. Sympathy with the two quarreling conservative leaders lags behind and is even surpassed by the sympathy expressed for Erhard Jakobsen (CD).

Figure 3.9. shows the map that can be derived from the sympathy data for party leaders. It fits the data acceptably well (Unweighted $R^2 = 0.61$). As can be seen at once, it bears a striking resemblance to the map of the perceived party system in Figure 3.1. The position of the party leaders on the map closely reflects the position of their parties in the perceived party space.

The arrangement of the party leaders in the horizontal direction on the map expresses their position on the left-right dimension. As can be seen once more, Glistrup is not perceived as being especially rightist. Of the three Socialdemocratic leaders, Anker Jørgensen is perceived to be the most leftist and Orla Møller to be the most centrist. Of the two conservative leaders, Haunstrup-Clemmensen is perceived to be closest to the center. The respondents thus appear surprisingly well oriented with respect to the internal discussions in the Socialdemocratic and the Conservative Party.

Fig. 3.9.: Perception of party leaders 1973

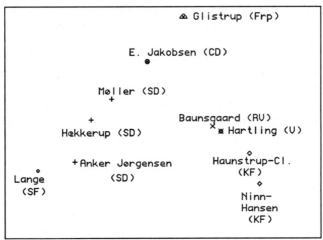

The vertical direction offsets the leaders of the two new parties, CD and Frp, from the leaders of the "old" parties in the same way as their parties are offset from the "core" of the party system. Thus there seems no doubt that the same two 'ideological' dimensions were structuring the perception of both parties and party leaders in 1973.

Turning next to the question of distrust in politicians, we are once more confronted with the problem of lack of comparability between the thermometer grades from 1971 and 1973. Moreover, the scores for three political leaders only (Baunsgaard (RV), Ninn-Hansen (KF) and Hartling (V)) can be directly compared, since for them thermometer scores were obtained in both 1971 and 1973. While nothing can be done about the second problem, the first one can be tackled in the same way as was done with respect to the parties' thermometer grades.

If the median distances between the respondents' "ideal points" and the positions of the party leaders in the maps from 1971 and 1973 are compared,[36] it turns out that, as far as party leaders are concerned, there was no uniform decline in the level of sympathy between 1971 and 1973. Ninn-Hansen (KF) lost sympathy between 1971 and 1973, his median distance to the respondents' "ideal points" in 1973 being slightly above his median distance in 1971 (2 pct.).[37] On the other hand both Baunsgaard (RV)[38] and Hartling (V) gained in sympathy between 1971 and 1973, their median distances to the respondents' "ideal points" being 14 pct. and 35 pct., respectively, below their median distances in 1971.

Moreover, all three Socialdemocratic party leaders were perceived more favorably in 1973 than Krag was in 1971, Hækkerup and Orla Møller outperforming Anker Jørgensen in this respect. Not unexpectedly, Morten Lange (SF) was perceived far less positively than his immensely popular precedessor as the leader of the Socialist Peoples' Party, Aksel Larsen.

When these results are combined with the results on the changes in sympathy for political parties between 1971 and 1973 presented above, it seems that the patterns of reaction exhibited by the respondents were far more differentiated than would appear from an analysis of responses to the "distrust"-items in the survey. Though there certainly was a certain amount of estrangement between voters and the "old" parties, there was still much sympathy left in the electorate for several of the party leaders.[39]

Finally we shall turn to the question concerning the role of the personality of party leaders in the vote decision in 1973. With 1971-data strong indications were found that voters voted for parties rather than persons (party leaders).

If the median sympathy grades for parties in Table 3.2. are compared to the median sympathy grades for party leaders in Table 3.7., it is seen that in all but one case those who voted for a particular party gave a higher median sympathy grade to the party than to the party leader(s). The sole exception is Erhard Jakobsen, who received a slightly higher median sympathy grade by CD-voters than did his party. Thus, as in 1971, those who voted for a particular party in 1973 tended to be on average more sympathetic towards the party itself than towards its leader. In that respect the huge difference in the median sympathy score between the Progress Party (47.79) and its

---

[36] Once more after suitable normalization to ensure that the maps are on the same scale.

[37] This figure is almost certainly an underestimate of the actual loss in sympathy, attributable to the less than perfect fit of the model from which the distances are derived.

[38] It appears that Baunsgaard had turned more sympathetic to especially SD-voters than he was in 1971 when he was the leader of a liberal-conservative government. On the other hand his standing within his own constituency - Radical Liberal voters - had weakened.

[39] Thus to speak of the rise of an "uncivic culture" (Nielsen and Sauerberg, 1976) in this connection seems a bit farfetched.

leader Mogens Glistrup (27.08) is particularly interesting. It indicates that the success of the Progress Party was far less dependent on the charisma of its founder and leader than was the success of the Center-Democrats.

If one looks at the proportion of voters for a party that gave a higher thermometer grade to the party leader than to the party, these proportions appear small in 1973 and do not vary much between parties, cf. Table 3.8. If the proportions in Table 3.8. are compared to the corresponding proportions from 1971 in Table 2.5., one finds that the election of 1973 was in fact far less person- or leader-oriented than was the election of 1971!

Table 3.8.:   Percentage of voters giving higher thermometer grade to party leader than to party 1973

	Party						
	SD*	RV	KF*	SF	CD	V	Frp
Pct. of voters	7.1	6.6	7.7	0	5.4	3.9	7.8

*with respect to the party leader who received the highest thermometer grade

This result is confirmed by Table 3.9. Its first row shows how many times the voters for a party gave a higher sympathy grade to a party leader from another party than to the leader of the party they voted for, while at the same time giving a lower sympathy grade to this other party than to the party they voted for. Thus the figures in the first row tell how many times party sympathy clashed with party leader sympathy - and party sympathy won. The second row shows how many times the voters for a party gave a lower sympathy grade to the party they voted for than to another party, while at the same time giving a higher sympathy grade to the leader of the party they voted for than to the leader of the other party. Percentages are relative to the total number of possible "overrulings" of this type.

Table 3.9.:   Party and party leaders in the vote decision 1973

	Party						
	SD**	RV	KF**	SF	CD	V	Frp
Party overrules* party leader							
Pct.	1.3	1.6	1.4	5.4	2.7	0.8	4.0
(N)	13	9	3	14	9	6	24
Party leader over-rules* party							
Pct.	0	0.2	0	0	1.8	0.3	0.2
(N)	0	1	0	0	6	2	1

*see text for explanation
**with respect to the party leader who was given the highest thermometer grade

Two things stand out clearly from the figures in Table 3.9. In the first place, conflicts between sympathy for parties and sympathy for party leaders occurred far less frequently in 1973 than in 1971. In 1973, the bulk of the voters for a party gave higher sympathy scores to both their party and to its leader (or at least one of its leaders) than to any other party and party leader. In the second place, when sympathy for parties clashed with sympathy for party leaders, the vote was most often cast according to party sympathy.

With regard to sympathy for the various parties and party leaders and to the vote there was much more "order" and consistency in the "landslide"-election of 1973 than there had been in 1971. From that perspective, one might even be tempted to talk about a higher state of stability having been attained in 1973. But from a different point of view, the 1973-situation could as well be interpreted as polarized and deadlocked, the voters being more firmly entrenched in their various "camps" in 1973 than they had been in 1971.

3.4. The impact of party identification, party vote, class, and party behavior on the perception of the party system 1973

The aim of the following section is to confront our propositions 2.1. and 2.2. with data concerning the perception of the party system in 1973. We shall examine the influence by various factors on this perception, primarily by way of testing if they make for systematic differences with regard to the goodness of fit of our model to the sympathy data from various subgroups in the survey.

In Table 3.10., the overall fit for the model of the perceived party space in 1973 has been broken down according to party vote and party identification. In a number of respects, the table exhibits the same patterns as the corresponding table in section 2.4. (Table 2.8.). As in 1971, the fit of the model to the sympathy data from voters for the Socialdemocrats, the Socialist Peoples' Party, and the Justice Party is poorer than average, most strikingly so for DR-voters. The fit is also slightly below average for DKP-, VS- and Frp-voters, while voters for Krf (who were also fitted poorer than average in 1973) are on average in 1973.

The extremely poor fit of the model to the sympathy grades administered by Justice Party-voters once more seems attributable to their "marching to a different tune", compared to the rest of the respondents. Obviously their belief system was very different from that of the other respondents. The fact that respondents identifying with the Justice Party are represented even poorer than non-identifiers (while normally identifiers are represented better than non-identifiers, cf. below) would seem to support this explanation.

Table 3.10.: R^2 for perceived party space 1973, broken down by party identification and party voted for

Voted	R2		
for	Party identifiers	Non-identifiers	All
SD	0.62	0.61	0.62
RV	0.74	0.67	0.69
KF	0.77	0.79	0.78
DR	0.05	0.22	0.17
SF	0.68	0.58	0.61
DKP	0.66	0.63	0.64
CD	0.68	0.65	0.66
Krf	0.72	0.64	0.66
V	0.80	0.74	0.78
VS	0.63	0.64	0.64
Frp	0.63	0.63	0.63
All	0.67	0.64	0.66

The below average figures for SD-, SF-, DKP-, VS-, and Frp-voters on the other hand presumably reflect a higher proportion of respondents being relatively low in political resources among respondents reporting a vote for these parties, thus making for a higher level of "noise" in the data: These parties had the lions share of the working class-vote in 1973, and - as can be seen below - the perception of working class respondents once more tends to be represented somewhat poorer than average by the model.

Turning to the differences between party identifiers and non-identifiers it can be seen that identifiers tend to be represented slightly better than non-identifiers. There is no difference with voters for SD and Frp, while the perception of non-identifiers is represented better than the perception of identifiers among voters for KF, DR and VS. With KF- and VS-voters the difference is small, however. Once more, the generally better fit obtained for party identifiers may be attributable to their greater interest in and knowledge about politics which makes for less "noise" in the data.

It may be concluded that both party preference (party vote) and party identification can be seen to have influenced the respondents' perception of the party system in 1973. A multiple classification analysis (MCA) with the individual R^2-values as the dependent and party preference (reported party vote) and party identification as the independent variable accounts for 18.6 pct. of the variance in individual fit. This represents a substantial increase over the corresponding value from 1971, but still the contribution of these variables to the overall variance in individual goodness of fit appears marginal. Moreover, it appears - with voters for the Justice Party as the only exception - that party preference and party identification influenced, how clearly the structure of the party system was seen, rather than what kind of structure was seen. So far then, proposition 2.1. can be considered confirmed.

In Table 3.11. the overall measure of fit for the model has been broken down according to the respondents' class and party identification. As mentioned above, the 1973-data do not allow us to classify respondents in exactly the same way as was done for 1971. Thus, housewives cannot be classified according to husband's class; they therefore have been left out. Wives assisting their husbands have been classified as self-employed. The group of respondents not in the labor force does only contain pensioners in 1973; unemployed are classified according to last occupation.[40]

Table 3.11.: R^2 for perceived party space 1973, broken down by class and party identification

	Working class	Middle class	Self-employed	Out of labor force	Under education	All
Party identifiers	0.61	0.69	0.79	0.66	0.63	0.67
Non-identifiers	0.58	0.66	0.70	0.64	0.68	0.64
All	0.60	0.67	0.76	0.65	0.67	0.66

As can be seen, self-employed respondents are represented somewhat above and working class respondents somewhat below average, as was also the case in 1971. Other deviations from average fit are very small. The pattern remains practically unchanged when party identification is controlled for.[41]

In comparison with the corresponding figures in Table 2.9., the goodness of fit for respondents from the working and the middle class has dropped between 1971 and 1973, relatively to the average, while there has been a certain upsurge for respondents under education. Still the most plausible explanation of the variations between groups remains the difference in political resources available to people in different social classes.

In any case the influence of class on goodness of fit of the model to sympathy data from the various subgroups of respondents is marginal, too. A multiple classification analysis (MCA) with individual R^2-values as the dependent variable and class, party vote and party identification as the independent variables accounts for 21.6 pct. of the variance in the R^2-values. Thus proposition 2.1. may be considered confirmed for 1973-data.

Turning to proposition 2.2., we shall finally examine the relationship between the perception of the party system by the respondents in 1973 and

---

[40] Since unemployment was still low in 1973, this probably does not matter much.
[41] The same is true when party vote is introduced as controlling variable.

the patterns in the parties' legislative behavior that turn up when the roll call-data from the legislative period 1971-1973 are scrutinized. For proposition 2.2. to be confirmed a strong resemblance should exist between the relationships among the parties as exhibited in their roll call-behavior and the relationships among the parties as perceived by the respondents. Figure 3.10. shows the map of the party system derived from the parties' stand in roll calls at the final reading of government bills 1971-73 (the "legislative party space"). This map has been superimposed on the map of the perceived party space in 1973, cf. Figures 3.1. and 3.2.

Fig. 3.10.: Legislative party space 1971-73 (bold symbols) superimposed on perceived party space 1973

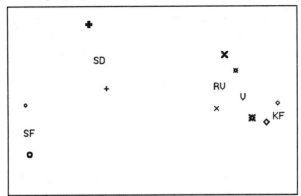

The map of the legislative party space fits the roll call-data very well ($R^2 = 0.99$). It can also be seen to be structured in the same way as the map of the perceived party system in 1973. The measure of agreement between the two maps is quite high (M = 0.78).

On closer inspection an interesting difference between the two maps becomes visible: Obviously the respondents perceived the Socialdemocrats and the Socialist Peoples' Party to be much closer to each other in 1973 than they actually were when judged from the stands taken by the two parties in roll call-divisions in the Folketing. This discrepancy probably reflects the effect of the much publicized "move to the left" of the Socialdemocrats in the wake of the referendum on the EEC-issue, a move that may seem to have been effected in words rather than in (legislative) deeds.[42]

Given the strong resemblance between the patterns in the legislative and the perceived party system in 1973, proposition 2.2. can be considered confirmed, too. It must be kept in mind, however, that this resemblance extends

---

[42] When roll call data from 1971-72 and 1972-73 are analyzed separately, distances between the Socialdemocrats and the Socialist Peoples' Party actually turn out to have grown a bit from 1971-72 to 1972-73, while in the same period distances between the Socialdemocrats and the liberal-conservative opposition have diminished!

to just five out of the 11 parties running in the election of 1973. Thus a considerable part of the respondents' perception of the party system in 1973 - and, not the least, their assessment of the position of the Center-Democrats and the Progress Party in the party system - must have been derived from other sources than recorded legislative behavior.

The most likely alternative source appears to be party communication, especially during the electoral campaign. Siune (1982, p.222) gives figures for the number of positive, neutral and negative references made by the parties to each other in television and radio broadcasts prior to the election. From these figures "distance indices" can be computed for each pair of parties in much the same way as from the figures on their stands on legislative roll calls (cf. section 1.5.).

When these "communication distance indices" are compared to the distances between the parties on the map of the perceived party system, they turn out to fit the distances acceptably well, as measured by the the coefficient of determination (R^2 = 0.61). Thus the relationship (or distance) between the parties as seen by the respondents agrees rather well with the relationship expressed through the way the parties make references to each other.[43]

3.5. Perception of the party system and voting behavior: Reactive voting in 1973

In the previous sections it has been established that the respondents in 1973 did have a clear perception of the party system and of the position of the parties in it. It has also been shown (to the extent possible) that the respondents' perception of the party system agreed well with the actual legislative behavior exhibited by the parties. It thus appears that the informational requirements for making a deliberate choice among the competing parties were fulfilled.

What remains to be shown is that the respondents did in fact act in accordance with their perception of the party system and reacted to the changes they perceived to have occurred from 1971 to 1973, as stipulated in proposition 3. The aim of the present section is to test the hypothesis of reactive (or retrospective) voting contained in this proposition. This will be done following the logic laid down in section 1.4. above.

---

[43] Siune (1982, pp.226-227) did herself derive maps of the party system from her data. As can easily be seen, they differ quite a lot from the maps presented in figures 3.1. and 3.2. Two factors may account for these difference: In the first place, Siune considered positive and neutral references only. In the second place, Siune tacitly assumed that the parties' preference functions with respect to other parties are single-peaked. This is probably not a realistic assumption (cf. the discussion in Lantermann and Feger, 1980, pp.375-377), and it has been dropped in the present context.

Table 3.12. gives the non-zero regression coefficients obtained when the model is applied to each of the 11 parties running in the 1973-election. As can be seen, for all parties but one the probability of voters moving to this particular party in 1973 is related - in the expected way - to at least a subset of the characteristics of the perceived party space and the perceived party movements in this space.

Table 3.12.: Regression coefficients for reactive voting model 1973. (Standard errors in parentheses)

	Intercept b_0	DISTij b_1	DISTjj b_2	NCLOSE b_3	DIST3 b_4	VPROP b_5
SD	5.43620 (2.10076)	-2.78760 (1.28010)	1.59002 (0.60175)		1.76366 (3.48304)	0.31914 (0.63153)
RV	4.24111 (0.56808)	-2.00968 (0.22747)			2.60324 (1.33279)	
KF	7.93939 (2.15813)	-1.86932 (2.71248)		-0.33914 (0.27138)	13.24519 (6.03222)	
DR	4.58547 (1.10144)				3.64850 (2.86022)	
SF	5.49328 (2.07421)	-1.92308 (0.44358)			5.37628 (6.17332)	0.48040 (0.66862)
DKP	5.29312 (1.26450)				5.39475 (3.35764)	
CD	3.43851 (1.07860)	-1.53069 (0.66359)				0.26621 (0.29276)
Krf	6.87777 (3.22955)		1.61956 (1.61591)	-4.95269 (3.15164)		0.32035 (1.15638)
V	3.73749 (0.84435)	-6.06831 (0.78503)	2.00042 (0.70380)			0.51930 (0.70000)
VS	2.76583 (1.57249)				0.68507 (3.80560)	
Frp	4.02105 (0.09849)	-0.13606* (0.19622)				

* with respect to the horizontal direction only

The Progress Party (Frp) constitutes the only exception. For this party no subset of variables in the model can be found that fulfills the constraints on the signs of the coefficients. Thus the model of reactive voting in its proposed form cannot account for the propensity to move to the Progress Party in 1973.

This should probably come as no major surprise. In section 2.5. above the complex interaction between the left right- and the "backlash"-dimension in determining the propensity of voters to move to the Progress Party in 1973 has been touched upon. But if we change the definition of the first variable in the model slightly, making it "the distance between the location of the Progress Party in 1973 and the location of party (j) in 1971, measured with respect to the first dimension (the left-right dimension) only", then we find a relationship of the kind expected: The closer the Progress Party in 1973 is located to the 1971-locations of the other parties with respect to the first dimension, the greater the proportion of voters it succeeds in picking up from these parties.

Table 3.13.: Observed and expected voter movements 1971 - 1973 in percentages of all respondents (n = 462). Observed percentages in parentheses.

Party	Party 1971								
1973	SD	RV	KF	DR	SF	DKP	Krf	V	VS
SD	27.7	0.4	0.4	0.2	0.2	0.0	0.0	0.4	0.0
	(27.7)	(0.9)	(0.0)	(0.0)	(0.0)	(0.0)	(0.4)	(0.4)	(0.0)
RV	1.5	8.4	1.5	0.0	0.0	0.0	0.0	1.1	0.0
	(1.3)	(8.2)	(1.7)	(0.2)	(0.0)	(0.0)	(0.0)	(1.1)	(0.0)
KF	0.4	0.2	4.1	0.0	0.0	0.0	0.0	0.6	0.0
	(0.4)	(0.2)	(4.1)	(0.0)	(0.0)	(0.0)	(0.0)	(0.6)	(0.0)
DR	1.3	0.4	0.2	0.0	0.2	0.0	0.0	0.2	0.0
	(0.0)	(0.9)	(0.0)	(0.9)	(0.6)	(0.0)	(0.0)	(0.0)	(0.0)
SF	2.4	0.2	0.0	0.0	3.0	0.0	0.0	0.0	0.0
	(2.4)	(0.0)	(0.2)	(0.0)	(3.0)	(0.0)	(0.0)	(0.0)	(0.0)
DKP	1.7	0.4	0.2	0.0	0.2	0.0	0.0	0.0	0.0
	(0.4)	(0.0)	(0.0)	(0.0)	(1.3)	(0.6)	(0.0)	(0.0)	(0.2)
CD	5.0	0.9	0.4	0.2	0.2	0.0	0.2	0.9	0.0
	(5.2)	(1.1)	(0.0)	(0.0)	(0.6)	(0.0)	(0.2)	(0.4)	(0.0)
Krf	0.2	1.1	0.4	0.4	0.0	0.0	0.4	0.9	0.0
	(0.4)	(1.1)	(0.0)	(0.0)	(0.0)	(0.0)	(1.1)	(0.9)	(0.0)
V	0.2	0.9	1.3	0.0	0.0	0.0	0.0	14.1	0.0
	(0.2)	(0.9)	(1.3)	(0.0)	(0.0)	(0.0)	(0.0)	(14.1)	(0.0)
VS	0.2	0.0	0.0	0.0	0.0	0.0	0.0	0.0	0.0
	(0.0)	(0.4)	(0.0)	(0.0)	(0.2)	(0.0)	(0.0)	(0.0)	(0.0)
Frp	5.4	2.6	1.1	0.2	0.9	0.0	0.2	2.6	0.0
	(3.9)	(2.8)	(3.2)	(0.2)	(0.9)	(0.0)	(0.0)	(2.4)	(0.0)

In comparison with the Progress Party, the pattern of voter movements to the other "upshot"-party of the 1973-election, the Center-Democrats, appears much more regular. As can be seen from Table 3.12., variations in the propensity to move to the Center-Democrats are inversely related to the distance between the perceived location of this party in 1973 and the perceived location of the other parties in 1971. There is a small contribution as well from the variable indicating how many voters there were to be picked up in the various regions of the space, but it appears rather insignificant.

Table 3.12. also shows a clear difference between the five "old" parties (SD, RV, KF, SF, and V) in the party system and the small and/or new parties with regard to which variables are related to the propensity of the voters to move to these parties in 1973. For all "old" parties, the probability of picking up voters in 1973 is clearly (and inversely) related to the distance between the perceived location of these parties in 1973 and the perceived party locations in 1971. Among the small and/or new parties, this relationship exists only for the Center-Democrats (and for the Progress Party, if the model is reformulated as described above).

Table 3.13. shows the expected voter movements between parties from 1971 to 1973 (in percentages of all respondents) as computed from the model of reactive voting. The voter movements computed from the 1971- and 1973-waves of the panel are given in parentheses underneath the corresponding expected figures.

Visual inspection of the table indicates that the agreement between observed and computed movements is quite good. This impression is confirmed by the value of the index of non-similarity (NS = 0.10), which shows that just about 10 pct. of the proportions would have to be moved in order to construct the observed proportions from the computed ones (or vice versa).

In general, the figures in Table 3.13. show a tendency for the voter movements to the "old" parties in 1973 to be somewhat better accounted for than are movements to the small and/or new ones. There are, however, exceptions to that rule.

Thus a rather clear relationship between the propensity of the voters to move to the various parties competing in 1973 and a number of characteristics of the perceived party spaces in 1971 and 1973 and of the perceived movements of parties within these spaces appears. Although it is not the same set of characteristics that has been found to be relevant in predicting the movements to all parties, and although the relative importance of the relevant variables varies between parties, as can be seen in Table 3.12., the performance of the model of reactive voting may be considered a relative success. The reservation is mainly due to the model's problems in accounting for the movement to the Progress Party, which could only be overcome by a partial redefinition of one variable.

The relative success of the model of reactive voting in accounting for the voter movements in 1973 carries implications for the substantive interpretation of this election as well. Hypotheses of changes in the voters' orientations and attitudes - like an upsurge of political distrust between 1971 and 1973, or a "rightist tide wave" sweeping away the voters - are obviously needed to account for only some part of the "landslide" in 1973. Another part can be ascribed to changes and continuities in the party system, i.e. the sudden emergence of two new parties on the arena and changes or lack of changes in the positions of the existing parties perceived to have occurred between 1971 and 1973.

By the same token, it also shows that in one important respect the result of the 1973-election did not constitute that disruptive change in Danish voting behavior it has often been described as: Since a sizeable part of the voter movements that occurred between 1971 and 1973 can be accounted for without assuming any changes at all in the voters' attitudes and orientations between 1971 and 1973, it follows that to some extent the attitudinal pre-requisites of the "landslide" in 1973 must have existed in 1971 already. Thus the result of the election in 1973 appears as the continuation of a develop-ment that - although largely unrecognized[44] - had been on its way for some time before finally becoming manifest in 1973.

---

[44]One of the rare exceptions can be found in Tonsgaard (1984, p.102).

4. Aftermath: The general election of January 1975

4.1. Background, campaign, and outcome

The "narrow" Agrarian government formed in the aftermath of the 1973-election did not last long. After 13 months and another election - which ironically was won by the Agrarians - it was forced to resign and give way to a Socialdemocratic minority government.

During the whole of its existence the Agrarian government had to cope with the extremely difficult parliamentary situation created by the outcome of the 1973-election. It was wholehearted supported by the Center-Democrats and the Christian Peoples' Party only. Whenever necessary, the Radical Liberals and the Conservatives went grudgingly along as well. But between them, these five parties held only 79 of the Folketing's 179 seats. Thus to have its legislation passed, the government had to rely on either the Socialdemocrats or the Progress Party to vote for its bills - or at least to abstain from voting.

Quite early it became clear that the Progress Party was not going to guarantee the survival of a bourgeois government in any way, and that it was even prepared to join forces with the Socialdemocrats and left-wing parties if it deemed fit.[1] The clearest example came in September 1974, when on the same day the government managed to survive four motions of non-confidence. In one of the divisions it was saved only by a break occurring in the Progress Party: Four members voted against the motion, the rest - together with the Socialdemocrats and the socialist parties - voted for non-confidence in the government. Thus at any time the Progress Party constituted a rather incalculable threat to the government's continued existence.

As a consequence, the Agrarian government's short period in office became characterized by a quick succession of "package deals" or comprehensive compromises arrived at with varying partners.[2] The first one in early 1974 (on measures to curb inflation and reduce the deficit in the balance of payments) the Agrarians concluded with the Socialdemocrats (and, of course, with the Center-Democrats and the Christian Peoples' Party). The next one, once more on measures to put brakes on an overheated economy, brought together the Agrarians, the Conservatives and the Radical Liberals, alongside with the Center-Democrats and the Christian Peoples' Party. The

---

[1] In the final divisions, the Progress Party voted against government bills in 36 out of 110 divisions. This number was only surpassed by the Communists who voted against in 47 cases, cf. Meyer (1984, p.75).

[2] This situation seems to provide the most natural explanation for a finding reported in Paldam and Schneider (1980): While up to 1973 the "responsibility hypothesis" is sustained by the data, the government being held responsible for the development in the economy, the situation changes in 1973. Given the degree of fragmentation in the Folketing after 1973 and the shifting patterns of cooperation, it may not have been easy to find out whom to blame and whom to reward for the state of the economy.

necessary majority was this time secured by the Progress Party. The following month a deal on housing policy was concluded between the parties that had worked out the previous compromise, but this time with the inclusion of the Socialdemocrats as well. Finally, in September 1974 the Agrarians and their loyal supporters, Center-Democrats and Christian Peoples' Party, agreed with Conservatives, Radical Liberals and the Justice Party on still another economic package deal, this time in order to stimulate the economy (which by then had been hit by the international recession following the first oil crisis) by a 7 billion kr. tax cut to become effective in 1975.[3] The passage of this legislation was secured by the Socialdemocrats abstaining in the final division, when an attempt to overthrow the government through a motion of non-confidence had failed.

To judge from the opinion polls conducted and published regularly, the voters approved of the government's endeavors and gave the Agrarians credit for doing a difficult job: The party improved its standing dramatically, compared to its meager results in the 1973-election. With the popularity in the polls the temptation grew to cash the chips by calling new elections.

Against the advice of its supporters, especially the Center-Democrats, who had good reasons to fear the voters' verdict, as their popularity had dropped markedly in the polls, the government seized the opportunity on the 5th December and called new elections to be held on the 9th of January 1975. Two days earlier, it had presented a "comprehensive plan" ("Helhedsplanen") for the economic policy in 1975. After an initial debate on the 5th of December, the government concluded that no sufficient support of the plan had been forthcoming and that new elections were the only way out.

The same 11 parties that had run in the 1973-election participated in the 1975-election as well.[4] Due to the Christmas holidays the campaign became a short one. The parties concentrated on labor marked-issues (including unemployment which had begun to rise steadily), taxes, and the economy. These issues were also perceived to be the most central ones by the voters.[5]

Opinion polls prior to the election had made it clear that a return to a more tranquil parliamentary situation was not to be expected. They proved correct. Table 4.1. shows the outcome of the 1975-election.

As expected from the opinion polls, the Agrarians were the big winners, almost doubling their number of seats in the new Folketing. But except for the Christian Peoples' Party which managed to increase its representation by two seats all parties which more or less enthusiastically had supported the "narrow" Agrarian government suffered severe losses. The Center-Democrats fared worst, being just able to pass the 2 pct.-threshold this time.

---

[3] At the same time it was agreed to reduce public spending by about 6.7 billion kr. in 1975.

[4] The Schlesvigian Party (Slp) continued its cooperation with the Center-Democrats and got one candidate elected on their ticket.

[5] Cf. Siune (1982, p.147, 177).

114

The Conservatives were - for the second time - almost reduced to half their strength in the previous Folketing, and the Radical Liberals for the second time in a row lost seven seats. The Justice Party did not obtain any seats at all.

Table 4.1.: Electoral results 1975 (with 1973 for comparison)

Party	4.12.1973		9.1.1975	
	votes (pct.)	seats	votes (pct.)	seats
SD	25.6	46	29.9	53
RV	11.2	20	7.1	13
KF	9.2	16	5.5	10
DR	2.9	5	1.8	0
SF	6.0	11	5.0	9
DKP	3.6	6	4.2	7
CD	7.8	14	2.2	4
Krf	4.0	7	5.3	9
V	12.3	22	23.3	42
VS	1.5	0	2.1	4
Frp	15.9	28	13.6	24

The Progress Party was weakened a bit, losing four seats and its position as the second largest party in the Folketing with them. But - as the other non-socialist parties were to experience soon after the election - it still remained a force to be reckoned with.

On the other side of the political spectrum, the Socialdemocrats re-covered somewhat, but were still far from their normal, pre-1973 strength. After their unsuccessful attempts in 1971 and 1973 the Left Socialists finally obtained representation in the Folketing again.

Thus there were 10 parties in the new Folketing, as there had been in the previous one. Together, the four "old" parties had regained some strength, increasing their number of seats from 104 to 118. Nevertheless, fractionalization in the new Folketing was still high.

Proclaiming itself victorious, the "narrow" Agrarian government con-tinued in office. Few weeks after the elections, however, it was forced to give up by a motion urging the government to resign in order to allow negotiations on the formation of a broadly based government to take place. The motion was supported by the Socialdemocrats, the Radical Liberals and the left-wing parties (86 seats) and opposed by the Agrarians, the Con-servatives, the Progress Party and the Christian Peoples' Party (86 seats). The draw to be expected in the division on the motion allowed the Center-Democrats to air their bitterness against the Agrarians by abstaining with-out (as they thought) endangering the government's life. But the defection of one conservative member turned the draw into a one vote majority against the government.

An attempt to form a four party government of Agrarians, Conserva-tives, Christian Peoples' Party and Center-Democrats was called off in a very late stage, when it became clear that the Progress Party would not guarantee to give such a government a chance. Instead Anker Jørgensen formed a Socialdemocratic minority government, which appeared to be the only constellation not being opposed by a majority in the Folketing from the very beginning.[6]

4.2. Perception of the party system 1975

In the present section, propositions 1.1. and 1.2. concerning the informational aspects of the vote decision shall be put to their third test. We shall try to demonstrate that also in 1975 the voters did possess a clear perception of the party system, structured by a relatively simple belief system.

Contrary to 1973, there were no new parties running in the elections in 1975. Moreover, 10 of the 11 parties presenting themselves to the voters did have a recent parliamentary record in 1975, having been represented in the previous Folketing. Given the unstable parliamentary situation and the frequently changing party constellations this need not have been conductive to a clear perception of the party system and of the parties' whereabouts prior to the 1975-election, however. Table 4.2., giving the median sympathy scores for the parties in 1975 by reported vote, conveys a first impression of the voters' reactions.

Table 4.2.: Sympathy scores by reported vote 1975 (medians).
(Bold: most preferred party; italic: next most preferred party)

Voted for	Sympathy scores for										
	SD	RV	KF	DR	SF	DKP	CD	Krf	V	VS	Frp
SD	**86.3**	*25.5*	1.6	6.4	16.3	-22.5	-0.2	10.8	10.4	-13.5	-56.0
RV	27.0	**82.2**	11.5	3.9	-54.9	-95.9	6.0	27.0	*44.4*	-83.0	-17.2
KF	4.2	18.8	**91.1**	5.1	-77.2	-96.6	20.9	58.8	*65.5*	-96.3	20.0
DR	20.0	23.5	4.8	**92.7**	-13.0	-33.0	4.3	24.2	*27.0*	-20.0	-15.3
SF	*54.1*	9.8	-22.8	10.7	**89.2**	19.2	-33.0	4.3	24.2	27.0	-80.0
DKP	53.5	7.1	-61.4	2.5	*56.5*	**86.1**	-90.5	-53.0	-93.3	56.5	-83.5
CD	40.0	14.8	11.6	7.2	-50.0	-94.4	**92.0**	*41.8*	33.7	-63.3	6.0
Krf	19.5	24.2	21.8	8.3	-53.6	-96.7	21.7	**93.3**	*69.4*	-94.0	8.9
V	1.7	21.1	35.5	2.3	-75.7	-97.7	16.9	*54.2*	**94.8**	-95.2	28.0
VS	36.5	16.9	-56.0	14.4	*60.0*	25.8	-72.0	-2.6	-34.4	**86.7**	-72.0
Frp	9.8	10.2	26.6	6.0	-60.5	-93.7	5.3	33.4	*45.5*	-85.9	**87.0**
All	34.6	21.4	12.4	5.7	-20.7	-81.7	6.5	26.3	45.0	-58.5	9.4

---

[6]Cf. Kaarsted (1988).

As can be seen in the bottom line of Table 4.2., all but the three left-wing parties (SF, DKP, and VS) were perceived positively in 1975, obtaining median sympathy grades above zero. The Communists still rank as the on average most disliked party in the Danish party system. The Progress Party, which had a median score below zero in 1973, did succeed in moving above that mark in 1975.

The bottom line also shows that by 1975 the Agrarians had taken over as the most popular party, outperforming both the Socialdemocrats and the Radical Liberals. The Christian Peoples' Party also appears to have improved its standing with the voters, ranking third in median sympathy in 1975. The remaining rows in Table 4.2. exhibit much the same patterns as are present in the corresponding table from 1973 (Table 3.2.).[7]

But it should be noticed that by 1975 the Christian Peoples' Party had taken over from the Socialdemocrats as the second most preferred party for CD-voters. This indicates a shift in the position of the Center-Democrats in the perceived party system between 1973 and 1975. Figure 4.1. shows the map of the perceived party space in 1975 as derived from the respondents' thermometer grading of the parties.

Fig. 4.1.:   Perceived party system 1975

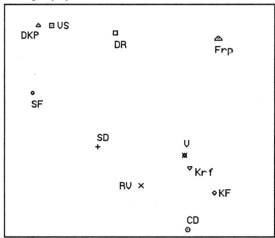

Compared to the 1973-map, both differences and similarities are evident. In the lower right corner of the map one finds once more a four-party cluster consisting of bourgeois parties (KF, CD, Krf, and V). As mentioned above it was this "four-leaved clover" that came together in the abortive attempt to form a broadly based government, when the "narrow" Agrarian govern-

_____

[7] Due to differences in the calibration of the thermometers used, the 1975 sympathy data cannot be compared to the sympathy grades from either 1971 or 1973.

ment had been forced to resign.

The Radical Liberals have moved out of the four-party cluster and the Center-Democrats have taken their place. In fact it is the difference in the perceived position of the Center-Democrats between 1973 and 1975 that is really dramatic. It is tempting to ponder some kind of relationship between this large, perceived change in position and the party's poor showing in the elections. We shall revert to this question later.

In the perception of the respondents, the Radical Liberals in 1975 had obviously turned their back at the liberal-conservative bloc to which they had clearly belonged in both 1971 and 1973, cf. Figures 2.1. and 3.1. The party was seen on its way back to its traditional centrist position between the Socialdemocrats and the liberal-conservative parties - and apparently leaving some of its voters behind it in the process.

Compared to the situation in 1973, the Progress Party had become isolated in the party system, now occupying a region entirely of its own on the map. If the horizontal direction on the map can be interpreted as a left-right dimension, as it could in 1971 and 1973, then the respondents in 1975 saw the Progress Party just a bit farther to the right than the liberal-conservative parties in the "four-leaved clover". This constitutes a change from the 1973-situation, when the Progress Party was not perceived to be the right-most party in the party system.

Fig. 4.2.:   Parties and "ideal points" in perceived party space 1975*

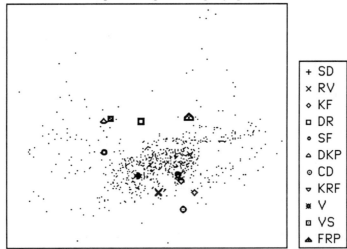

*17 outliers removed.

In Figure 4.2. above, the respondents' "ideal points" have been added to the map. As on the 1973-map, there is a tendency for the distribution of the "ideal points" to be oriented in a north-eastern direction. This implies that

118

the perceived position of the respondents vis a vis the parties in 1975 tends to be jointly determined by both the horizontal and the vertical direction on the map.

The position of the parties and of the respondents' "ideal points" in Figure 4.2. at once suggests the reason for the severe losses suffered by the Conservatives and the Center-Democrats in the 1975-elections: With respect to the main concentration of "ideal point"-positions, these two parties were quite literally standing in the shadow of the Agrarians (and, to a lesser degree, of the Christian Peoples' Party as well).

The fit between map and data is approximately the same as for the 1973-data (unweighted $R^2 = 0.67$; weighted $R^2 = 0.81$) and hence again quite good on this criterion. The "hindcasted" distribution of votes that can be obtained from the map under the assumption that the respondents vote for the party closest to their "ideal point" is given in Table 4.3. Despite numerous minor deviations, the "hindcast" appears to capture the main trends in the electoral outcome - the upsurge of the Agrarians and the heavy losses of the Center-Democrats - very well, although the value of the index of non-similarity (NS = 0.11) between the reported and the "hindcasted" distributions is poorer than it was with the 1973-data.

Table 4.3: Reported and "hindcasted" distribution of votes 1975

| Party | Distribution of votes | |
	reported (n=1143)	"hindcasted" (n=1156)
SD	29.5	28.6
RV	6.9	4.4
KF	5.7	6.0
DR	2.1	2.0
SF	3.7	7.8
DKP	3.9	2.3
CD	1.0	1.2
Krf	6.3	2.1
V	26.6	30.6
VS	1.5	0.3
Frp	12.7	14.7

Finally, 76.0 pct. of the party votes at the individual level are reproduced correctly in the "hindcast". Although lower than the comparable figures from 1971 and 1973, this proportion of correctly "hindcasted" individual party votes is still satisfactory. In part the decrease in the proportion of party votes "hindcasted" correctly parallels the increase in the proportion of respondents reporting a vote for a party different from the party that was given the highest thermometer grade. This proportion rose from 6.7 pct. in 1973 to 9.6 pct. in 1975.

On the basis of all three criteria we may conclude that the map fits the data well enough to allow us to consider it evidence of a clear perception of the party system and of the parties in it existing in 1975. Thus, once more, proposition 1.1. is confirmed.

The next task is to identify and interpret the structure of the map of the perceived party system of 1975. Its likeness to the corresponding map from 1973 strongly suggests that the horizontal direction represents a left-right dimension in the voters' belief system, while the vertical direction represents a "backlash"-dimension. We shall try to validate this interpretation using once more the respondents' issue positions on a number of issues (viz. the median "ideal points" in each of the categories on a number of scales measuring the respondents' attitudes towards a series of issues) as the central "clues".

From 1971 onwards, responses evoked by a number of economic items could be shown to be closely related to the left-right dimension. In the 1975-survey three of the economic items used in 1973 do reappear.[8] Figure 4.3. shows the distribution of the respondents' median "ideal points" in each category on the three scales belonging to these three items. For ease of reference, the median "ideal points" corresponding to the neutral categories have been left out, and only a "zoom"-view of the relevant part of the map in Figure 4.1. is shown.

Fig. 4.3.:   Perceived party space and issue positions on three economic issues 1975

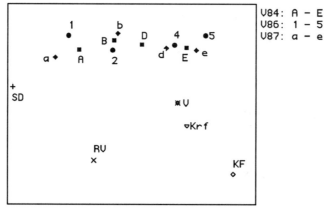

A, a, 1: Agree completely; B, b, 2: Do agree in part; D, d, 4: Do disagree in part;
E, e, 5: Disagree completely

As can be seen from Figure 4.3., support for positions favoring economic equality, state control of private investments, and higher taxes on high incomes tends to decrease as one moves horizontally from the left to the

---

[8] V84 ("In politics one should strive to make economic conditions equal for all, regardless of education and job"), V86 ("There is too little state control with private investments"), and V87 ("High incomes should be taxed harder than today").

right across the map of the perceived party system. Thus it appears plausible that the horizontal direction does indeed represent a left-right dimension in 1975, the content of which is at least in part economic.

Besides the three economic items mentioned above, eight additional economic items were presented to the respondents in 1975.[9] All of these refer to various economic measures taken by the government or proposed by it prior to the elections.

The issue positions on four of the eight economic items (V72 on incomes policy, V73 on equal amounts of CoL-regulations, V74 on a price freeze, and V76 on cuts in child allowances) do not exhibit any clear pattern.[10] The median "ideal points" of the respondents in each of the categories on the scales belonging to the remaining four items (V69 on wage rises, V70 on the Folketing interfering with tariff negotiations, V71 on increasing subsidies to building and construction work, and V75 on the government's "comprehensive plan") are shown in Figure 4.4.

As can be seen from this figure, the issue positions tend to be arranged horizontally across the map. As one moves from the left to the right, support tends to increase for the view that wage rises cannot be afforded in the present situation (V69) and that the government's "comprehensive plan" is the best proposal for a solution to the country's economic worries (V75), while support tends to decrease for the opinion that the Folketing should not interfere with the ongoing tariff negotiations (V70) and that state subsidies to building and construction work should be increased in order to create new jobs (V71).

As can also be seen from the lower part of Figure 4.4., the distribution of the issue positions for items V71 and V75 appears a bit deflected into the north-eastern direction. This was not the case with the issue positions on the three "recurring" economic items, cf. Figure 4.3. Here the deviations from a purely horizontal arrangement do look random. The interpretation of this difference could be that positions on general, basic economic issues, like

---

[9] V69 ("We cannot afford wage rises in the present economic situation"), V70 ("Under no circumstances should the Folketing interfere with the ongoing tariff negotiations"), V71 ("In order to create jobs for more people, state subsidies to building and construction work should be increased substantially"), V72 ("The state should conduct income policy by regulating prices, wages and revenues"), V73 ("All wage-earners should have the same amount of money as CoL-regulation of their wages"), V74 ("There should be a complete freeze on prices and revenues"), V75 ("Everything taken into account, the governments "comprehensive plan" is the best proposal for a solution of the country's present economic problems"), and V76 ("It would be wrong to cut child allowances").

[10] In two cases, the wording of the item may have contributed to this: V72 (on income policy) is multidimensional. It would be perfectly reasonable to be in favor of e.g. state regulation of wages, but against interference with prices and revenues. Respondents agreeing only with one or two of the three different measures mentioned in the wording of the item may have split more or less randomly between the various response alternatives. The Danish wording in the documentation of V74 (on a price freeze) is ambiguous (which is not brought out by the translation). It is not clear from the wording whether it says that a total freeze on prices and revenues should be introduced or will be introduced, which may have caused confusion.

121

economic equality or the role of the state in the economy, are solely determined by the left-right dimension, while positions on concrete economic issues taken from the ongoing political debate are at least "tinted" a bit by the dimension corresponding to the vertical direction (i.e. the presumed "backlash"-dimension) on the map as well.

Fig. 4.4.: Perceived party space and positions on four economic items 1975

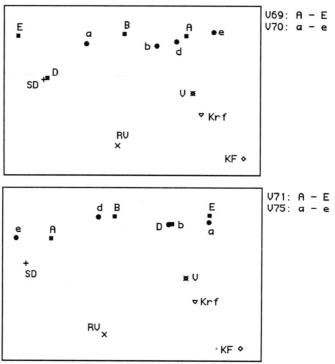

A, a: Agree completely; B, b : Do agree in part; D, d: Do disagree in part; E, e: Disagree completely

We shall conclude the discussion of the horizontal direction on the map with a brief look at the NATO- and the EEC-issue.[11] As was shown in previous chapters, positions on the NATO-issue tend to be structured by the left-right dimension, while attitudes towards EEC-membership in 1971 and 1973 were related to, but not entirely determined by this dimension.

As can be seen from Figure 4.5. below, issue positions on the NATO-issue are once more strung out roughly in the horizontal direction on the map in 1975. Issue positions on EEC-membership exhibit the same pattern:

---

[11] V66 ("If there were a referendum on the EEC today, would you vote for or against membership?") and V82 ("We should leave NATO as soon as possible").

Support of EEC-membership tends to increase as one moves horizontally from the left to the right.

Fig. 4.5.: Perceived party space and issue positions on NATO- and EEC-issue 1975

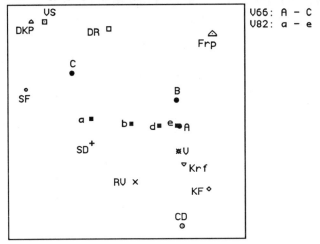

A: Would vote for membership; B: Would abstain; C: Would vote against membership
a: Agree completely; b: Do agree in part; d: Do disagree in part; e: Disagree completely

The direction defined by the issue positions on the EEC-issue is deflected in the north-western direction, as was also the case in 1971 and 1973, but the issue positions are still related to the left-right dimension. There is not much empirical support in this finding for the above-mentioned view of the EEC-issue "cutting across" the traditional left right-cleavage in Danish politics.[12]

With 1973-data, the vertical dimension of the perceived party space was found to correspond to a second 'ideological' dimension in the respondents' belief system, representing in a number of respects a backlash against the established parties, politicians, and policies. It was found that issue positions evoked by various items dealing with different aspects of trust in politicians were strung out in the vertical direction of the map or showed an ordering strongly co-determined by the vertical direction.

Thus trust (or distrust) in the regime turned out to be related to the vertical distribution of the respondents' "ideal points" on the map of the perceived party system in 1973, when it was measured by an item dealing with the possibility of having a strong man taking power in an economic crisis.[13] As can be seen from Figure 4.6. the same item once more produced vertically structured median "ideal points" in 1975.

---

[12] Cf. Borre (1981; 1982); Worre (1987, p.69).
[13] VAR123 ("It would be reasonable to have a strong man take power in an economic crisis"). In the 1975-survey, the item reappears (with the same wording) as V85.

Though, as suggested by the close clustering of the median "ideal points" in Figure 4.6., the discriminatory power of this item is not very strong, distrust in the regime (in the Eastonian sense) appears to be one of the defining features of the vertical direction on the map of the perceived party space in 1975 as well, despite the fact that the proportion of respondents agreeing to the item went down from 1973 to 1975.

Fig. 4.6.: Perceived party space and issue position on "strong man"-item 1975

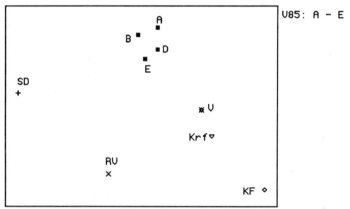

A: Agree completely; B: Do agree in part; D: Do disagree in part; E: Disagree completely

But while a small majority (8.1 pct.) of respondents with "ideal points" above the median of the vertical direction endorsed the view expressed in item V85, a still slighter majority (0.8 pct.) of respondents with "ideal points" below the median had turned against it by 1975. In 1973, there had been a clear majority endorsing the viewpoint in all four quartiles of the distribution of "ideal points" in the vertical direction.

Of the three items used to measure trust in authorities in 1973, only one reappears in the 1975-survey.[14] It failed to produce clearly structured issue positions in 1975, however.

The analysis of 1973-data revealed a number of items the positions on which were simultaneously related to the horizontal (i.e. the left-right dimension) and the vertical direction on the map of the perceived party system. Among those belonged another "distrust in politicians"-item, dealing with politicians spending the taxpayers' money too lavishly.[15] Moreover, the stand taken on this item was clearly related to the stand taken

---

[14] V77 ("Politicians usually do care too little about what the voters think").

[15] VAR134 ("The politicians spend the taxpayers' money too lavishly"). In the 1975-survey, the item reappears as V78.

on a "social benefit"-item.[16] Figure 4.7. shows that the responses to these two items in 1975 were structured in basically the same way as they had been in 1973.

Fig. 4.7.: Perceived party space and issue positions on distrust- and "social benefit"-item 1975

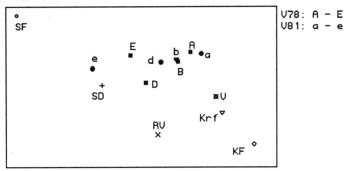

A, a: Agree completely; B, b : Do agree in part; D, d: Do disagree in part; E, e: Disagree completely

As had also been the case in 1973, the type of distrust and dissatisfaction tapped by these items is not independent of the respondents' position with respect to the left-right dimension. Concern about how the politicians handle money clearly increases as one moves from the left towards the right on the map. But at the same time, it also increases as one moves from the bottom towards the top. Obviously these two items tap a specific "rightist" component of dissatisfaction or distrust.

A similar pattern - only this time running in the north-western direction - was in 1973 found for another "distrust in politicians"-item, dealing with politicians having to give up their principles to make it to the top.[17] As can be seen from Figure 4.8. the same pattern once more emerges in 1975, but this time with a different distrust item: In 1975, it is an item dealing with trust in the politicians' ability to make the right decisions[18] that defines a special "leftist" component of the distrust.

Thus a "backlash"-interpretation of the vertical dimension in the map of the perceived party space does suggest itself again. On a number of issues dealing with trust in politicians, there is a tendency for respondents to be-

---

[16] VAR121 ("Too many people get social benefits without really needing them"). In the 1975-survey, this item reappears as V81.

[17] VAR136 ("People wanting to make it to the top in politics are forced to give up most of their principles"). In the 1975-survey, this item reappears as V79.

[18] V79 ("In general one can trust our political leaders to make the right decisions for the country"). In 1973, when the same item was used (as VAR135), it failed to produce any clear pattern at all.

come more distrustful as one moves from the bottom towards the top of the map of the perceived party space. Attitudes towards some of these issues cut across the left right-dimension, meaning that the attitudes expressed by the respondents do not appear to be influenced by their position with respect to the left-right dimension. Attitudes towards the item referring to the politicians using the taxpayers' money too lavishly, on the other hand, are clearly dependent on both the horizontal and the vertical dimension, people to the right being most distrustful of politicians in that respect.

Fig. 4.8.: Perceived party space and issue positions on distrust-item 1975

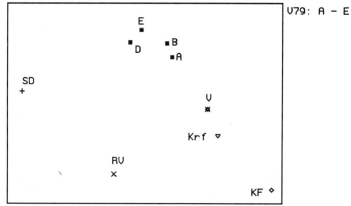

A: Agree completely; B: Do agree in part; D: Do disagree in part; E: Disagree completely

As was shown in the preceding chapter, the second dimension in the perceived party space of 1973 was also related to attitudes evoked by an item with bearing on tolerance towards deviant points of view, lifestyle etc. In the 1975-survey, the item on Christiania was not repeated, but an item on the "moral development in society" was included.[19] Moreover, an item dealing with "indoctrination in schools" was introduced.[20]

The ordering of issue positions produced by the indoctrination-item is shown in Figure 4.9. As can be seen, their location is determined by the left right-direction only and is entirely independent of the vertical direction. "Indoctrination in schools" was a clear left-right issue in 1975.

The morality item has only two response categories. One should expect a tendency for people considering the moral development reason for concern to be located nearer to the top of the map than respondents who did not profess such a point of view. This is indeed the case, but the difference is very slight: This item does not have much discriminatory power in 1975, while the item on killing extremist views by silence does not produce any

---

[19] V67 ("The moral development in our society has been discussed quite a lot. Do you think there is reason to be concerned or do you think there is no reason for concern?")

[20] V88 ("We must be more vigilant about indoctrination occurring in schools").

clear ordering of issue positions at all.

Despite the fact, that a number of items that in 1973 produced an ordering of issue positions clearly structured by the vertical dimension in the map fail to do so in 1975, the items that do produce sensible orderings of issue positions nevertheless allow us once more to interpret the vertical direction as a "backlash"-dimension in the perception of the party system in 1975 - and hence in the belief system of our respondents.

Fig. 4.9.: Perceived party space and issue positions on indoctrination-item 1975

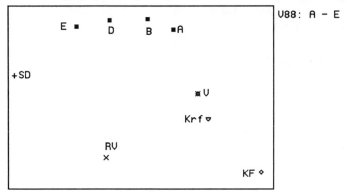

A: Agree completely; B: Do agree in part;; D: Do disagree in part; E: Disagree completely

Finally we shall turn to the "social basis" of the two dimensions in the respondents' belief system. Once more the left-right dimension can be expected to reflect the "labor vs. capital" cleavage in society, while the results from 1973 suggest that the "backlash"-dimension might be related to some kind of polarization between public and private employees (including the self-employed). Figure 4.10. shows the median "ideal points" for respondents in various occupational groups. Respondents have been classified according to their own class. Married women not in the labor force have been classified according to their husbands' class.

As can be seen from Figure 4.10., the horizontal dimension does indeed correspond to the labor-capital cleavage. Workers do generally place themselves to the left and self-employed to the right, with white collar groups between them. It should be noticed that white collar personnel in the public sector is placed in about the same position on the left-right dimension as are workers, both public and private. This finding agrees well with other results showing workers to have been moving to the right and public white collar employees to the left in the seventies (Goul Andersen, 1984).

With regard to the vertical dimension, the picture is blurred somewhat by the position of workers employed by the public. Except for this group, one finds the same pattern as in 1973: The median "ideal points" of those groups depending on the public - in one way or the other - for their income (marked by squares in Figure 4.10.) are positioned closer to the bottom of the map than the median "ideal points" of those deriving their income from the private sector (marked by dots). Although it is not as clear in 1975 as it was in 1973, there is still a tendency for the respondents to array themselves along the vertical direction in the map in accordance with which sector of the economy they base their existence on.

In conclusion it appears that propositions 1.1. and 1.2. can be considered confirmed again: The respondents did have a rather clear and well-structured perception of the party system and of the position of the parties with respect to the main dimensions of this party system in 1975. Their perception was primarily structured by two 'ideological' dimensions, a left-right dimension related to the labor capital-cleavage in society and a "backlash"-dimension related (albeit less clearly in 1975 than in 1973) to a cleavage between public and private employees (including the self-employed).

Fig. 4.10.: Perceived party space and class 1975

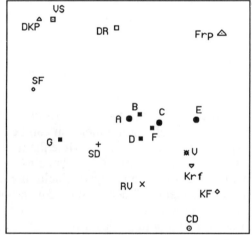

Working class, priv. : A
Working class, publ. : B
White collar, priv.: C
White collar, publ.: D
Selfemployed: E
Out of workforce: F
Under education: G

Compared to the results from 1973, the perception of the party system in 1975 is almost as clear and well-structured as it was in 1973. This may be surprising, since one might have expected that the confusing parliamentary situation described above would provide weaker clues for the respondents to make use of in their attempts to orientate themselves in the new party system that had been created by the outcome of the 1973-election. If this were indeed the case, then we should expect the agreement between the legislative and the perceived party space in 1975 to be lower than it was in 1971 and 1973. We shall revert to this question below.

4.3. The impact of party identification, party vote, class, and party behavior on the perception of the party system 1975

Having established how the respondents perceived the party system in 1975, we shall continue by investigating the influence on this perception from various factors. The theoretically most important of these are party identification and social class: Both of them appear as possible conditioning agents in the literature, while our proposition 2.1., which so far has been confirmed by data from 1971 and 1973, ascribes only marginal influence to them. Once more this proposition shall be tested primarily by checking if the potentially influencing factors make for systematic differences with regard to the goodness of fit of our model to the sympathy data from relevant subgroups in the survey.

In Table 4.4., the overall fit of the model of the perceived party space in 1975 has been broken down according to reported party vote and party identification. The R^2-values used are the unweighted coefficients. As can be seen in the tables below, a number of familiar-looking patterns appear.

Table 4.4.: R^2 for perceived party space 1975, broken down by party identification and party voted for

Voted for	R2		
	Party identifiers	Non-identifiers	All
SD	0.65	0.59	0.63
RV	0.73	0.69	0.71
KF	0.74	0.67	0.72
DR	0.46	0.51	0.49
SF	0.69	0.64	0.67
DKP	0.69	0.64	0.67
CD	0.52	0.66	0.64
Krf	0.81	0.79	0.80
V	0.84	0.76	0.80
VS	0.72	0.53	0.59
Frp	0.70	0.64	0.66
All	0.71	0.64	0.68

In the first place, the variation in fit depending on party preference (reported vote) exceeds the corresponding variation between party identifiers and non-identifiers, although the latter is more marked than it was in 1973 or 1971. Voters for the Justice Party once more turn out to have the poorest fit, and - contrary to the general trend - the fit obtained for identifiers with this party is poorer than the fit obtained for non-identifiers. Three other parties (SD, SF, and Frp) the voters of which were found to be fitted poorer than average in 1973 are once more below average in this respect in 1975.

But in 1975, sympathy data from the voters for three other parties - DKP, CD, and VS - turn out to be fitted poorer than average, too. In the case of the Center-Democrats we are dealing with extremely small numbers (7 respondents, only one of these being an identifier), so the result is highly unreliable.[21]

Discarding CD (and the voters for the Justice Party) we find that it is the perception of the party space by respondents reporting a vote for one of the "workers' parties" (SD, SF, DKP, VS, and Frp)[22] that seems to be consistently represented poorer than average by our model.

To check if there are any systematic deviations in the way voters for the "workers' parties" perceive the party system in 1975, a separate solution for working class respondents is obtained. This solution, superimposed on the map from Figure 4.1., is shown in Figure 4.11.

Fig. 4.11.: Perceived party space 1975 with separate solution for working class respondents (bold symbols)

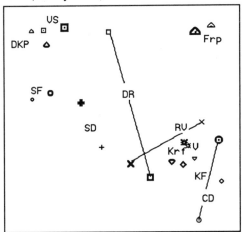

The separate solution fits the sympathy data from working class respondents somewhat better than did the common model in Figure 4.1. (unweighted R^2 = 0.67). Still the increase in goodness of fit is not dramatic.

The map obtained from the sympathy grades administered by this group of respondents alone resembles the map in Figure 4.1. in many respects. This is also reflected by the measure of agreement between the two maps (M = 0.67).

But there are two striking differences to be noticed as well. In the first

---

[21] If we include two respondents who reported a CD-vote but have missing values on the party identification question, the mean R^2-value for CD is in fact above average (0.68)!

[22] Between them, these five parties had 74.7 pct. of the working class vote in 1975. Moreover, they ranked highest among all parties with respect to the proportion of working class votes in their total constituencies: DKP received 66.7 pct., SD 44.0 pct., VS 31.6 pct., Frp 28.7 pct., and SF 23.9 pct. of their votes from working class voters.

place, the position of the Justice Party is widely different on the two maps. To the working class respondents the Justice Party is close to the bourgeois parties (as in fact it can be said to be in a number of respects due to for example its pronounced liberalistic stand). But this is not how all respondents see it.

In the second place, the "four-leaved clover" parties (KF, CD, Krf and V) are seen as closer to each other by the working class respondents than they are on the common map, while working class respondents perceive the Socialdemocrats to be farther away from the bourgeois parties. This way of looking at other parties is faintly reminiscent of a "we against the others"- or "Lager"-attitude which one would expect to find, when the perception of the party system is conditioned by, e.g., party preference or party identification.

Despite these differences there are some strong structural similarities between the two maps. It therefore appears sensible to say that the maps of the perceived party system in Figures 4.1. and 4.2. do not systematically misrepresent the perception of working class respondents.

In conclusion it thus appears that the conditioning influence of party preference and party identification on the perception of the party system was about the same in 1975 as it was in connection with the two previous elections. This impression is confirmed by a multiple classification analysis (MCA) with the respondents' R^2-values as the dependent and party preference and party identification as independent variables: With the 1975-data, party preference and party identification account for 13.8 pct. of the variation in the goodness of fit (as against 18.6 pct. in 1973).

Table 4.5.: R^2 for perceived party space 1975, broken down by class and party identification

	Working class	Middle class	Self-employed	Out of labor force	Under education	All
Party identifiers	0.66	0.74	0.82	0.69	0.71	0.72
Non-identifiers	0.52	0.63	0.75	0.72	0.55	0.64
All	0.60	0.68	0.78	0.69	0.61	0.68

In Table 4.5. the overall measure of fit for the model has been broken down according to the respondents' class and party identification. As has been the case with both 1971- and 1973-data, the average fit values for working class respondents are below the overall average fit obtained for the model in 1975 as well, while the best fit is once more obtained for self-employed respondents. The average fit for young people under education is below the overall average too, but since this group numbers only few respondents, not too much should be made of that finding.

A multiple classification analysis (MCA) with individual R^2-values as dependent and party preference, party identification, and class as independent variables accounts for 17.4 pct. of the variance in the individual fit-values. This is below the level found in 1973, and may clearly be called marginal.

Finally we shall shortly examine the relationship between how the respondents perceived the party system in 1975 and the patterns of party relationships as they surface in the parties' legislative behavior from 1973 and 1975. From the outset one would expect this relationship to be weaker in 1975 than it was in both 1971 and 1973, due to the confusing parliamentary situation that existed prior to the election in 1975.

Fig. 4.12.: Legislative party space 1973-75 (bold symbols) with perceived party space 1975 superimposed

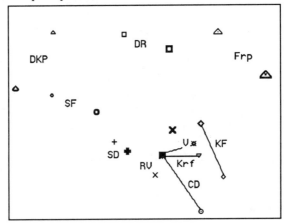

Figure 4.12. shows the map of the "legislative party system", derived from the parties' stand in roll calls on government bills in the 1973-75 legislature and superimposed on the map of the perceived party system in 1975 (from Figure 4.1.). This map of the "legislative party system" fits the roll call data extremely well ($R^2 = 0.96$). Moreover, the agreement between the two maps is quite satisfactory (M = 0.66). Obviously the respondents had managed somehow to keep a realistic picture of what was going on between the parties.

But there are nevertheless some systematic differences between how the party system in 1975 looked to the respondents and how it looks when judged from the parties' actual legislative behavior. Obviously the distance between the parties backing the "narrow" Agrarian government (CD, Krf, and V) and the Socialdemocrats is perceived to be larger by the respondents than it appears to be when judged from the parties' legislative behavior. The same tendency exists for the distance between the governments' "backing

132

group" and the Radical Liberals. On the other hand, the respondents tend to underrate the distance between the parties supporting the government and the Conservatives.

With regard to the two parliamentary debutantes, the Center-Democrats and the Progress Party, Figure 4.12. shows that the respondents were quite able to reappraise the previous perception of the position of these two parties with an eye to their recorded parliamentary behavior. It may be said that they did not perceive the full extent of the Progress Party's move to the right (relative to its position in the perceived party space in 1973), but still the change between the perceived positions of this party in 1973 and 1975 is in the direction indicated by its parliamentary record. As for the Center-Democrats the change in perceived position between 1973 and 1975 - from a position as kind of a right-wing Socialdemocratic party to a position in the bourgeois "four-leaved clover" - appears to closely reflect the actual parliamentary behavior of this party.

In conclusion it can be said that the influence from the hypothetically conditioning factors - party preference, party identification and class - on the respondents' perception of the party system in 1975 was about the same size as in 1973, and that the relationship between the respondents' perception of the party system and the parties' legislative behavior showed the same strength as in 1973. Once more, propositions 2.1. and 2.2. appear to have been confirmed.

4.4. Perception of the party system and voting behavior: Reactive voting in 1975

In this section we shall finally examine to what extent the voter movements between parties occurring from the 1973- to the 1975-election can be accounted for as simple reactions to changing party positions in the perceived party space or to other characteristic developments in this space. We shall do this by testing our model of reactive voting, which is based on two fundamental assumptions, viz. that voters vote for the party closest to their "ideal point" in the perceived party space, and that the voters' "ideal points" in the perceived party space remain fixed between any two elections.

Table 4.6. gives the non-zero regression coefficients obtained when the model is applied to each of the 11 parties running in the 1975-election. As can be seen, for all parties the probability of voters moving to this particular party in 1975 is related - in the stipulated way - to at least a subset of the characteristics of the perceived party space and to the movements of the parties in this space from 1973 to 1975, as these movements were perceived by the respondents.

Table 4.6.: Regression coefficients for reactive voting model 1975. (Standard errors in parentheses)

	Intercept b_0	DISTij b_1	DISTjj b_2	NCLOSE b_3	DIST3 b_4	VPROP b_5
SD	4.32721 (0.17813)	-1.19555 (0.89409)	0.09874 (0.35904)	-0.50567 (0.14171)	0.85395 (0.58385)	
RV	3.74366 (0.42097)	-1.53970 (2.31089)	0.62616 (0.91696)	-0.42840 (0.20958)	2.17811 (2.79648)	
KF	1.60112 (0.43256)		2.45121 (0.46949)	-0.47720 (0.06979)	2.87231 (0.53472)	
DR	3.33841 (0.53656)	-3.94783 (2.34326)	2.75394 (1.15160)	-0.24449 (0.43577)		
SF	3.23296 (0.37310)			-0.53926 (0.08707)	0.40193 (1.11974)	
DKP	1.31088 (1.13946)	-1.94668 (1.39495)		-0.34631 (0.15619)	10.31880 (3.48845)	
CD	-0.35405 (0.89078)	-0.39217 (0.70281)	4.64519 (1.28256)			
Krf	3.39569 (0.88108)	-3.63422 (1.92133)		-0.23768 (0.12638)	1.47000 (2.12592)	0.43376 (0.67068)
V	4.47084 (0.18935)	-2.48517 (0.18818)	2.04335 (0.22741)			5.48030 (0.69918)
VS	4.48130 (0.31331)	-4.19194 (1.00323)	4.10187 (1.03839)	-0.36049 (0.14525)		
Frp	4.08112 (0.28801)		0.32216 (0.44391)	-0.39628 (0.04574)	1.30982 (0.91092)	

In comparison with the corresponding figures from 1973 (Table 3.12. above), it can be seen that there is no longer any systematic difference between "old" and new and/or small parties as to the composition of the relevant subset of variables. Only for three parties - two of which belong to the "old" parties in the party system - the distances between their location in the perceived party space of 1975 and the location of other parties in the perceived party space of 1973 is not related to their chances of picking up voters from these other parties in 1975.

It can also be seen that the variable indicating how many parties were closer to the perceived location of party (j) in 1973 than was a party (i) (NCLOSE) appears much more frequently in the relevant subset of variables in 1975 than it did in 1973. The same is true of the variable measuring the distance between the perceived location of party (j) in 1973 and 1975, respectively (DISTjj). This indicates that in 1975 the chances of picking up voters from other parties (as well as the party's core voters) were much more dependent on the movements of other parties than they had been in 1973.

Table 4.7. shows the expected voter movements between parties that should have occurred between 1973 and 1975 according to the model of reactive voting. The actual voter movements computed from the 1975-survey data, using the recall-question, are given in parentheses beneath the corresponding expected figures.

Visual inspection of Table 4.7. reveals that the deviations between expected (from the model of reactive voting) and observed voter movements are greater in 1975 than they were in 1973. The value of the non-similarity index bears out this impression (NS = 0.14), being about 50 pct. above the 1973-value. Still this is not an expression of poor fit, however, meaning that only about 14 pct. of the proportions would have to be moved to make the expected and observed figures equal.

Inspection of the figures in Table 4.7. further suggests that the model of reactive voting is particularly successful in predicting which other parties a certain party was *not* able to get voters from: Out of a total of 53 cases, where no voter movement has been observed between two parties, 44 are correctly "predicted" by the model. Moreover, the model is most often very close to the mark in predicting the proportion of voters who voted for the same party in both the 1973- and the 1975-election. In 7 out of the 11 cases, the figure returned by the model is accurate (to one decimal).

In other respects, the models "predictions" are less accurate. This can be seen easily by examining the "predictions" of voter movements to the Agrarians. Here the influx of former voters for the Socialdemocrats, Center-Democrats, Christian Peoples' Party, and Progress Party is exaggerated, while the attractiveness of the Agrarians to former voters for the Radical Liberals and the Conservatives is underestimated, as is the ability of the Agrarians to hold on to their own 1973-voters. On the other hand, the model captures quite well where - in a broad sense - the many new voters for the Agrarians in 1975 came from, and where they did not come from.[23]

It is obvious, then, that the model of reactive voting is able to account for a lesser part of the voter movements between the 1973- and 1975-elections than between the 1971- and 1973-elections. There are at least two possible explanations for this difference, one purely technical, the other substantial.

The technical explanation would ascribe the differences in the fit of the models for the 1973- and 1975-elections, respectively, to differences in data quality. While the observed party shifts from 1971 to 1973 can be computed from panel-data, the observed party shifts from 1973 to 1975 are obtained from the recall-question in the 1975-survey. There is little doubt that the 1973-75 data contain more noise than do the 1971-73 data, and naturally

---

[23] In contrast the losses of the Center-Democrats are well accounted for by the model. They obviously reflect a reaction to the perceived movement of this party from a position between the Socialdemocrats and the center to a position close to the liberal and conservative parties.

this will have an adverse effect on the goodness of fit obtainable with the 1973-75 data.

Table 4.7.: Observed and expected voter movements 1973 - 1975 in percentages of all respondents (n = 1132). Observed percentages in parentheses.

Party 1975	Party 1973										
	SD	RV	KF	DR	SF	DKP	CD	Krf	V	VS	Frp
SD	24.3	1.0	0.5	0.2	0.4	0.2	0.4	0.2	1.1	0.0	0.9
	(24.3)	(0.8)	(0.0)	(0.1)	(0.6)	(1.1)	(0.4)	(0.4)	(0.4)	(0.0)	(1.1)
RV	0.3	5.7	0.3	0.0	0.0	0.0	0.1	0.0	0.4	0.0	0.0
	(0.4)	(5.7)	(0.1)	(0.0)	(0.0)	(0.0)	(0.3)	(0.0)	(0.3)	(0.0)	(0.2)
KF	0.0	0.0	3.6	0.0	0.0	0.0	0.4	0.0	0.7	0.0	1.1
	(0.0)	(0.0)	(4.7)	(0.3)	(0.0)	(0.0)	(0.2)	(0.1)	(0.4)	(0.0)	(0.3)
DR	0.1	0.0	0.0	1.8	0.0	0.0	0.2	0.0	0.0	0.0	0.0
	(0.0)	(0.0)	(0.0)	(1.8)	(0.2)	(0.0)	(0.2)	(0.0)	(0.0)	(0.0)	(0.0)
SF	0.6	0.1	0.1	0.0	2.4	0.1	0.0	0.0	0.2	0.0	0.2
	(0.4)	(0.4)	(0.0)	(0.3)	(2.4)	(0.1)	(0.1)	(0.0)	(0.0)	(0.1)	(0.0)
DKP	0.9	0.0	0.0	0.6	0.7	1.5	0.0	0.0	0.0	0.1	0.0
	(0.4)	(0.0)	(0.0)	(0.2)	(0.1)	(2.6)	(0.0)	(0.0)	(0.0)	(0.0)	(0.0)
CD	0.0	0.0	0.2	0.0	0.0	0.0	0.6	0.0	0.1	0.0	0.0
	(0.0)	(0.0)	(0.0)	(0.0)	(0.0)	(0.0)	(0.7)	(0.0)	(0.2)	(0.0)	(0.0)
Krf	0.2	0.2	0.1	0.0	0.0	0.0	0.2	4.1	1.1	0.0	0.3
	(0.0)	(0.3)	(0.3)	(0.0)	(0.0)	(0.0)	(0.0)	(4.1)	(1.1)	(0.0)	(0.3)
V	3.7	0.7	0.9	0.0	0.0	0.0	3.4	1.6	13.2	0.0	3.3
	(0.6)	(1.8)	(2.6)	(0.0)	(0.0)	(0.0)	(1.1)	(0.7)	(17.3)	(0.0)	(2.5)
VS	0.2	0.0	0.0	0.0	0.4	0.4	0.3	0.0	0.0	0.5	0.0
	(0.0)	(0.0)	(0.0)	(0.1)	(0.4)	(0.3)	(0.3)	(0.0)	(0.1)	(0.5)	(0.0)
Frp	0.6	0.3	0.4	0.1	0.1	0.1	0.3	0.1	0.4	0.0	11.1
	(0.4)	(0.2)	(0.6)	(0.2)	(0.2)	(0.0)	(0.2)	(0.2)	(0.3)	(0.0)	(11.1)

On the other hand a substantial explanation cannot be excluded. The poorer fit of the "reactive voting"-model in 1975 may seem to closely parallel the breakdown of the "responsibility"-hypothesis, when this hypothesis is applied to Danish data from 1973 onwards (Paldam and Schneider, 1980). The authors propose that this breakdown might be related to the confusing parliamentary situation following the 1973-election, which may have made it difficult to the voters to find out whom to blame for the state of the economy and whom to reward.

The same logic could be applied to the present case, meaning that due to the intricacies of the parliamentary situation leading up to the election in

1975, the respondents found it harder than in 1973 to apply the deliberate strategy of party shift described by the model of "reactive voting". Some support for this view can be taken form the observation above (sec. 4.2.) that the percentage of respondents reporting a vote for a party different from the party (or parties) they had given the highest thermometer grade increases between 1973 and 1975.

It should also be noticed that the poorest fit between observed and expected voter movements occurs with the Agrarians, meaning that the upsurge of this party in 1975 is difficult to account for by our model of reactive voting. This suggests that to a considerable degree shifts to the Agrarians in 1975 may not simply have been reactions to a perceived change of location of this party relative to the "backlash"- and the left-right dimension, but may reflect the working of some kind of "valence dimension" not captured by our models.

Still it should be remembered that we are not faced here with anything resembling a breakdown of the "reactive voting"-model (as was the case with the "responsibility"-hypothesis tested by Paldam and Schneider). For most parties, the model still fits the variations in the recorded party shifts from the 1973- to the 1975-election rather well. But the poorer overall fit of the "reactive voting"-model suggests that the 1975-election rather than the much epithetized "landslide election" of 1973 may constitute a deviant case as far as the patterns of voter movements between parties are concerned.

5. Intermezzo: The general election of February 1977

5.1. Background, campaign, and outcome

The Socialdemocratic minority government that took over from the "narrow" Agrarian government in 1975 found itself in much the same situation as the Agrarians in the preceding 13 months. With the Folketing still strongly fragmented after the latest election, the task of building a stable coalition was almost impossible and finding majorities was extremely difficult.

Under these circumstances, the government's greatest asset turned out to be the animosity between the non-socialist parties which practically barred the danger of a common non-socialist opposition overthrowing the government. After having pulled the rug from beneath the feet of a new bourgeois government in 1975, the Progress Party was generally considered a bunch of political outcasts by the other non-socialist parties; under the penalty of losing its reputation as a "responsible" party, none of them dared or wanted to cooperate with them. Thus 24 of the non-socialist parties' 102 votes in the Folketing were effectively neutralized. Besides that, neither the Conservatives nor the Radical Liberals had forgotten what had appeared to them the extraordinary rudeness shown by the Agrarians in connection with the formation of the "narrow" Agrarian government in 1973, while the Center-Democrats felt antagonized by Hartling's decision in 1975 to call elections at a time when it was clear from the opinion polls that this might possibly mean the exit of the Center-Democrats altogether - a fate from which in the end they had barely managed to escape.

In this situation, the Socialdemocratic government turned primarily to the three small non-socialist parties - Radical Liberals, Center-Democrats, and Christian Peoples' Party - for support of its legislation. Together with the Socialdemocrats, these three parties could muster only 79 seats, however - not enough to pass a bill, even provided the members elected on Greenland and the Faeroe Islands abstained, which usually they could be expected to do if the bill was of no specific concern to their regions.

But in a number of situations the government succeeded in enlisting the necessary support of one or both of the "old" non-socialist parties as well. This was typically done by negotiating "package deals" consisting of a number of bills targeted at some particular issue. The period from 1975 to 1977 saw its share of them, so many in fact that they came to be christened after the month in which they were concluded.

In the spring of 1975, the Folketing intervened in the ongoing tariff negotiations to hinder strikes. Working conditions and tariff regulations were fixed by law. All non-socialist parties, except for the Progress Party, supported this measure. In September of the same year, a number of expansive economic measures were passed, primarily to fight unemployment. This time the Agrarians joined the three small non-socialist parties, and a package deal on housing policies concluded in 1976 was supported by both the Conservatives and the Agrarians. In august 1976, it had once more become time to do something about the economy. This time, restrictive measures were called for. A package deal supported by one or both of the two big non-socialist parties proved unfeasible this time, but the Conservatives voted for most of the proposals nevertheless.

In an attempt to strengthen the governments' position prior to the final stage of another round of difficult tariff negotiations in the labor marked and to soften the opposition's increasingly intransigent stand, Prime Minister Anker Jørgensen - without being forced to do so by a parliamentary defeat - decided to call for new elections to be held on February 15, 1977. In this situation he acted much in the same way his precedessor Hartling had done two years earlier.

This time 12 parties were running in the election.[1] Besides the parties that had participated in the 1975-election, a newly founded Pensioners' Party (Pens) was presenting itself to the voters, mainly appealing to the votes from the about 200.000 pensioners.

The central issues of the campaign were unemployment and incomes policy. Unemployment had been rising steadily and was now close to 10 pct.. It was acknowledged by all parties to be a serious social problem, but the proposed solutions varied widely. Incomes policy also divided the parties - from the left-wing parties rejecting such a thing out of hand to the bourgeois parties accusing the government of being afraid to use this instrument effectively.

As can be seen from Table 5.1., the outcome of the election was primarily a success for the Socialdemocrats. With 37 pct. of the votes and 65 seats in the new Folketing, they were finally back at their pre-1973 strength.

Table 5.1.: Electoral results 1977 (with 1975 for comparison)

| Party | 9.1.1975 | | 15.2.1977 | |
	votes (pct.)	seats	votes (pct.)	seats
SD	29.9	53	37.0	65
RV	7.1	13	3.6	6
KF	5.5	10	8.5	15
DR	1.8	0	3.3	6
SF	5.0	9	3.9	7
DKP	4.2	7	3.7	6
CD	2.2	4	6.4	11
Pens	-	-	0.9	0
Krf	5.3	9	3.4	6
V	23.3	42	12.0	21
VS	2.1	4	2.7	5
Frp	13.6	24	14.6	26

---

[1]The Schlesvigian Party was again running on the Center-Democrats' ticket.

Also gaining were the Conservatives, the Center-Democrats and the Progress Party. With their leadership crisis finally resolved, the Conservatives managed to increase their number of seats in the Folketing from 10 to 15. The Center-Democrats jumped from 4 to 11 seats,[2] while the Progress Party, obtaining 26 seats, was only two seats from its stunning 1973-success and was back as the second largest party in the new Folketing. Finally, the Justice Party managed to stage a successful comeback.

The big losers were the Agrarians, who were not able to hold on to what they had gained in 1975, but lost it all. Another big loser were the Radical Liberals, for the second time in a row losing seven seats.[3]

The new Folketing was still very fragmented, and the parliamentary situation had not been changed significantly by the electoral outcome. But the Socialdemocrats' morale had been boosted considerably, and the government simply continued in office without negotiations, confident (rightly) that even though there still was a majority of non-socialist parties in the new Folketing, these parties would not be able to get together to overthrow the government.

5.2. Perception of the party system 1977

In the following section we shall examine the perception of the party system that is supposed to have been lying at the bottom of the respondents' vote decision in 1977. Again the main interest will be focused on how clearly the respondents perceived the alternatives at hand and which dimensions did structure their perceptions for them.

---

[2] After the election, the Center-Democrats' leader, Erhard Jakobsen, was almost universally credited for the spectacular recovery of his party, which was ascribed to his performance in the final party leader debate in TV. Erhard Jakobsen managed to partly monopolize this debate by suddenly bringing up the issue of indoctrination in schools, backed by concrete examples. According to commentaries he had won scores of votes by thus "pulling a white rabbit out of his hat".

At first glance data seem to support this point of view: 53.2 pct. of those voting CD in 1977 reported to have decided to do so only in the last days before the election. But if data from 1975 are scrutinized it turns out that the proportion of CD-voters who reported to have made up their mind very late in the campaign was high in that election, too: Here 44.4 pct. (the highest proportion among all parties) reported to have decided to vote for the Center-Democrats only in the last days prior to the election in 1975.

[3] A leadership crisis may have contributed to the Radical Liberals' poor showing in the 1977-election. Their leader, former prime minister Baunsgaard, had announced his resignation from the leadership, partly because a wing in the party opposing his line and advocating closer cooperation with the Socialist Peoples' Party was gaining some momentum.

The Socialist Peoples' Party was in a crisis itself, having just purged its wing of "Larsenists", adherents of the late founder of the party, who supported closer cooperation with the Socialdemocrats. Predictably, the Socialist Peoples' Party lost votes and seats as well.

Table 5.2. shows the median sympathy grades for the parties in 1977, broken down by reported vote. As can be seen from the bottom line, the three left-wing parties (SF, DKP, and VS) once more received median thermometer grades below zero in 1977. The same did the new Pensioners' Party and the Progress Party. The latter even took over from the Communists as the on average most disliked party in the Danish party system. As Table 5.2. shows, it got a negative median grade from voters for all other parties. In comparison to the thermometer grades it received in both 1973 and 1975, this drop constitutes a significant change in the overall evaluation of the Progress Party and indicates its increasing isolation in the party system.[4] But still the majority of parties in the party system was - on average - perceived positively.

Table 5.2.: Sympathy scores by reported vote 1977 (medians).
(Bold: most preferred party; italic: next most preferred party)

Voted for	Sympathy scores for											
	SD	RV	KF	DR	SF	DKP	CD	Pens	Krf	V	VS	Frp
SD	**91.6**	*28.3*	14.2	8.4	6.6	-21.9	20.1	-9.7	-0.7	-6.0	-19.7	-91.6
RV	*51.1*	**83.0**	26.7	10.0	-9.0	-48.6	23.0	-5.5	6.4	18.8	-35.0	-92.4
KF	30.7	3.2	**82.2**	-0.9	-57.7	-91.9	45.2	-40.0	30.6	37.5	-90.7	-16.7
DR	48.2	30.0	8.5	**83.6**	2.3	-30.0	5.0	-36.7	-5.4	-1.7	-26.7	-90.0
SF	*54.8*	18.2	-52.5	19.0	**89.6**	39.1	-62.5	-9.0	-62.0	-47.0	38.8	-96.4
DKP	*52.5*	0	-5.7	31.4	45.7	**94.1**	-90.7	-55.0	-96.5	-92.0	47.0	-95.2
CD	*53.5*	2.5	22.7	-20.0	-50.7	-85.7	**77.9**	-52.5	33.0	36.5	-75.0	-8.8
Pens	*40.0*	0	15.0	40.0	-30.0	-30.0	30.0	**80.0**	-30.0	0	-30.0	-20.0
Krf	38.0	30.0	40.0	10.0	-30.0	-77.1	41.8	-5.0	**94.7**	*48.0*	-52.5	-37.5
V	37.8	12.0	*46.3*	-12.9	-53.9	-93.4	43.2	-8.4	32.7	**90.0**	-88.4	-2.6
VS	50.0	15.7	-63.3	20.6	*54.0*	30.0	-78.9	-1.8	-56.3	-43.3	**85.0**	-93.8
Frp	26.9	3.2	23.8	5.5	-40.0	-80.0	*37.5*	-8.6	14.8	15.8	-58.3	**88.6**
All	59.2	16.7	19.9	5.7	-6.9	-39.4	27.4	-9.8	6.2	11.0	-30.7	-44.3

The Socialdemocrats stand out as the most popular party of the 1977-election. Compared to the median grades from 1975 (Table 4.2. above), it can be seen that the party improved its standing with the voters for almost all other parties. Moreover, while in 1975 it was the second most preferred party for voters for the Socialist Peoples' Party only, in 1977 it was the second most preferred party for voters for six parties. Of these, two were left-wing parties (SF and DKP), the rest were non-socialist parties. Thus by 1977 the Socialdemocrats obviously had acquired a central position in the party system which made the party widely acceptable in the electorate.

---

[4] This finding is paralleled by another one, to be reported below, which shows that - beginning in 1977 - the perception of the party system by voters for the Progress Party is represented considerably poorer than average by a common model of the perceived party system. This indicates that the appeal and the recruitment basis of the Progress Party had shrunk, compared to previous elections, and from 1977 onwards contained a rather high proportion of voters with quite peculiar perceptions of the party system.

The Agrarians, on the other hand, which had been the most popular party in 1975 were confronted with a heavy loss in sympathy. In 1977 they ranked only fifth in median sympathy among all respondents, and they received lower grades than in 1975 from voters for most other parties. And while in 1975 they had been the second most preferred party for voters for five other parties, in 1977 they were the second most preferred party for voters from the Christian Peoples' Party only; voters for the Radical Liberals and for the Justice Party now had the Socialdemocrats as their second most preferred party, while voters for the Conservatives and the Progress Party had transferred that rank to the Center-Democrats. Thus in 1977 the Agrarians appear to have become rather marginal in the perception of the respondents.

Table 5.2. also indicates that the change in the perceived position of the Radical Liberals in the party system that had emerged in 1975 was continuing: Respondents voting for this party in 1977 can be seen to be more sympathetic to the Socialdemocrats and to show a less negative attitude towards the left-wing parties (SF, DKP, and VS) than RV-voters had exhibited in 1975. This change in attitude was evidently not paralleled by a corresponding change in the attitude of voters for these parties towards the Radical Liberals, however. But it obviously did cost the Radical Liberals sympathies with voters for the non-socialist parties (with the exception of voters for the Justice Party and the Christian Peoples' Party).

The general perception of the new Pensioners' Party was negative, as can be seen from its median score in the bottom row of Table 5.2., which is well below zero. The party received negative median grades from all voters but its own. Closer inspection reveals striking differences in the perception of the newcomer, however.

The party's own voters appear to have seen the Pensioners' Party as some kind of centrist party with a leaning to the non-socialist camp. They have the Socialdemocrats and the Justice Party as their second most preferred parties. But, as a whole, they are more sympathetic towards the non-socialist than towards the socialist parties, and only voters for three parties (V, CD, and KF) are less negative towards the Progress Party than are voters for the Pensioners' Party.

On the other hand, the Pensioners' Party receives its least negative grading from voters for the Left Socialists and its most negative grading from communist voters. This is paralleled in the non-socialist camp by a not very negative grading of the party by voters for the Agrarians and the Christian Peoples' Party, alongside with grades below -50 degrees from voters for the Center-Democrats and the Conservatives.[5]

Figure 5.1. shows the map of the perceived party system in 1977 as derived from the respondents' thermometer grading of the parties. The map brings out the existence of two clusters of parties in the perceived party

---

[5]For proper representation, the Pensioners' Party might in fact need a dimension of its own. But since the party matters very little, it has been preferred to stick to a two-dimensional representation.

system of 1977: Near the left edge there is a cluster of socialist parties (SF, DKP, and VS). On the opposite side, a "four-leaved clover" of non-socialist parties (KF, CD, Krf, and V) can be found. None of these clusters is very tight, however.

Fig. 5.1.: Perceived party system 1977

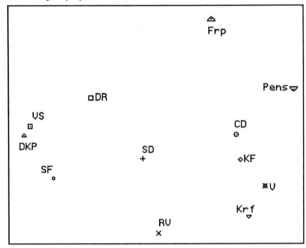

Fig. 5.2.: Parties and "ideal points" in perceived party space 1977*

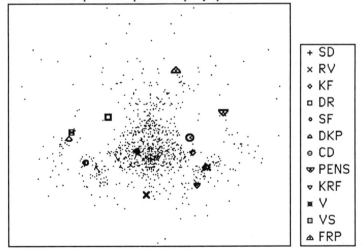

*12 outliers removed.

The Socialdemocrats occupy the middle ground between the two clusters, while the Radical Liberals appear suspended in the middle of nowhere. As was to be expected, the Progress Party is still fairly isolated, but is still not seen as markedly rightist. The Pensioners' Party's position reflects that it is rejected by voters for all other parties, but least so by voters for the non-socialist parties.

In Figure 5.2. the respondents' "ideal points" have been added to the map. Contrary to what was found in both 1973 and 1975, the arrangement of the bulk of "ideal points" is almost circular around the center of the map in 1977. Thus the variance (over respondents) is about the same with respect to both dimensions.

The fit of the map to the thermometer data from 1977 is somewhat poorer than for the corresponding maps from the preceding elections (weighted $R^2 = 0.79$; unweighted $R^2 = 0.60$). In part at least, this poorer fit is a consequence of the increased number of parties to be fitted (12 in 1977 as against 11 in 1973 and 1975, and 9 in 1971). Moreover, the very varied perceptions of the new Pensioners' Party found in the data undoubtedly accounts for some part of the deterioration in fit.

The "hindcasted" distribution of votes that can be obtained from the maps - under the assumption that the respondents vote for the party closest to their "ideal point" on the map - is given in Table 5.3.

Table 5.3.: Reported and "hindcasted" distribution of votes 1977

| Party | Distribution of votes | |
	reported (n=1241)	"hindcasted" (n=1435)
SD	44.3	48.8
RV	3.1	4.3
KF	7.7	6.0
DR	3.5	1.5
SF	5.9	5.8
DKP	2.4	2.8
CD	5.2	4.2
Pens	0.6	1.3
Krf	2.4	3.8
V	12.9	9.7
VS	2.0	1.8
Frp	9.4	9.7

As can be seen from Table 5.3., the "hindcast" picks up the main trend of the 1977-election - the upsurge of the vote for the Socialdemocrats and the heavy losses of the Agrarians. In fact, these tendencies are even somewhat exaggerated by the "hindcast". The recovery of the Center-Democrats is likewise brought out, but the "hindcast" fails to detect the come back of the Justice Party. Altogether the deviations from the reported distribution of votes are small (NS = 0.08).

Despite the numerous small deviations between the reported and the "hindcasted" distribution of votes in 1977, the percentage of votes "hindcasted" correctly (79.4 pct.) remains quite high. Thus, although the models fit is the poorest so far, it is still good enough to allow us to consider proposition 1.1. confirmed also by the data from 1977.

Turning to the problem of identifying the basic structuring features in the respondents' perception of the party system in 1977, an answer is immediately suggested by the maps in Figures 5.1. and 5.2. The existence of a cluster of socialist parties opposite - in the horizontal direction - a cluster of non-socialist parties indicates that the horizontal direction on the map once more corresponds to a left-right dimension in the respondents' perception of the party system. As far as the vertical arrangement of the location of parties on the map is concerned, a separation between the new and minor parties, located nearer to the top of the map, and the "old" parties, located nearer to the bottom of the map (with the sole exception of the Christian Peoples' Party that mingles with the "old" parties), indicates that the vertical direction may signify the continued existence of a "backlash"-dimension in the respondents' perception of the party system. We shall attempt to validate this interpretation in the familiar manner, using the distribution of the respondents' issue positions on various issues as clues to an understanding of the substantial meaning of the axes on the maps in Figures 5.1. and 5.2.

Fig. 5.3.: Perceived party space and issue positions on two economic items 1977

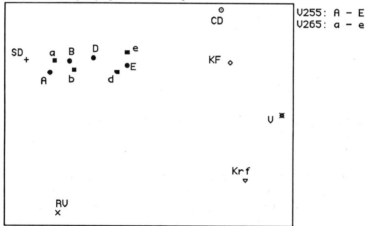

A, a: Agree completely; B, b : Do agree in part; D, d: Do disagree in part; E, e: Disagree completely

In the previous analyses economic issues have invariably tended to elicit responses the patterns of which are structured by the left-right dimension. In the 1977-survey, three of the economic items that were used in 1973 and

1975 as well reappear.[6] Both V255 (on economic equality) and V265 (on harder taxation of high incomes) produce median "ideal points" that are strung out in a horizontal direction, cf. Figure 5.3. Item V250 (on state control with private investments) fails in 1977.

The remaining economic items in the 1977-survey concern two major economic issues of high political actuality: Three items deal with incomes policy,[7] while two items deal with issues bearing on housing policy.[8]

Figure 5.4. shows the median "ideal points" in each of the non-neutral categories on the scales belonging to the three items pertaining to the incomes policy issue. As can be seen, the median "ideal points" are strung out in a horizontal direction on the map.

Fig. 5.4.: Perceived party space and issue positions on incomes policy-items 1977

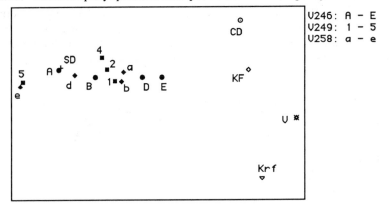

A, a, 1: Agree completely; B, b, 2: Do agree in part; D, d, 4: Do disagree in part; E, e, 5: Disagree completely

On comparison, there is an interesting difference between Figures 5.3. and 5.4.: The most leftist issue positions on the general economic items are located somewhat to the right of the position of the Socialdemocrats; agreement (or lip service) to the points of view expressed by these items thus extends into the center of the political spectrum. With regard to the

[6] V250 ("There is too little state control with private investments"), V255 ("In politics one should strive to make economic conditions equal for everybody, regardless of education and job"), and V265 ("High incomes should be taxed harder than today").

[7] V246 ("Under no circumstances should the Folketing interfere with tariff negotiations"), V249 ("The Folketing, and not interest organizations, must have the final responsibility for income development in this country"), and V258 ("We cannot afford wage rises in the present economic situation"). V246 and V258 were also used in the 1975-survey.

[8] V263 ("Homeowners' tax advantages should be abolished") and V266 ("There must be a freeze on further raises in rents").

more "tangible" content of the items dealing with incomes policy, the most leftist positions are clearly located to the left of the Socialdemocratic position. Thus the borderline between left and non-left is not fixed, but depends very much on the issue at hand, even with regard to economic issues.

Of the items dealing with the policy of housing, only item V263 (on abolishing the tax advantages of house owners) produces clearly structured issue positions. They are shown in Figure 5.5.

As Figure 5.5. shows, the issue positions on item V263 tend to be bent upwards in a north-eastern direction. Thus they are related to both the horizontal and the vertical dimension. The "pull" upwards is primarily due to voters for the Center-Democrats, the platform of which always contained a point on defending house owners against increased tax burdens.

Fig. 5.5.: Perceived party space and issue positions on housing policy item 1977

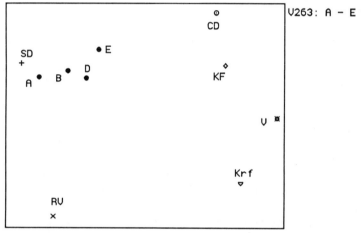

A, a: Agree completely; B, b : Do agree in part; D, d: Do disagree in part; E, e: Disagree completely

In all previous analyses the horizontal direction also turned out to structure issue positions on two foreign policy-items, one on leaving NATO as soon as possible and the other on EEC-membership. Both items were included in the 1977-survey as well.[9] Figure 5.6. shows the median "ideal points" in each of the non-neutral categories on the scale belonging to these two items.

From the figure it appears that support for membership of NATO and of the EEC obviously tends to increase, as one moves horizontally from the left to the right across the map. Thus we have the same relationship between

_____

[9] V209 ("If there were a referendum on EEC-membership today, would you vote for or against?") and V262 ("We should leave NATO as soon as possible").

foreign policy issue positions and the horizontal direction in the map of the perceived party system as in 1975.

Fig. 5.6.: Perceived party space and issue positions on NATO- and EEC-item 1977

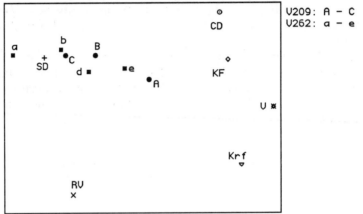

A: Would vote for membership; B: Would abstain; C: Would vote against membership
a: Agree completely; b: Do agree in part; d: Do disagree in part; e: Disagree completely

The structuring of issue positions brought out by economic and foreign policy items is then largely the same as was found in previous analyses. Together with the observed clustering of parties, it strongly supports the interpretation of the horizontal direction in the maps in Figures 5.1. and 5.2. as an 'ideological' left-right dimension in the respondents' political belief system.

This leaves the vertical direction to be identified. In previous analyses it turned out to be related to various kinds of "distrust", especially distrust in the regime and in the authorities. In the 1977-survey items relevant to both aspects of distrust were included.

Five items deal with distrust in or discontent with the democratic regime and its way of working.[10] With three of them - V257 (On a strong man taking power), V260 (On parliamentarism being better than any alternatives), and V267 (On democracy failing in a situation of crisis) - Table 5.4. shows a growth in the probability of getting an answer reflecting

---

[10] V247 ("It is through elections the people really determines how things shall be done in this country"), V252 ("The decision made by some majority in the Folketing is not necessarily the most democratic one"), V257 ("It might be very reasonable to have a strong man take power in an economic crisis"), V260 ("Parliamentarism is better suited to solve the country's problem than would be any other system"), and V269 ("Democracy fails when the country is confronted with really serious problems"). V257 (On a strong man taking power) was also used in the preceding surveys.

distrust or discontent as one moves from the bottom of the maps in Figures 5.1. and 5.2. towards the top.[11]

Table 5.4.: Net majorities agreeing to three "distrust"-items in each quartile of the vertical distribution of the "ideal points" in 1977

	V257	V260	V267
1. quartile	22.0	39.5	51.4
2. quartile	-2.7	46.5	25.3
3. quartile	-9.2	62.0	12.0
4. quartile	-26.5	63.0	7.4

Thus among those with their "ideal point" located in the upper quartile of the vertical dimension in the maps, a net majority of 22 pct. agrees to the idea of having a strong man taking power in an economic crisis. As one moves downwards in the vertical direction, an steadily increasing majority of the respondents having their "ideal points" located in the second, third or fourth quartile can be seen to oppose this idea. Likewise, a net majority of 39.5 pct. among those with their "ideal points" located in the upper quartile agree to parliamentarism being superior to other systems, as against a net majority of 63.0 pct. among those with their "ideal points" in the lowest quartile. And while a net majority of 51.4 pct. among those with their "ideal points" in the upper quartile doubt that democracy can handle a situation of crisis, this majority dwindles to 7.4 pct. among those with their "ideal points" in the lowest quartile. Thus there is no doubt that the vertical direction on the maps in Figures 5.1. and 5.2. once more is related to distrust or discontent, viz. distrust in the regime.

Four items relevant to the question of distrust in politicians were presented to the respondents in 1977. All of the items had been used in previous surveys as well.[12] The median "ideal points" in each category on the scales belonging to two of these items - V259 (On the politicians spending the taxpayers' money too lavishly) and V256 (On political leaders making the right decisions for the country) - turn out to be structured by the vertical direction in Figures 5.1. and 5.2., as can be seen from Figure 5.7.

---

[11] The two items failing to produce clearly structured response patterns are V247 and V252. As can be seen in the preceding note, their wording refers to rather abstract principles of democracy and representation, whereas the three items that do produce structured response patterns all refer to the ability of democratic systems to handle situations of crisis. Given the prevailing economic and political conditions in Denmark at the time of the survey, these three items may well have appeared less abstract and more salient to the respondents, thus making for higher reliability of the responses.

[12] V245 ("People wanting to make it to the top in politics are forced to give up most of their principles"), V254 ("Politicians usually do care too little about what the voters think"), V259 ("Politicians do spend the taxpayers' money too lavishly"), and V256 ("Usually one can trust our political leaders to make the right decisions for the country").

Fig. 5.7.: Perceived party space an issue positions on two "distrust in politicians"-items 1977

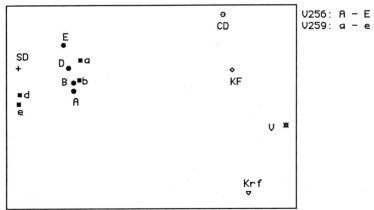

A, a: Agree completely; B, b : Do agree in part; D, d: Do disagree in part; E, e: Disagree completely

While the issue positions produced by item V256 are strung out roughly in parallel to the vertical direction, the issue positions produced by item V259 (On the politicians spending the taxpayers' money too lavishly) are arranged in a north-eastern direction, indicating that the stand taken on this item is determined both by the horizontal dimension - viz. the left-right dimension - and the vertical dimension: Those agreeing to the item tend to be both rightist and relatively distrustful. This pattern was found in previous analyses as well.

Finally we shall turn to three items relevant to other aspects of distrust or discontent than the "systemic" aspects. These items have been designed to tap a "moralist" attitude. All three items were used in previous surveys as well. In analyses of these data item V251 (on indoctrination in schools) turned out to be a "pure" left right-item in 1975, while item V264 (on having TV and radio kill extremist views by silence) did not produce a well-structured response pattern. Figure 5.8. shows the location of the median "ideal points" in the non-neutral response categories on the scales belonging to these two items in 1977. Moreover, it shows the median "ideal points" of the respondents answering that the moral development in society was a cause for concern, not a cause for concern, or undecided, respectively.[13]

As can be seen from Figure 5.8., issue positions on the "moralism"-items are strongly influenced by the left-right dimension. In general, concern about moral development in society and indoctrination in schools as well as support for having TV and radio kill extremist views by silence (i.e., a kind

---

[13] V210 ("The moral development in our society has been debated, e.g. pornography or the film on Jesus. Do you consider this development a cause for concern, or do you think it is not a special cause for concern?")

of censorship) increases as one moves from the left towards the right on the maps in Figures 5.1. and 5.2. But in the case of both the indoctrination- and the censorship-item, the locations of the median "ideal points" appear deflected a bit upwards in the north-eastern direction, indicating that the second dimension is structuring the positions on these items as well.

Fig. 5.8.: Perceived party system and issue position on "moralism"-items 1977

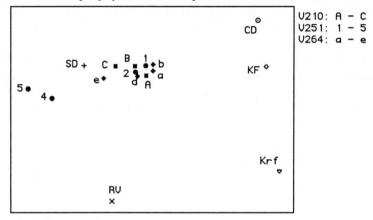

A: Cause for concern; B: It depends; C: Not a cause for concern
1,a: Agree completely; 2,b: Do agree in part; 4,d: Do disagree in part; 5,e: Disagree completely

Fig. 5.9.: Perceived party space and issue positions on "social benefits"-item

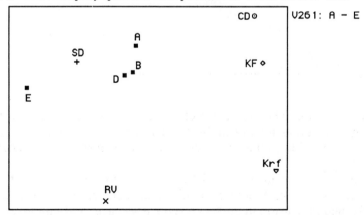

A: Agree completely; B: Do agree in part; D: Do disagree in part; E: Disagree completely

The same picture emerges if the item on social benefits is considered.[14] As has been the case in earlier analyses, the median "ideal points" of the respondents in each category of the scale belonging to this item are structured by both the horizontal and the vertical dimension, cf. Figure 5.9.

Thus the vertical direction in Figures 5.1. and 5.2. can once more be seen to be strongly related to attitudes of distrust, discontent and moralism. There is no reason to doubt that also in 1977 a "backlash"-dimension was present in the respondents' political belief system, and that this dimension is represented by the vertical dimension in the maps of the perceived party system. At the risk of boring the reader, proposition 1.2. can again be considered confirmed.

Finally, we shall shortly examine the relationship between the left-right dimension in the maps in Figures 5.1. and 5.2. and the class cleavage in 1977. Figure 5.10. shows the median "ideal points" of respondents belonging to the various classes according to their occupational status.

Fig. 5.10.: Perceived party space and class 1977

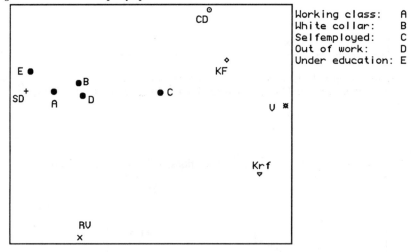

```
Working class:      A
White collar:       B
Selfemployed:       C
Out of work:        D
Under education:    E
```

Women not in the labor force are classified according to their husbands' class. Other respondents not in the labor force (O.A.P.'s etc.) are made a special group.[15] The same are students and other respondents under education.

As can be seen from Figure 5.10., the location of the median "ideal points" for respondents belonging to different social classes is structured by the horizontal dimension in the perceived party space: Self-employed are to

---

[14] V261 ("Too many people get social benefits without really needing them").
[15] Unfortunately, there is no data on mode of employment (private/public) in the 1977-survey.

the right, workers to the left, with white collar employees between them. Once more students and other respondents under education turn out to be the most leftist respondents in 1977.

Summing up the results of the preceding analysis we may conclude that propositions 1.1. and 1.2. concerning the perception of the party system in 1977 and the structuring of this perception have been confirmed: The respondents did indeed approach the election with a reasonably clear picture of what there was to choose from, and this picture was determined by a "backlash"- and a left-right dimension. Together, these two dimensions made up the grid used by the respondents to cut down the complexities of the political situation to a manageable size.

5.3. The impact of party identification, party vote, class, and party behavior on the perception of the party system 1977

In the following, the influence of a number of factors that might be suspected to have conditioned the respondents' perception of the party system shall be briefly examined. Moreover, we shall compare the perceived party system as derived from the thermometer gradings of the parties by the respondents with the legislative party system derived from the parties' legislative behavior between the elections of 1975 and 1977.

Table 5.5.: R^2 for perceived party space 1977, broken down by party identification and party voted for

Voted for	R2		
	Party identifiers	Non-identifiers	All
SD	0.63	0.64	0.63
RV	0.62	0.58	0.60
KF	0.70	0.67	0.69
DR	0.44	0.55	0.49
SF	0.69	0.54	0.63
DKP	0.63	0.68	0.65
CD	0.68	0.71	0.70
Pens	0.21	0.43	0.40
Krf	0.74	0.65	0.70
V	0.66	0.66	0.66
VS	0.63	0.61	0.62
Frp	0.44	0.46	0.45
All	0.63	0.58	0.61

In Table 5.5., the overall fit of the model of the perceived party space in 1977 (unweighted R^2) has been broken down according to reported party vote (party preference) and party identification. The table indicates that the perception of the party system held by voters for three out of the 12 parties is represented significantly poorer than average. The parties involved are the Justice Party (as usual), the new Pensioners' Party, and the Progress Party.

This finding is not surprising as far as the Justice Party is concerned. Voters for this party regularly show a perception of the party system which is not compatible with the way the overwhelming majority of the respondents sees it.

The finding is not surprising either with respect to voters for the Pensioners' Party. A look at the median thermometer grades in Table 5.1. above revealed that respondents reporting a vote for this party tended to feel simultaneously close to parties other respondents tend to perceive as very different. The explanation for this difference is probably that the Pensioners' Party was a single-issue party, and in that respect more like an interest organization than a party. Hence respondents preferring the Pensioners' Party may well have judged the "closeness" between it and other parties according to their stands on specific Pensioners-issues rather than according to their position with respect to the general 'ideological' dimensions that have been shown to structure the perception for the party system for the bulk of the respondents.

No such easy explanation seems available for the poor fit of the perception of the party system held by voters for the Progress Party. In previous analyses it was found that voters for the Progress Party were normally fitted just a bit below average, due mainly to a quite large number of respondents with relatively few political resources in its constituency. It appears tempting to relate the clear decrease in the goodness of fit of a common model of perception to the perception of Progress Party-voters to the continuing and increasing isolation of this party in the party system, which might have turned it into a party for voters with somewhat idiosyncratic political viewpoints.

Reverting for a moment to the sympathy scores in Table 5.2. above, one figure pointing in that direction can be found. As can be seen, voters for the Progress Party were quite sympathetic to the Socialdemocratic Party in 1977 - in fact it was the third-most preferred party for those voters. Obviously this perception does not agree too well with the general perception of the party system in 1977 which saw these two parties distances away from each other.

Following this lead, Table 5.6. presents the median sympathy scores administered to the parties by two groups of Progress Party voters in 1977: Those whose perception is represented below average and those whose perception is represented above average by the common model of the perceived party system in Figure 5.1. (as measured by the unweighted R^2).

Table 5.6. exhibits a clear tendency: Progress Party-voters who have their perception represented below average by the common model of the perceived party system, turn out to be those who as a group are more sympathetic to all socialist parties in the party system (SD, SF, DKP, and VS) than are those whose perception is represented above average. Obviously these respondents perceived the distance between the Progress Party and the socialist parties to be considerably smaller than did the rest of the respondents. There was then in 1977 a systematic difference between how a group of Progress Party-voters saw the party system and how it appeared to most other respondents.

Table 5.6.: Sympathy scores from Frp-voters 1977, broken down according to fit of the common model (medians).

Fit	Sympathy scores for											
	SD	RV	KF	DR	SF	DKP	CD	Pens	Krf	V	VS	Frp
< av.	39.1	0.1	20.2	-0.1	0	-59.3	40.0	-15.8	19.0	0.1	-19.4	80.2
≥ av.	20.5	0.3	40.4	20.9	-58.6	-100.0	50.0	-0.1	1.0	20.1	-79.4	99.9

Even though the maps in Figures 5.1. and 5.2. do not fit the perception of the party system among voters for the Justice Party, the Pensioners' Party, and the Progress Party too well, the influence of party preference and party identification on goodness of fit remains marginal. A multiple classification analysis (MCA) shows that party preference and party identification together account for about 10 pct. of the variance in the R^2-values.[16]

In Table 5.7., the R^2-values are broken down according to class and party identification. The picture emerging from this break-down is quite familiar from previous analyses.

Among those in the labor force we once more have the best fit for self-employed and the poorest for working class-respondents, with the white collar-group in between. The differences are rather small, however. It appears that in 1977 the influence of class on the perception of the party system was even more marginal than it was found to be in preceding elections.

Table 5.7.: R^2 for perceived party space 1977, broken down by class and party identification

	Working class	Middle class	Self-employed	Out of labor force	Under education	All
Party identifiers	0.62	0.63	0.64	0.64	0.56	0.63
Non-identifiers	0.54	0.61	0.63	0.55	0.56	0.58
All	0.58	0.62	0.63	0.61	0.56	0.61

---

[16] The exact value is $R^2 = 0.097$.

This impression is confirmed by a multiple classification analysis (MCA) with party preference, party identification, and class as independent variables. It turns out that class does not make an independent contribution to the variance in R^2-values above the contribution from party preference and party identification: Together the three factors account for exactly 10 pct. of the variance in the R^2-values.

While the influence of party preference, party identification, and class on the perception of the party system in 1977 can safely be assumed to have been marginal, this perception is very clearly related to developments in the legislative party system, i.e. the pattern of cooperation and conflict exhibited by the parties between the elections of 1975 and 1977. Figure 5.11. shows the legislative party system, derived from the stand taken by the parties in the final reading on government bills, with the perceived party system superimposed for easy comparison.

Fig. 5.11.: Legislative party space 1975-77 (bold symbols) with perceived party space 1977 superimposed

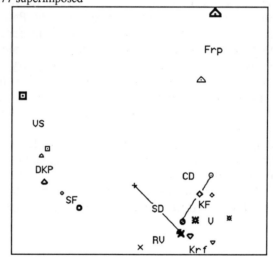

The agreement between the two maps is rather close (M = 0.78). Basically the structure in both maps appears to be the same. But there are also some clearly visible differences.

Most important, the distance between the Socialdemocrats and the non-socialist parties it had to cooperate with in the Folketing 1975-77 (RV, KF, CD, Krf, and V) is perceived by the respondents to be considerably larger than it turns out to have been in legislative work. The same is true for the distances between the non-socialist parties. One might be tempted to conclude that the respondents were fully aware of the fact that the cooperation between these parties in many cases was brought about by the necessity to build a majority for some decision rather than by the closeness of the parties' policy positions.

Another feature of the map in Figure 5.11. worth noticing is the tendency on the part of the respondents to underrate the distance between the extreme parties and the rest, as compared to the distance between the parties exhibited in the legislative arena. Especially the Progress Party was far more isolated in the Folketing than it was perceived to be in the perceived party system.

Concluding with respect to propositions 2.1. and 2.2., data from the 1977-survey tend to support them both: The influence of party preference, party identification, and class on the goodness of fit of a common model of the perceived party system is sufficiently marginal to allow one to infer that the way the respondents saw the alternatives to choose among in 1977 was only marginally affected by their party preference, party identification, or class. On the other hand, the resemblance between the perceived and the legislative party system is strong enough to suggest that - with some characteristic deviations - the perceived party system reflected the legislative party system in 1977.

5.4. Perception of the party system and voting behavior: Reactive voting in 1977

Finally we shall once more subject the model of reactive voting - and hence our proposition 3 - to an empirical test. Table 5.8. gives the non-zero regression coefficients obtained by fitting the model to data from 1975 and 1977.

As can be seen from the second column in Table 5.8., $DIST_{ij}$ (i.e. the distance from the (perceived) location of party (i) at time (t) to the (perceived) location of party (j) at time (t-1)) in most cases plays a role for the variation in the proportion of voters which party (i) succeeds in picking up from other parties. Also the distance from the (perceived) location of party (j) at time (t-1) to the (perceived) location of this party at time (t) contributes to the variation in most cases .

Table 5.9. shows the voter movements between parties that should have occurred from 1975 to 1977 according to the model of reactive voting (with the coefficient values from Table 5.8.). As for 1975, the "observed" voter movements are computed from the survey data, using the recall-question of "party voted for in 1975".

On visual inspection, the deviations in Table 5.9. between "observed" and "expected" voter movements appear about the same size as in 1975. This is confirmed by the value of the index of non-similarity (NS = 0.12), which once more is satisfactory.

Table 5.8.: Regression coefficients for reactive voting model 1977. (Standard errors in parentheses)

	Intercept b_0	DISTij b_1	DISTjj b_2	NCLOSE b_3	DIST3 b_4	VPROP b_5
SD	4.67303 (0.14194)	-3.49411 (0.80299)		-0.11050 (0.08944)	1.58524 (0.37864)	
RV	5.17424 (0.21189)	-2.37110 (0.69303)	6.12651 (0.95286)			
KF	14.00817 (1.29525)	-15.95267 (2.23226)	3.55162 (0.44751)		36.41227 (5.03240)	
DR	2.99981 (0.48095)	-3.86681 (0.43097)	0.45343 (0.53448)			
SF	2.96811 (0.12469)	-1.66473 (0.12608)				
DKP	5.27066 (1.43006)	-8.20483 (1.53292)		-2.02168 (1.21779)		3.61386 (1.38836)
CD	13.61652 (1.87639)	-2.22930 (1.58459)	6.07705 (0.93444)	-5.56288 (1.15307)	12.65495 (2.98539)	0.56621 (0.43494)
Pens	5.03030 (2.01804)		1.33632 (1.40562)		5.29682 (4.30110)	0.13516 (0.41718)
Krf	3.93132 (0.67056)	-0.97647 (1.01747)	2.24368 (1.18613)			
V	5.16243 (0.22403)	-9.89233 (0.72773)				5.48851 (0.51477)
VS	2.72987 (0.18998)			-0.51582 (0.05540)		
Frp	8.10386 (1.77727)	-6.02617 (1.36114)	7.29175 (2.34250)		1.02798 (0.66765)	1.02369 (0.73553)

As with the data from 1975, the model of reactive voting is rather successful in 1977 as well in accounting for where the parties did pick up their voters in 1977, and where they did not: Out of 66 cases in which no voter movement is observed between a pair of parties 50 are correctly "expected" by the model to exhibit no voter movement. But contrary to what was found for 1975, the model is less successful in accounting for the ability of the various parties in 1977 to hold on to their voters: Only in three cases (SD, CD, and Frp) does the model return the exact figures.

Table 5.9.: Observed and expected voter movements 1975 - 1977 in percentages of all respondents (n = 1143). Observed percentages in parentheses.

Party 1977	Party 1975										
	SD	RV	KF	DR	SF	DKP	CD	Krf	V	VS	Frp
SD	39.2	1.2	0.3	0.9	1.0	0.2	0.2	0.2	1.3	0.1	1.0
	(39.2)	(1.2)	(0.7)	(0.5)	(1.6)	(0.0)	(0.2)	(0.2)	(1.0)	(0.0)	(0.9)
RV	1.4	0.8	0.1	0.0	0.0	0.0	1.0	0.1	0.2	0.0	0.0
	(0.3)	(2.6)	(0.0)	(0.0)	(0.0)	(0.0)	(0.0)	(0.0)	(0.5)	(0.0)	(0.0)
KF	0.2	1.4	1.9	0.0	0.0	0.0	0.4	0.2	2.6	0.0	0.8
	(0.3)	(0.3)	(3.9)	(0.0)	(0.0)	(0.0)	(0.0)	(0.4)	(2.1)	(0.0)	(0.4)
DR	0.6	0.0	0.0	2.0	0.1	0.2	0.0	0.0	0.2	0.2	0.0
	(0.2)	(0.2)	(0.2)	(2.3)	(0.2)	(0.0)	(0.0)	(0.2)	(0.1)	(0.0)	(0.1)
SF	0.9	0.1	0.0	0.1	3.9	0.1	0.0	0.0	0.2	0.1	0.1
	(0.1)	(0.0)	(0.0)	(0.2)	(3.8)	(0.8)	(0.1)	(0.0)	(0.3)	(0.1)	(0.0)
DKP	0.0	0.0	0.0	0.0	0.3	1.8	0.0	0.0	0.0	0.1	0.0
	(0.0)	(0.0)	(0.0)	(0.0)	(0.3)	(1.9)	(0.0)	(0.0)	(0.0)	(0.0)	(0.0)
CD	0.4	0.3	0.6	0.0	0.0	0.0	2.1	0.1	1.2	0.0	0.4
	(0.4)	(0.2)	(0.7)	(0.0)	(0.0)	(0.0)	(2.1)	(0.1)	(1.2)	(0.0)	(0.4)
Pens	0.4	0.0	0.0	0.0	0.0	0.0	0.1	0.0	0.0	0.0	0.1
	(0.4)	(0.1)	(0.0)	(0.1)	(0.0)	(0.0)	(0.0)	(0.0)	(0.0)	(0.0)	(0.1)
Krf	0.7	0.4	0.3	0.0	0.0	0.0	0.5	0.2	0.5	0.0	0.0
	(0.2)	(0.0)	(0.3)	(0.0)	(0.0)	(0.0)	(0.0)	(2.0)	(0.0)	(0.0)	(0.0)
V	0.7	0.0	0.9	0.0	0.0	0.0	0.0	0.1	11.7	0.0	0.0
	(0.3)	(0.1)	(0.1)	(0.0)	(0.0)	(0.0)	(0.0)	(0.3)	(12.4)	(0.0)	(0.1)
VS	0.2	0.0	0.0	0.0	0.1	1.2	0.0	0.0	0.1	0.7	0.0
	(0.1)	(0.1)	(0.0)	(0.1)	(0.2)	(0.3)	(0.0)	(0.0)	(0.1)	(1.6)	(0.0)
Frp	0.3	0.1	0.1	0.0	0.0	0.0	0.3	0.1	0.4	0.0	7.3
	(0.3)	(0.1)	(0.0)	(0.2)	(0.2)	(0.0)	(0.4)	(0.1)	(0.4)	(0.0)	(7.3)

If we look at the big winners of the 1977-election, the Socialdemocrats and the Center-Democrats, the influx of voters from other parties to them seems to be quite well accounted for by the model. With the big loser, the Agrarians, the picture is different: Here the deviations between observed and expected voter movements are sizeable. The same is true for the Radical Liberals.

In conclusion it appears that the model of reactive voting proposed above performs acceptably well with data from 1977 also. Despite differences in the accuracy of the numbers of "expected" voter movements, compared to the "observed" numbers, the variation in the ability of the parties in the 1977-survey to pick up voters can be well accounted for by the model: In large measure, the voters reacted to perceived shifts in party positions between two elections by transferring their votes to another party, if the party they had preferred in the previous election was perceived to have moved away from their "ideal points", or if another party was perceived to have come closer to them.

6. Finale: The general election of October 1979

6.1. Background, campaign, and outcome

After its victory in the 1977-election, the Socialdemocratic government headed by Anker Jørgensen continued in office, but still as a minority government. For its existence it had mainly to rely on support from the parties that had backed the government in the previous Folketing, viz. the Radical Liberals, the Center-Democrats, and the Christian Peoples' Party. But together, the four parties were now close to a majority, commanding 88 of the 179 seats in the new Folketing.

In this situation any development that might lead to the defection of one of its supporting parties constituted a serious danger to the government's existence. Therefore Anker Jørgensen reacted swiftly, when in the first half of 1978 the Center-Democrats and the Christian Peoples' Party began moving closer to the Conservatives and the Agrarians, establishing a co-operation named the "four-leaved clover cooperation".

As a counter-measure, Anker Jørgensen aired the possibility of a coalition government consisting of Socialdemocrats, Radical Liberals, and Agrarians. Commanding a majority, such a government would be able to bring political stability and would have the political muscle to take the necessary - and probably rather painful - measures needed to alleviate the problems in the Danish economy, which by then threatened to become chronic: Huge deficits in the budget and in the balance of payments, a constant high level of unemployment, high inflation, and low economic growth rates.

The hope was that having the two parties - the Socialdemocrats and the Agrarians - with the closest relations to the best organized interests in Danish society, viz. trade unions and the Agrarian interest organizations, respectively, in government together would be accepted by these groups as some kind of guarantee of a built-in evenhandedness in the government's approach to the solution of the economic problems. This might induce both groups to accept sacrifices, knowing that the other side would not be spared.

The Agrarians reacted cautiously but positively to the proposal from the Socialdemocrats; they made it clear from the outset, however, that they were not prepared to have the Radical Liberals participate. Thus, after painful and protracted negotiations, a Socialdemocratic-Agrarian coalition government under the leadership of Anker Jørgensen was agreed upon in August 1978.

Very soon, however, it became evident that this bold initiative was bound to end in a failure. The trade union movement had denounced the new government even before its formation, and its attitude put a heavy strain on the relationship between the Socialdemocrats and the labor movement. Moreover, a number of members of the Socialdemocratic parliamentary group sided with the trade unions and were openly opposed to the formation of the coalition government, too.

Under such circumstances, reconciling the different viewpoints of Socialdemocrats and Agrarians became almost impossible from the start: Soon after its inauguration, there were open clashes in the cabinet about how to interpret the coalition agreement. And when the second oil crisis hit Denmark in 1979, threatening to cause still another worsening of the balance of payment problem, the government found itself unable to come to terms about how to respond to this situation. After 13 months, the government collapsed, and for the fifth time in just eight years the voters were summoned to the polls.

As in 1977, 12 parties entered the electoral contest. The Pensioners' Party had disappeared from the arena, while a small left-wing party, the Communist Workers' Party (KAP), made its first appearance. It announced itself the representative of the pure doctrine of Marxism-Leninism, as against the various revisionist versions allegedly marketed by other left-wing parties. It had the communist parties of Maoist China and Albania as its leading examples, and it called upon the Danish working class to prepare for armed struggle.

The campaign was dominated by economic issues. Unemployment, inflation, and the country's growing foreign debts were also the three issues considered most pressing by the voters.[1] Not surprisingly, the counter-measures advocated by the various parties still differed widely, not only between socialist and non-socialist parties, but also within each camp. The electoral campaign revealed that the "four-leaved clover" parties were deeply divided on a number of issues, while at the same time being separated from the Radical Liberals on the one side and the Progress Party on the other by strong differences of opinion. Thus once more the voters were not presented with a credible bourgeois alternative to the Socialdemocrats.

Opinion polls suggested that the Progress Party was going to lose in the ensuing election, while the Conservatives stood to gain. The Christian Peoples' Party was in danger to lose its representation altogether, being close to the minimum threshold of 2 pct. of the votes in a number of polls, which also most often had the Center-Democrats below their 1977-result.

In many respects, the results of the election of October 23 agreed with what could be predicted from the opinion polls, but there were some surprises, too.

Table 6.1. shows the outcome of the election, with the results from 1977 for comparison. Both the Socialdemocrats and the Agrarians gained votes and seats, although the gains were modest indeed for the Agrarians. Thus the two parties were not "punished" by the voters, neither for having tried a coalition government together, nor for having failed. As expected, the Progress Party lost, while the Conservatives gained quite heavily. The

---

[1] When asked about the most important political task in the coming years in the 1979-survey, 26 pct. mentioned "to reestablish full employment", 23 pct. "to stop the growth in foreign debts", and 15 pct. "to fight inflation".

Radical Liberals and the Socialist Peoples' Party also gained votes and seats. Thus all five "old" parties in the party system regained strength. With 74.6 pct. of the votes they reached their highest percentage since 1973, regaining about 10 pct. compared to the all-time low of 1973.

Table 6.1.: Electoral results 1979 (with 1977 for comparison)

Party	15.2.1977		23.10.1979	
	votes (pct.)	seats	votes (pct.)	seats
SD	37.0	65	38.3	68
RV	3.6	6	5.4	10
KF	8.5	15	12.5	22
DR	3.3	6	2.6	5
SF	3.9	7	5.9	11
DKP	3.7	6	1.9	0
CD	6.4	11	3.2	6
Krf	3.4	6	2.6	5
KAP	-	-	0.4	0
V	12.0	21	12.5	22
VS	2.7	5	3.6	6
Frp	14.6	26	11.0	20

The two parties formerly supporting the Socialdemocratic minority government - Center-Democrats and the Christian Peoples' Party - both fared badly at the hand of the voters, but retained a reduced representation in the new Folketing, as did the Justice Party. The Communists lost their six seats. Thus, with the exception of the Left Socialists, all the "new" parties lost votes and seats in 1979.

The outcome of the election led to the formation of still another Social-democratic minority government, headed by Anker Jørgensen. Its main parliamentary support now became the Radical Liberals. This constellation, too, represented the return of well-known patterns of cooperation in Danish politics. Together with either the Socialist Peoples' Party or with the Center-Democrats and the Christian Peoples' Party, a majority for the government's bills could usually be established.

6.2. Perception of the party system 1979

In the following section we shall for the last time examine the perception of the party system as it appeared to the voters - now at the time of the 1979-election. Our main interest in relation to propositions 1.1. and 1.2. is how clearly the respondents perceived the alternatives provided to them and which dimensions did structure their perception of the similarities and dis-similarities between the various parties.

Table 6.2. shows the median sympathy grade for the parties in 1979, broken down according to reported vote. If this table is compared to the corresponding table in section 5.2., both differences and similarities become visible.

The Socialdemocrats retained the position as the on average most sympathetic party they had held in 1977, but in comparison lost sympathy with voters for all the other parties (as well as with their own voters). Thus their surprising gains in the election may well have reflected the absence of a plausible alternative rather than a genuine improvement in the general assessment of the party's own merits.

The Agrarians recovered from their 1977-drop in popularity to reclaim the position as the second most liked party in 1979. Here the picture is almost exactly the opposite from what can be found with the Socialdemocrats, however: Compared to 1977, the Agrarians gained sympathy with voters for all parties, except those for the Left Socialists - and with their own voters.

Table 6.2.: Sympathy scores by reported vote 1979 (medians).
(Bold: most preferred party; italic: next most preferred party)

Voted for	Sympathy scores for											
	SD	RV	KF	DR	SF	DKP	CD	Krf	KAP	V	VS	Frp
SD	**85.0**	*42.8*	-1.0	3.0	21.2	-35.6	-21.9	-14.1	-68.8	12.0	-3.9	-92.6
RV	48.2	**80.0**	10.6	3.2	2.9	-62.9	-12.7	-8.1	-85.0	26.8	-28.2	-83.3
KF	23.7	9.8	**85.7**	-8.3	-39.4	-91.4	21.3	11.8	-94.6	*53.7*	-73.5	-8.1
DR	*43.3*	24.3	0	**80.0**	15.0	-33.3	-46.0	-38.0	-50.0	2.0	-5.0	-80.0
SF	*44.1*	17.2	-41.5	3.0	**87.4**	15.8	-68.6	-57.1	-5.7	-9.5	31.3	-94.7
DKP	25.0	-2.0	-74.0	-1.4	56.3	**92.1**	-92.1	-90.0	-25.0	-56.7	*47.5*	-98.6
CD	33.5	12.5	40.0	-16.3	-46.7	-92.9	**72.0**	22.0	-94.5	*42.1*	-88.0	-7.0
Krf	40.0	30.0	35.7	7.3	-30.0	-80.0	26.7	**94.2**	-90.0	*52.2*	-50.0	-2.7
KAP	-30.0	-20.0	-60.0	-6.7	25.0	10.0	-73.3	-75.0	**65.0**	-66.7	*40.0*	-95.0
V	29.3	12.0	*41.8*	-9.4	-41.3	-92.5	17.8	17.9	-94.1	**87.5**	-76.5	-22.7
VS	13.6	5.0	-72.0	7.7	*48.4*	20.7	-90.3	-78.6	14.2	-53.3	**87.0**	-97.2
Frp	8.0	4.7	*30.0*	-3.1	-30.0	-87.7	14.3	2.4	-86.0	25.6	-38.8	**85.6**
All	51.6	25.8	14.1	-0.7	2.9	-54.4	-4.1	-3.6	-77.0	26.8	-16.4	-72.2

Despite their gains in the election, the overall median sympathy for the Conservatives was lower in 1979 than in 1977. The figures indicate that the party got higher sympathy grades primarily from voters for the Center-Democrats and for the Progress Party - besides from its own voters - while it lost sympathy with voters for the other parties. This pattern suggests that - at least in part - the gains of the Conservatives were obtained by trespassing into the realms of the Progress Party.

The most dramatic change in opinion occurred for the Center-Democrats, however. In 1977, they were the on average second most liked party; in 1979, they received a negative median score from all respondents taken together. The Christian Peoples' Party's average sympathy grade dropped from a little above zero in 1977 to a little below in 1979, while the grade for the Socialist Peoples' Party exhibits the opposite trend. For all three parties, the development in voter sympathy is closely reflected in the electoral outcome.

Communists and the Progress Party receive extremely negative gradings, in 1979 joined - and surpassed in that respect - by the Communist Workers' Party (KAP). Compared to 1977, the standing of both Communists and Progress Party with the voters can be seen to have markedly deteriorated by 1979, which is also reflected in their electoral losses.

The patterns in Table 6.2. suggest the existence of at least three distinct clusters of parties in the perception of the party system in 1979. In the first place, the Socialdemocrats and the Radical Liberals obviously are rather close, since on average the voters for each of these parties have the other party as the second most preferred one. In the second place, there is a "four-leaved clover" cluster, consisting of the Conservatives, Center-Democrats, Christian Peoples' Party, and Agrarians; voters for one of these parties obviously tend to feel quite sympathetic to the rest as well. Finally, there is a cluster of socialist parties, consisting of the Socialist Peoples' Party, Communists, the Communist Workers' Party, and the Left Socialists. Again the existence of such a cluster is suggested by the fact that voters for one of these parties tend to be relatively sympathetic towards the others as well.

Figure 6.1. shows the map of the perceived party system in 1979 as derived from the respondents' thermometer gradings of the parties.[2] As can easily be seen, the map brings out the existence of the three above-mentioned party clusters.

Fig. 6.1.:   Perceived party system 1979

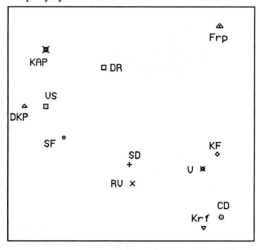

[2] The map is based on the thermometer grades administered by 1825 respondents who gave valid grades to at least two of the 12 parties in this analysis.

But the map also brings out a number of patterns that would be somewhat more difficult to detect just by visual inspection of Table 6.2. Thus it can be seen that the "four-leaved clover" cluster consists of two sub-clusters, one composed of the Conservatives and Agrarians, the other of Center-Democrats and the Christian Peoples' Party. This may well be a trace of the disagreement between the "four-leaved clover" parties that surfaced on several occasions prior to the election. Moreover, Conservatives and Agrarians are perceived to be closer to the Socialdemocratic - Radical Liberal cluster than are Center-Democrats and the Christian Peoples' Party.

The Progress Party once more appears in an isolated region in the perceived party space. But - if we may assume that the horizontal direction on the map represents a left-right dimension, as has been the case with all maps so far - the party is still not perceived as (radical) rightist by the respondents, being located in about the same position with respect to the horizontal direction as the Conservatives and the Center-Democrats.

The other party outside the clustering of parties is the Justice Party which, however, is closest to the cluster of socialist parties. Once more, this position may be mainly attributable to the party's marked anti-EEC stand.

In Figure 6.2. the respondents "ideal points" have been added to the map. The bulk of respondents is found near the center of the map, a little to the right and above the position of the Socialdemocrats. The resemblance with the corresponding map from 1977 is close.

Fig. 6.2.: Parties and "ideal points" in perceived party space 1979*

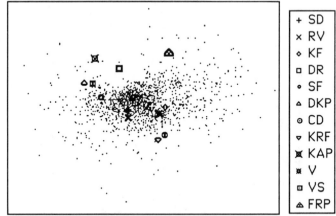

+	SD
×	RV
◇	KF
□	DR
•	SF
▲	DKP
⊙	CD
▽	KRF
✖	KAP
✳	V
▫	VS
△	FRP

*26 outliers removed.

Figure 6.2. shows that by 1979 the Center-Democrats and the Christian Peoples' Party have become marginal in the respondents' perception of the party system. In their position they are effectively screened off from the bulk of "ideal points" by the Conservatives and the Agrarians. The figure also suggests that the Conservatives achieved at least part of their recovery by raiding into Progress Party "territory".

The map fits the thermometer data well (unweighted $R^2 = 0.73$).[3] This represents a clear improvement over the fit obtained with the 1977-data, although the number of parties to be fitted is the same. At least in part the difference may be explained by the absence of the Pensioners' Party in 1979; as was mentioned in section 5.2. above, this party generated some "noise" in the perception of the party system in 1977.

The "hindcasted" distribution of votes that can be obtained from the maps under the assumption that the respondents vote for the party closest to the location of their "ideal point" on the map is shown in Table 6.3.

As can be seen from Table 6.3., the "hindcasted" distribution of votes in 1979 comes rather close to the reported distribution (NS = 0.06). The greatest deviation occurs with the Socialist Peoples' Party; here the "hindcast" overestimates the party's result by about 50 pct., obviously at the expense of the Left Socialists the strength of which is somewhat underrated by the "hindcast". In a similar way part of the underestimation of the proportion of Socialdemocratic votes may be due to a certain overestimation of the strength of the Radical Liberals.

Table 6.3.: Reported and "hindcasted" distribution of votes 1979

| Party | Distribution of votes | |
	reported (n=1632)	"hindcasted" (n=1825)
SD	40.3	39.1
RV	5.5	6.0
KF	14.2	15.3
DR	2.0	2.5
SF	6.3	9.7
DKP	1.6	1.9
CD	3.1	1.7
Krf	2.0	1.5
KAP	0.3	0.6
V	14.2	13.3
VS	3.7	1.4
Frp	6.9	7.2

Despite such minor deviations between the reported and "hindcasted" distributions of votes, the agreement between the two distribution appears certainly good enough to allow us to consider proposition 1.1. confirmed by the 1979-data.

---

[3] No weighting of thermometer grades given to the most and second most preferred parties was performed in this case, since weighting was found to lead to an unacceptable drop in the unweighted R^2-value, cf. the discussion in section 1.6. above.

The next task is to put labels on the axes of the maps in Figures 6.1. and 6.2., i.e. to identify the basic structuring features in the respondents' perception of the party system and to examine some of their attitudinal correlates. The appearance of the 1979-maps as well as the result from previous chapters strongly suggest that the main 'ideological' dimensions defining the respondents' belief system or "mental grid" in 1979 were a "backlash"- and the left-right dimension, as has indeed been the case throughout the seventies.

In the 1979-survey the respondents were asked to place themselves on a left-right scale with ten positions, presented to the them as a row of boxes numbered from 1 to 10. Box no. 1 was marked "farthest to the left" and box no.10 "farthest to the right".[4] If the horizontal dimension on the maps in Figures 6.1. and 6.2. represents a left-right dimension in the respondents' perception of the party system, then we must expect the median "ideal points" of the respondents in each of the positions on the left-right scale (V303) to be arranged roughly parallel to the horizontal dimension on the maps. Moreover, these median "ideal points" should appear in the correct order: The median "ideal point" of the respondents in box no.1 should be located farthest to the left and the median "ideal point" of the respondents in box no.10 farthest to the right on the map, while the remaining median "ideal points" should be located in between the extreme ones and should appear in accordance with the numerical order of the boxes.

Fig. 6.3.:   Perceived party space and self-placement on left right-scale 1979

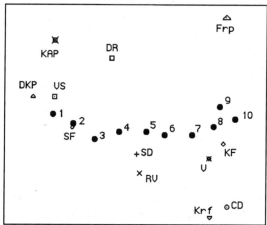

In Figure 6.3. the median "ideal points" of the respondents in each of the 10 boxes on the left right-scale (V303) have been added to the map in Figure

[4] V303 ("In politics one often speaks of "left" and "right". Where would you locate yourself on such a scale?").

6.1. The median "ideal points" are labeled 1 to 10 in accordance with the numbering of the corresponding boxes on the left right-scale.

Figure 6.3.shows that the median "ideal points" of the respondents in each of the ten boxes on the left right-scale presented to the respondents are indeed located in the correct order on the map. They are also arranged roughly parallel to the maps' horizontal axis. This clearly validates the interpretation of the horizontal dimension as an 'ideological' left-right dimension in the respondents' perception of the party space in 1979.[5]

It should be noticed that the arrangement of median "ideal points" in Figure 6.3. shows a tendency to "curl up" a bit: It is bent at the endpoints. This implies that there is a relationship between being extremely placed with respect to the left-right dimension and being extremely placed with respect to the second dimension. Respondents belonging (in their own opinion) to the "farthest left" or the "farthest right" also tend to be closer to the top end of the second dimension. This should come as no surprise, however, if the relationship between the second dimension and attitudes of distrust and dissatisfaction is kept in mind: In previous chapters a specific "left distrust" and a specific "right distrust" appeared on several occasions as shown by distrust items which produced orderings of median "ideal points" running in a north-western and a north-eastern direction, respectively. Nor is the rejection of the values and tenets of pluralist democracy a privilege of the far right as witnessed by, e.g., the platform of the Communist Workers' Party presented in the 1979-campaign.

In previous chapters attitudes towards a number of economic issues have invariably turned out to be related to the left-right dimension: With many items the median "ideal points" in each of the non-neutral categories of the five-point scale used to record the respondents' attitudes towards the particular item were strung out parallel to the horizontal axis on the map of perceived party locations and "ideal points". We shall examine the relationship between attitudes towards different economic issues and the left-right dimension in the 1979-survey as well.

In the 1979-survey, 15 items concerning economic policies were presented. One group of items concerns attitudes towards general economic questions, like economic equality or the role of the state in the economy. Another group of items deals primarily with incomes policy and its implementation.

Among the items in the first group there are three items which have been used continuously in all surveys since 1973.[6] All of them - V204 (on state

---

[5] The left-right selfplacement question also tends to corroborate the present results concerning the role of an 'ideological' left right-dimension in the respondents' belief system in a more indirect way: It appears that only quite few respondents had difficulties in handling the task of placing themselves on the left-right scale. It obviously was not a strange or unfamiliar concept to them. The proportion of "don't know", missing, or erroneous responses on this item is only about 11 pct..

[6] V204 ("There is too little state control with private investments"), V208 ("In politics one should strive to make economic conditions equal for everybody, regardless of education and job"), and V217 ("High incomes should be taxed harder than today").

control with private investments), V208 (on economic equality, and V217 (on harsher taxation of high incomes) - produce median "ideal points" in the non-neutral categories on their scales that are strung out in a horizontal direction, cf. Figure 6.4. For the sake of clarity, only a "zoom view" of the relevant part of the map is presented, and the locations of the neutral categories have been omitted.

Fig. 6.4.: Perceived party space and issue positions on three economic items 1979

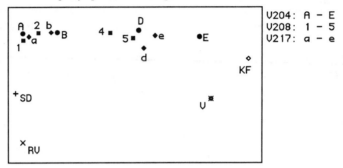

A, a, 1: Agree completely; B, b, 2: Do agree in part; D, d, 4: Do disagree in part; E, e, 5: Disagree completely

Besides these three items, four other items dealing with general economic questions[7] were presented to the respondents in 1979. The form of presentation chosen with these items differed from the form used with the items encountered so far: Instead of confronting the respondents with one statement and recording their professed degree of agreement or disagreement to it, the respondents were confronted with to contradictory positions on the same issue, labeled A and B, and asked to indicate which position they felt most in agreement with. Three of these items - V265 and V267 (on socialization), and V268 (on state control with business and industry) - deal with the role of the state in the economy, while the last - V266 (on differences with regard to income and living conditions) - deals with economic equality.

---

[7] V265 ("A says: The Folketing should pass a bill to make the state take over banks and big industries. B says: Banks and big industry should continue to be private enterprises"), V266 ("A says: Differences in income and living conditions are still too big in our country. Therefore people with small income should have their living conditions improved more rapidly than people with higher income. B says: Equalization of incomes has gone far enough. The differences that exist today should by and large continue to exist"), V267 ("A says: Besides big industry, all other important industries should be nationalized too. B says: It would be wrong to nationalize all important industries"), and V268 ("A says: People in business and industry should have greater freedom of action in conducting their business. B says: The state should control and coordinate economic activity. At the very least, state control should not be weaker than it is today").

Table 6.4. shows the net majorities agreeing to the "leftist" position[8] among the respondents having their "ideal points" located in each of the four quartiles of the horizontal distribution of "ideal points" on the map in Figure 6.2.

Table 6.4.: Net majorities agreeing to "leftist" position on four economic items in each quartile of the horizontal distribution of "ideal points" in 1979

	V265	V266	V267	V268
1. quartile	-84.3	-51.1	-90.1	-37.5
2. quartile	-79.7	1.0	-85.5	-2.9
3. quartile	-64.0	36.5	-71.4	28.1
4. quartile	5.9	66.9	-28.5	48.0

As can be seen in Table 6.4., net majorities agreeing to "leftist" positions on all four items tend to increase as one moves from the right side of the map in Figure 6.2. (1. quartile) towards the left side, confirming the relationship between the horizontal axis on the map and an 'ideological' left-right dimension in the respondents' belief system. Once more, agreement to an egalitarian economic position turns out to reach well into the center of the political spectrum in Danish politics: A small majority supporting greater economic equality (V266) is even found in the quartile next to the most rightist one.

Fig. 6.5.: Perceived party space and issue positions on three incomes policy items 1979*

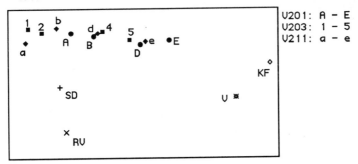

*Polarity of items V203 and V211 reversed.

A, a, 1: Agree completely; B, b, 2: Do agree in part; D, d, 4: Do disagree in part; E, e, 5: Disagree completely

---

8 With items V265, V266, and V267: Position A. With item V268: Position B.

Owing, of course, to the rather destitute economic situation in 1979, the question of incomes policies and their implementation played an important role in political discussions and during the electoral campaign, as had also been the case in 1977. A number of items presented in the 1979-survey deal with this issue, and three of them had been used in the 1977-survey as well.[9] The median "ideal points" in each of the non-neutral categories on the scales belonging to these items are shown in Figure 6.5., which again presents a "zoom-view" of the relevant part of the map of the perceived party system in 1979 only.

Clearly issue positions on these three items are structured by the horizontal axis on the map of the perceived party space, as was also the case in 1977 (cf. Figure 5.4.), once more validating its identification as a left-right dimension. In comparison with Figure 6.4., it should be noted that the left-most positions on two of the three incomes policy items (V203 on the Folketing having final responsibility for the development in incomes, and V211 on wage rises being unaffordable in the present situation) are located to the left of the position of the Socialdemocrats on the map, while the left-most positions on the general economic items are located a bit to the right of the Socialdemocratic position. Thus as a whole, the respondents tend to be more "leftist" on the general economic issues of state intervention in the economy and economic equality than on the more specific issues of incomes policies.[10]

Fig. 6.6.: Perceived party space and issue positions on two economic items 1979

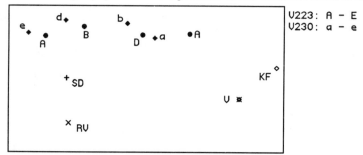

A, a: Agree completely; B, b : Do agree in part; D, d: Do disagree in part; E, e: Disagree completely

---

[9]V201 ("Under no circumstances should the Folketing interfere with tariff negotiations"), V203 ("The Folketing, and not interest organizations, must have the final responsibility for income development in this country"), and V211 ("We cannot afford wage rises in the present economic situation").

[10] The same result was found for 1977.

Three further items presented in 1979 deal with economic policies.[11] They reflect positions taken by various parties before and during the electoral campaign. A compulsory profit sharing scheme in which the wage earners' share would be administered for them by the trade unions (called "economic democracy") had been one of the Socialdemocratic claims in the negotiations with the Agrarians that finally led to the break down of the coalition government of these two parties; an unconditional freeze on wages had been the counter-claim of the Agrarians, and the Radical Liberals had contributed the idea of a kind of social contract, where labor and business organizations would share in the making of the economic policies.

The issue positions on the "corporatist" item V226 (On making economic policies in cooperation with labor and business organizations) do not exhibit any clear pattern. The issue positions on the other two items do, as can be seen in Figure 6.6. Again, the locations of the median "ideal points" in each of the categories on the scales belonging to these items are strung out parallel with the horizontal axis on the map of the perceived party system in 1979.

Finally there are two items of the "A says... B says..."-type that deal with economic policies.[12] Table 6.5. shows the net majorities agreeing to position A in each quartile of the horizontal distribution of "ideal points" on the map of the perceived party system in 1979.

Table 6.5.: Net majorities agreeing to position A on two economic policy items in each quartile of the horizontal distribution of "ideal points" in 1979

	V270	V274
1. quartile	9.1	-9.3
2. quartile	23.2	-25.0
3. quartile	49.7	-52.1
4. quartile	62.9	-68.5

As can be seen from Table 6.5., the majority of respondents that agrees to fighting unemployment, if necessary at the cost of higher inflation, increases as one moves from the right towards the left across the map of the perceived party system in 1979. But even among the most rightist respondents there is a majority endorsing such a policy. Likewise, the size of the majority that opposes the position that wage earners should accept a drop in

[11] V223 ("A compulsory profit sharing scheme should be introduced"), V226 ("The economic policies should be decided upon in cooperation with the big labor and business organizations"), and V230 ("A unconditional wage freeze is necessary").

[12] V270 ("A says: It is most important to fight unemployment, even if it should lead to higher inflation. B says: It is most important to fight inflation, even if it should lead to higher unemployment"), and V274 ("A says: In the present economic situation, wage earners should be willing to accept a drop in real wages. B says: Our economic problems must be solved in a way that does not result in lower real wages for ordinary wage earners").

real wages increases as one moves from the right towards the left across the map. Again it is seen that the idea of accepting lower real wages does not command a majority even among the most rightist respondents.[13]

Fig. 6.7.: Perceived party space and issue positions on NATO- and EEC-item 1979

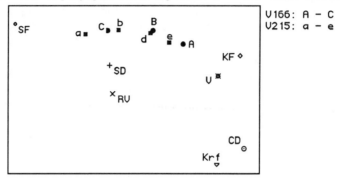

A: Would vote for membership; B: Would abstain; C: Would vote against membership
a: Agree completely; b: Do agree in part; d: Do disagree in part; e: Disagree completely

Thus the horizontal direction on the maps in Figures 6.1. and 6.2. is very strongly related to positions on economic policies. The patterns found and shown above clearly reinforce the interpretation of the horizontal dimension as an 'ideological' left-right dimension in the political belief system of the respondents in 1979.

In previous chapters, attitudes towards membership of NATO and of the EEC have regularly turned out to be related to the respondents' position relative to the horizontal axis on the map of the perceived party system, indicating that the 'ideological' left-right dimension in their belief system has a foreign policy-component as well.

With data from the 1979-survey,[14] the same picture emerges, cf. Figure 6.7. As one moves towards the left across the map, attitudes towards NATO- and EEC-membership tend to grow increasingly negative.

Comparison of Figure 6.7. to the corresponding Figure 5.6. in the preceding chapter shows that the location of the median "ideal points" of the respondents in the categories on the two scales are approximately the same. Thus these attitudes seem to be rather stable across time, both with respect to their mutual relationship and with respect to their being tied up with the left-right dimension.

The 1979-survey also contains two items that might be expected to tap attitudes towards "post-material values" in the respondents. One of these

---

[13] These attitudes may also be part of the explanation why conducting an efficient economic policy in Denmark is a very difficult task indeed.

[14] V166 ("If there were a referendum on EEC-membership today, would you vote for or against?") and V215 ("We should leave NATO as soon as possible").

items concerns the choice between continuously growing consumption and protection of the environment; the other concerns the introduction of nuclear power plants.[15] It is not without interest to examine, how the respondents' positions on these items relate to their positions on the left-right dimension. After all, "post-material values" are often supposed to create new cleavage lines in politics, cross-cutting the old ones - like the time honored left-right dimension. Figure 6.8. shows the median "ideal points" in each of the categories on the scales belonging to these two items.

Fig. 6.8.: Perceived party space and issue positions on two "post-material value"-items 1979

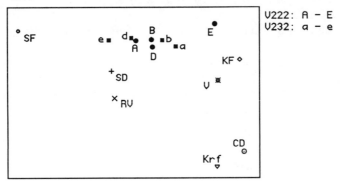

A, a: Agree completely; B, b : Do agree in part; D, d: Do disagree in part; E, e: Disagree completely

Figure 6.8. shows that the issue positions on item V222 (on environment versus consumption) and on item V232 (on nuclear power) follow the left-right dimension quite closely. There is in 1979 no sign of these two items defining a new cleavage line that might cross the existing ones.[16]

This finding indicates the strength of the 'ideological' left-right dimension in the political belief system - or political frame of reference - of the respondents in 1979. It also shows this dimension to be extremely "spacious", being able to "bundle" issues with very little, if any, necessary mutual relationship to each other.[17] Finally, this finding may give a hint as

---

[15] V222 ("We should create a more humane environment instead of increasing consumption continuously"), and V232 ("For Denmark to be able to satisfy the need for energy it will become necessary to introduce nuclear power plants").

[16] In this respect the situation in Denmark seems very different from the situation in, e.g., Norway, cf. Valen (1981, p.252).

[17] As noted by Paldam (1987, pp. 83-84): "It is often difficult to understand why certain attitudes are leftist or rightist, respectively, but it is practical. If ,e.g., we are against the EEC, then we we will also automatically be in favor of windmills". According to Paldam, this is practical because it brings down the cost of individual decision making.

to why ecologist parties (e.g. "The Greens" modelled after German inspiration) have been a very limited success in Denmark.

Next we turn to the interpretation of the vertical axis on the maps in Figures 6.1. and 6.2. In the previous chapters the distribution of "ideal points" in the vertical direction on the maps has been shown to be systematically related to, i.a., attitudes of dissatisfaction with and distrust in various levels of the political system, mainly the regime and the authorities (in the sense of Easton (1965)). Hence we shall start out by examining the relationship of the vertical distribution of "ideal points" in 1979 to attitudes of systemic dissatisfaction and distrust.

In the 1979-survey five items deal with the parliamentary system and its ability to handle situations of crisis as well as its participatory aspect.[18] These items refer to the regime-level of the political system. Four items deal with trust in politicians and political leaders, i.e. refer to the authority-level.[19]

On closer analysis only one item in each group - V210 (on a strong man taking power) and V212 (on politicians spending the taxpayers' money too lavishly) - turns out to produce issue positions structured by the vertical axis on the maps in Figures 6.1. and 6.2.

Table 6.6.: Net majorities agreeing to two "distrust"-items in each quartile of the vertical distribution of "ideal points" 1979

	V210	V212
1. quartile	16.7	81.6
2. quartile	-11.7	67.4
3. quartile	-22.8	58.2
4. quartile	-34.2	45.8

As can be seen from Table 6.6., there is a net majority among respondents having their "ideal points" located in the upper quartile of the vertical distribution of "ideal points" on the map in Figure 6.2. which agrees to the idea of a strong man taking power in an economic crisis. As one moves towards the bottom of the map, increasing net majorities oppose such an idea. Likewise, the net majority agreeing that politicians spend the taxpayers' money

---

[18] V210 ("It might be very reasonable to have a strong man take power in an economic crisis"), V213 ("Parliamentarism is better suited to solve the country's problem than would be any other system'), V218 ("Democracy fails when the country is confronted with really serious problems"), V224 ("By voting in the election one can really participate in deciding how the country should be run"), and V227 ("We must keep the existing parliamentary system at any cost"). All of these items were also used in 1975.

[19] V200 ("People wanting to make it to the top in politics are forced to give up most of their principles"), V207 ("Politicians usually do care too little about what the voters think"), V209 ("Usually one can trust our political leaders to make the right decisions for the country"), and V212 ("Politicians spend the taxpayers' money too lavishly"). All of these items have been used in previous surveys as well.

too lavishly diminishes as one moves from the top towards the bottom of the map (but still there is a net majority agreeing to this point of view, regardless of which quartile of the vertical distribution of "ideal points" is examined). Thus the interpretation of the vertical axis on the map as a "backlash"- or distrust-dimension i supported.

But when the net majorities agreeing to item V210 are compared to the corresponding Figures from 1977 (Table 5.4.), it becomes evident that the net majority in the first (upper) quartile agreeing to a takeover of power by a strong man has decreased, while the net majorities opposing such an idea have increased in the other three quartiles. If one goes back to 1973, the development in the net majorities becomes even more dramatic: In 1973 the idea of having a strong man take power found a net majority in all four quartiles, ranging from 44 pct. to about 11 pct., cf. Table 3.6. This, taken together with the diminished importance of the vertical dimension in the structuring of attitudes of political distrust (as witnessed by the small number of distrust-items that produce issue positions which are structured by it), suggests that by 1979 the importance of the distrust-aspect of the "backlash"-dimension as a structuring feature in the respondents' political frame of reference has declined considerably. Such interpretation also appears to fit nicely with the heavy losses incurred by the Progress Party in the 1979-election.

In 1975 the vertical dimension was found to play a role as well in the structuring of issue positions on what has been called "moralism"-items, indicating that there were other aspects to the dissatisfaction- or "backlash"-dimension than the purely systemic ones concerning distrust in and dissatisfaction with the regime and the authorities. The three "moralism"-items used in 1977 were re-used in 1979,[20] and two new items - V225 on pornography and V231 on the punishment of crimes of violence - were added.[21]

Table 6.7. shows the net majorities in each quartile of the vertical distribution of "ideal points" on the map in Figure 6.2. that agree to the various "moralism"-items.

Table 6.7.: Net majorities agreeing to "moralism"-items in each quartile of the vertical distribution of "ideal points" 1979

	V205	V216	V225	V231	V238
1. quartile	81.2	-17.0	10.5	92.0	30.0
2. quartile	77.0	-20.8	5.3	88.6	23.0
3. quartile	59.0	-40.3	-1.2	80.3	22.6
4. quartile	51.9	-44.9	-9.4	69.6	9.4

---

[20] V205 ("We must be more on guard against indoctrination in schools"), V216 ("TV and radio should kill extremist views by silence"), and V238 ("The moral development in our society has been debated. Do you consider the development a cause for concern, or do you think it is not a cause for special concern?").

[21] V225 ("Legalizing pornography was a mistake"), and V231 ("Crimes of violence should be punished much harder than today").

Table 6.7. demonstrates the existence of a clear relationship between "moralism"-attitudes and the vertical location of "ideal points": With all five items, agreement to a "moralistic" position increases as one moves from the bottom of the map (4. quartile) towards the top (1. quartile). On three items - V205 on indoctrination in schools, V231 on punishment for crimes of violence, and V238 on the moral development in society being cause for concern - there is a net majority agreeing to the position expressed in the wording of the item, regardless of the quartile of the distribution examined, but it diminishes in size as one moves towards the bottom of the map. There is a net majority opposing censorship in TV and radio, regardless of the quartile of the distribution considered, but it diminishes as one moves nearer to the top of the map. And finally, in the upper half of the distribution of "ideal points" we find a net majority considering the legalizing of pornography a mistake, while (growing) net majorities in the lower half of the distribution do not see it that way.

In conclusion we may consider the interpretation of the vertical axis on the maps in Figures 6.1. and 6.2. as the expression of a "backlash"-dimension in the respondents' political frame of reference validated by the relationships found between the vertical location of "ideal points" and the respondents' attitudes towards the regime- and authority-aspect of the political system on one hand and the moral development (in a very broad sense) in society on the other. It may seem, however, that the relative importance of these two aspects of the "backlash"-dimension have begun to change by 1979, the "moralism"-aspect gaining increasing weight: Issue positions that are structured by the vertical dimension were found only with two "distrust"-items, as against five "moralism"-items.

We shall conclude this investigation into the respondents' perception of the party system in 1979 and of their underlying belief system by examining the relationship between social class and location of "ideal points" with respect to the horizontal axis on the maps in Figures 6.1. and 6.2. Such a relationship has invariably been found in connection with the other elections in the seventies.

Fig. 6.9.: Perceived party space and class 1979

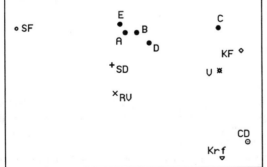

Figure 6.9. shows the median "ideal points" for respondents belonging to different classes in 1979.[22] The location of these median "ideal points" is indeed structured by the horizontal axis of the map: We find self-employed to the right, workers to the left, and white collar employees in between. Respondents under education remain the on average most leftist group when judged on the basis of the location of their "ideal points" on the map.

Summing up the results arrived at so far, it may be concluded that propositions 1.1. and 1.2., concerning the respondents' perception of the party system in 1979 and the mental "grid" (the belief system) structuring this perception, have been confirmed again. The respondents appear to have had a reasonably clear perception of the alternatives to choose from, and they conceived of the differences and similarities between them primarily in terms of an 'ideological' left-right dimension, supplemented by a "backlash"-dimension.

But it also seems that by 1979 a certain weakening of the saliency of the "backlash"-dimension had taken place, which primarily affected the distrust-aspect. In this respect, the situation in 1979 resembles the situation in 1971 to some extent, which agrees well with the electoral outcome of 1979 marking a certain renaissance of the five "old" parties, which together won back about 10 pct. of the electorate, compared to the fateful election of 1973.

6.3. The impact of party identification, party vote, class, and party behavior on the perception of the party system 1979

Turning to our propositions 2.1. and 2.2. next, we shall satisfy ourselves that the model of the perceived party system shown in Figures 6.1. and 6.2. does not systematically misrepresent the way, certain relevant subgroups of respondents perceived the parties and their relationships. From the outset, the goodness of fit obtained with a model built on the assumption of a common perception for all respondents may seem to provide some guarantee against any major-scale systematic misrepresentation. By examining the mean R^2-values in several relevant subgroups we can obtain more detailed knowledge about this aspect of the solution presented above.

In Table 6.8. the overall fit of the model of the perceived party system in 1979 (unweighted R^2) has been broken down according to reported party vote (party preference) and party identification. The table shows that the perception of the party system by voters for the Justice Party and for the Progress Party is represented substantially poorer than average by the common model in Figures 6.1. and 6.2. As far as the Justice Party is

---

[22] Women not in the labor force are classified according to their husbands' class. Other respondents not in the workforce (O.A.P.'s, unemployed, etc.) are made a separate group.

concerned this finding is in agreement with what has invariably been found before: Justice Party voters seem to view things in a different light from other respondents. This also agrees well with the fact that "true believers" in the tenets of the Justice Party orthodoxy are represented even poorer by a common model than are more loosely affiliated voters.

As far as Progress Party voters are concerned, their poor fit by a common model did emerge for the first time in 1977. In section 5.3. we suggested that the continuing and increasing isolation of the Progress Party in the party system might have increased its proportion of voters with highly idiosyncratic political viewpoints. The development between 1977 and 1979 with regard to the position of the Progress Party in the party system and the below average fit of a common model to the perceptions of its voters found once more in 1979 lend some further plausibility to this interpretation.

Table 6.8.: R^2 for perceived party space 1979, broken down by party identification and party voted for

Voted for	R^2		
	Party identifiers	Non-identifiers	All
SD	0.73	0.72	0.73
RV	0.76	0.70	0.72
KF	0.83	0.76	0.80
DR	0.60	0.68	0.65
SF	0.74	0.76	0.75
DKP	0.70	0.78	0.72
CD	0.75	0.73	0.74
Krf	0.71	0.71	0.71
KAP	0.76	0.78	0.77
V	0.80	0.79	0.79
VS	0.79	0.83	0.81
Frp	0.64	0.61	0.62
All	0.74	0.72	0.73

But even with the Justice Party and the Progress Party taken into account, the variations in goodness of fit between voters for the various parties as well as between party identifiers and non-identifiers remain small. A multiple classification analysis (MCA) with R^2-values as the dependent and party voted for and party identification as independent variables accounts for about 6 pct. of the variance in the R^2-values.[23] From this it would appear that the influence of party preference and party identification on the way in which the respondents perceived the party system in 1979 was indeed marginal.

---

[23] The exact value is $R^2 = 0.058$.

In Table 6.9. the R^2-values have been once more broken down, this time by class and party identification. From this, a by now quite familiar picture emerges.

Among respondents in the labor force we once more find the poorest fit with working class respondents. As has been shown earlier, the below average fit of the common model to the perception of the party system by working class respondents does not per se prove the existence of a particular "class perspective" on the party system: Whenever it was possible to derive a separate model for the perception of the party system by working class respondents, this model turned out to highly resemble the common model. It is rather the "noise level" in the data from working class respondents that appears to be somewhat higher than in the data from other groups.

Table 6.9.: R^2 for model of perceived party space 1979, broken down by class and party identification

	Working class	Middle class	Self-employed	Out of labor force	Under education	All
Party identifiers	0.69	0.78	0.77	0.74	0.76	0.74
Non-identifiers	0.65	0.76	0.73	0.72	0.70	0.72
All	0.67	0.77	0.76	0.73	0.72	0.73

If class is added to party preference and party identification as independent variables in a multiple classification analysis (MCA), the proportion of the variance in the R^2-values accounted for increases moderately to about 8 pct.[24] Hence the impact of class on the perception of the party system in 1979 should be considered marginal, too.

Having thus once more confirmed proposition 2.1., we shall turn to the relationship between the perceived party system in 1979 and actual party behavior as it surfaces in the voting patterns in the Folketing between 1977 and 1979. In doing this, we encounter one problem, however: As has been described in section 6.1. above, the parliamentary situation and the patterns of cooperation in the Folketing did change radically in august 1978, when the Socialdemocratic-Agrarian majority government took office. Which pattern of legislative party relationships, then - pre-August 1978 or post-August 1978 - shall we expect to have exerted its influence on the voters' perception of the party system and the parties' mutual relationships, when they were contemplating their choices in 1979?

If we compare the maps of the legislative party system prior to and after the taking office of the Socialdemocratic-Agrarian government, it turns out

---

[24] The exact value is $R^2 = 0.081$.

that the map showing the strongest resemblance to the respondents' perception is in fact the map of the legislative party system prior to august 1978: Its index of agreement is clearly higher (M = 0.82) than is the index of agreement for the map of the legislative party system after august 1978 (M = 0.70).

At first sight this may seem astonishing. After all, in tests of the "responsibility-hypothesis" it has normally been established that voters tend to forget rapidly: Their judgement of the government's economic performance is normally only marginally affected by economic developments more than three months in the past (Paldam and Schneider, 1980). Then why should the respondents' perception of the party system in 1979 show a clearer resemblance to the party relations as they existed a year ago than as they existed right up to the election?

A possible answer is that the respondents did not perceive any significant change in party relations to have occurred, despite the formation of a Socialdemocratic-Agrarian government. If this was the case, they can hardly be blamed: After all, Socialdemocrats and Agrarians continued to quarrel almost as intensely after the coalition government had taken office as they had done before, and ended breaking up. Thus although they kept up appearances in the final vote on the government's bills and preserved discipline in their ranks during the governments entire lifetime, the two parties may well have seemed as far away from each other as they had always been.

Figure 6.10. shows the map of the legislative party system 1977-78 with the map of the perceived party system (Figure 6.1. above) superimposed. As can be seen at once, the basic structure of the two maps is practically identical.

Fig. 6.10.: Legislative party space 1977-78 (bold symbols) with perceived party space 1977 superimposed

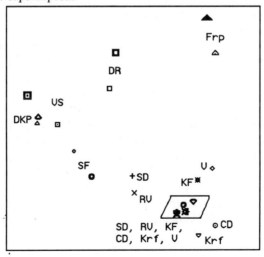

Figure 6.10. reveals another trait that was also found with the corresponding maps in 1977: There is a clear tendency for the respondents to underrate the distance between the extreme or marginal parties in the party system (DR, DKP, VS, and Frp) and the rest of the party system, compared to the distances displayed in legislative voting. On the other hand, there is a equally clear tendency to perceive the "central" parties (SD, RV, KF, CD, Krf, and V) as more different than may seem warranted by their legislative behavior alone.

On balance, however, the resemblance between the two maps appears strong enough to allow us to consider proposition 2.2. confirmed. To a considerable degree, the perception of the party system by the respondents seems to have been rooted in the parties' actual behavior.

6.4. Perception of the party system and voting behavior: Reactive voting 1979

We shall conclude this analysis of the 1979-election by examining to what degree the results of this election may be accounted for by the model of reactive voting.

Table 6.10. gives the non-zero regression coefficients obtained by fitting the model to the data on voter movements between 1977 and 1979.[25] The table shows that once more the distance between the perceived location of a party (i) in the party space of 1979 and the perceived locations of parties (j) in the party space of 1977 ($DIST_{ij}$) is needed in most cases (8 out of 12) to account for the variations in the proportion of voters switching parties between the elections: The greater this distance, the smaller the proportion of voters picked up by party (i) from party (j).

Besides this factor, the competitiveness variable (DIST3) also enters the model in 8 out of 12 cases: The greater the average distance between the perceived location of party (j) in 1977 and the perceived position of the three parties located closest to that spot in 1979, the greater the chance for party (i) to pick up former voters for party (j).

To judge the goodness of fit of the reactive voting model with the 1979-data, consider the figures in Table 6.11. They show the proportion of voters moving between parties that would be predicted by the model, together with the reported movements (in parentheses) computed from the responses to the recall question in the 1979-survey.

---

[25] The Pensioners' Party has been excluded from the analysis. The party did not run in the 1979-election and hence did not pick up votes from any party. Moreover, no respondent in our data reported a shift from the Pensioners' Party in 1977 to any other party in 1979.

Table 6.10.: Regression coefficients for reactive voting model 1979. (Standard errors in parentheses)

	Intercept b_0	DISTij b_1	DISTjj b_2	NCLOSE b_3	DIST3 b_4	VPROP b_5
SD	4.21075 (0.16337)			-0.68975 (0.02804)	0.51272 (0.39632)	
RV	3.55083 (0.30130)			-0.73475 (0.06356)	0.41207 (0.78038)	
KF	3.48365 (0.06817)	-2.08473 (0.12847)				
DR	2.96147 (0.47721)	-0.36340 (1.92962)		-0.71740 (0.41486)	0.58142 (1.37263)	
SF	4.22297 (0.75127)	-3.64864 (0.37944)	1.53415 (0.96202)		0.92556 (1.02851)	
DKP	7.36006 (1.92103)	-6.55976 (1.32915)	4.77351 (1.75721)		5.92645 (3.70477)	
CD	7.09818 (0.50657)		5.91768 (0.57768)		2.63911 (0.90914)	
Krf	5.14246 (0.85652)	-7.32718 (1.04097)			11.38599 (2.95236)	
KAP	2.72795 (3.76583)	-7.28346 (3.47361)	1.85581 (5.29592)			
V	14.03247 (0.91991)		11.01112 (0.92460)	-0.85478 (0.12370)		5.24443 (0.62292)
VS	9.93205 (4.13940)	-6.52690 (4.89777)	5.59217 (3.92676)	-0.21566 (0.67566)	6.38163 (4.34641)	1.37235 (0.70514)
Frp	3.93754 (0.36045)	-3.28625 (0.21506)	0.96393 (0.59122)			

On visual inspection the deviations in Table 6.11. between "observed" and "expected" voter movements appear about the same size as in 1975 and 1977. This is confirmed by the value of the index of non-similarity (NS = 0.13), which once more can be called satisfactory.

From Table 6.11. it is easily seen that shifts to a number of parties are captured with a somewhat lesser degree of accuracy. This is true, e.g., for the Socialdemocrats and the Agrarians. Considering the situation leading to the election, a possible explanation might well be that one or more valence dimensions entered into the perception of these two parties.

Table 6.11.: Observed and expected voter movements 1977 - 1979 in percentages of all respondents (n = 1483). Observed percentages in parentheses.

Party 1979	Party 1977										
	SD	RV	KF	DR	SF	DKP	CD	Krf	V	VS	Frp
SD	37.6	0.5	0.4	0.1	0.3	0.1	0.2	0.1	0.7	0.1	0.7
	(37.6)	(0.2)	(0.1)	(0.4)	(0.8)	(0.3)	(0.4)	(0.1)	(0.2)	(0.2)	(0.7)
RV	1.6	3.0	0.1	0.1	0.1	0.0	0.1	0.0	0.3	0.1	0.1
	(1.3)	(3.0)	(0.2)	(0.1)	(0.1)	(0.0)	(0.1)	(0.1)	(0.2)	(0.1)	(0.2)
KF	2.1	0.1	5.1	0.1	0.1	0.0	3.1	0.2	2.7	0.1	0.3
	(0.7)	(0.3)	(9.6)	(0.2)	(0.0)	(0.0)	(0.5)	(0.0)	(1.6)	(0.1)	(1.0)
DR	0.2	0.0	0.0	1.6	0.0	0.0	0.0	0.0	0.1	0.0	0.1
	(0.3)	(0.0)	(0.0)	(1.6)	(0.0)	(0.0)	(0.0)	(0.0)	(0.0)	(0.0)	(0.1)
SF	1.2	0.1	0.0	0.1	4.0	0.1	0.1	0.0	0.1	0.1	0.0
	(1.1)	(0.1)	(0.0)	(0.1)	(4.0)	(0.2)	(0.1)	(0.0)	(0.0)	(0.2)	(0.1)
DKP	0.0	0.0	0.0	0.0	0.0	1.3	0.0	0.0	0.0	0.1	0.0
	(0.1)	(0.0)	(0.0)	(0.0)	(0.1)	(1.3)	(0.0)	(0.0)	(0.0)	(0.0)	(0.0)
CD	0.1	0.1	0.0	0.0	0.0	0.0	2.2	0.0	0.5	0.0	0.2
	(0.0)	(0.1)	(0.2)	(0.0)	(0.0)	(0.0)	(2.4)	(0.0)	(0.2)	(0.0)	(0.3)
Krf	0.0	0.1	0.0	0.0	0.0	0.0	0.0	1.8	0.1	0.0	0.1
	(0.0)	(0.0)	(0.0)	(0.0)	(0.0)	(0.0)	(0.0)	(1.8)	(0.1)	(0.0)	(0.1)
KAP	0.0	0.0	0.0	0.0	0.0	0.1	0.0	0.0	0.0	0.1	0.0
	(0.0)	(0.0)	(0.0)	(0.0)	(0.0)	(0.1)	(0.0)	(0.0)	(0.0)	(0.1)	(0.0)
V	2.3	0.0	0.5	0.0	0.0	0.0	2.3	0.0	9.8	0.0	0.0
	(0.0)	(0.1)	(0.2)	(0.1)	(0.0)	(0.0)	(0.3)	(0.2)	(13.8)	(0.0)	(0.2)
VS	0.5	0.0	0.0	0.0	0.1	0.2	0.0	0.0	0.0	2.6	0.1
	(0.5)	(0.1)	(0.0)	(0.1)	(0.0)	(0.0)	(0.0)	(0.0)	(0.0)	(2.6)	(0.0)
Frp	0.3	0.0	0.1	0.0	0.0	0.0	0.1	0.0	0.1	0.0	5.8
	(0.2)	(0.0)	(0.1)	(0.1)	(0.0)	(0.0)	(0.1)	(0.0)	(0.2)	(0.0)	(5.8)

In conclusion it appears that our proposition 3 can be considered confirmed by the 1979-data also. Clearly, the variations in the propensity to move from one party in 1977 to one of the parties running in the 1979-election cannot fully be accounted for by the model of reactive voting: About 13 pct. of the proportions would have to be moved to make the tables of the "predicted" and the reported voter movements identical. But this number is sufficiently small - especially when the rather restrictive assumptions of the model are taken into account - to allow the conclusion that a considerable part of the voter movements occurring between the elections in 1977 and

1979 can be accounted for as reactions to perceived party movements (or lack of such movements), and without assuming any changes in the locations of the voters' "ideal points" to have taken place.

7. Conclusions

Having finished our tour de force through the Danish political landscape of the seventies, we shall stop to summarize and to contemplate where it has taken us. This will be done at two different levels.

In section 7.1. we shall try to draw together and review some of the empirical findings which have emerged from the preceding analyses and which are central to our interpretation of voting as an instrumental and re-active choice. In section 7.2. we shall turn to a discussion of some of the theoretical implications of these findings.

7.1. Summary of empirical findings: Behavioral volatility and perceptual stability

Seen in a long perspective, the seventies appear as a period of quite unusual instability and volatility in Danish electoral behavior. Figures on gross and net movements between parties clearly bear out that tendency: The average net change in party strength was 17 pct. in the elections in the seventies (as against 6 pct. in the fifties, 9 pct. in the sixties, and (so far) 12 pct. in the eighties),[1] while reported gross movements between parties ranged from a maximum of about 40 pct. (1971-73) to a minimum of about 16 pct. (1977-79).[2] Thus even in the most "stable" election in the seventies, one out of six voters reported a shift to a new party. Most parties thus had to get accustomed to sizeable and rapid changes in their parliamentary strength.

From this one might easily gain the impression of an electorate in con-siderable confusion, suffering from a near-total lack of orientation, and moving hither and dither without knowing where to go and where to stay. Such an interpretation would also fit well into the classical picture of "the floating voter" known from e.g. The People's Choice.[3]

The results presented in the preceding chapters have shown this type of interpretation to be untenable, however:[4] Underneath the observable sur-face volatility in the electorate we have found a perception of the party sys-tem - and of the parties comprising that system - which seems much more adequately characterized by notions like clarity, stability and continuity than by notions like confusion and disorientation.

The clarity of the perception of the party system has been demonstrated by the fit of a simple distance model to the thermometer data on party sym-

---

[1] Worre (1987, p.14).

[2] Cf. the figures in table 3.13, table 4.14, table 5.8, and table 6.12.

[3] Lazarsfeld et al. (1944).

[4] This also applies to Johs. Andersen's above-mentioned thesis on the elections' loss of political content and meaning to the electorate.

pathy. On all measures used, the model's fit to the data turned out to be satisfactory in connection with all elections. Table 7.1. summarizes the values of two fit criteria with data from the five elections in the seventies.

Table 7.1.: Fit values for model of the perceived party system 1971-79

Election	R^2	NS-index "hindcasted" - oberved distribution of votes
1971	0.76	0.05
1973	0.65	0.08
1975	0.67	0.11
1977	0.60	0.08
1979	0.73	0.06

The table indicates a varying, but consistently low level of "noise" in the data, and hence in the electorate's perception of the parties in the party system as well. Obviously, as a basis for grading the parties according to sympathy, the voters did possess a clear impression of the overall structure of the party system and of the relations between the parties, and they were able to relate their own political position (in terms of "ideological" dimensions) to the parties' positions. In short, they knew quite well what they were choosing from.

The perception of the party system found in the respondents in the seventies is not only remarkably clear; it is also quite accurate, when compared to the relationships between the parties as they manifest themselves in the parties' legislative behavior. Table 7.2. summarizes the close resemblance found between party relations as indicated in the parties' voting in the third reading of government bills in the legislative period preceding the election, and party relations as perceived by the electorate at election time.

Table 7.2.: Agreement between party relations in legislative voting and perceived party relations 1971-79 (M-values)

	1971	1973	1975	1977	1979
M-value	0.89	0.78	0.66	0.78	0.82

Thus clearly the perception of the party system by the electorate cannot just be browsed off as a fidget of the voters' imagination; it had a solid foundation in the political "reality" of the seventies.

The accuracy of the voters' perception also expressed itself in the data on the perception of party leaders. With data from 1973, a striking precision in the perception of the position of competing leaders for the Socialdemocrats and the Conservatives, respectively, could be found.

Taken together, the clarity and accuracy of the electorate's perception of the party system in the seventies does not only force us to abandon the idea of a general loss of orientation causing the electoral volatility of the seventies; it also seems to contradict the picture - well-known primarily from the social-psychological theory of voting - of the generally uninformed or poorly informed voter.

To a considerable part, this contradiction may be an apparent one, however. The verdict of poor or no information in the voters is usually arrived at by studying correlations between opinions, expressed on batteries of specific items. Such correlations do indeed tend to indicate low consistency (low correlations between the opinions expressed on related items) and low stability (low correlations between opinions expressed on the same item in successive studies) in the respondents' opinions.[5] In contrast, in the present study we have been looking at the respondents' use of some basic "ideological" dimensions to fathom and describe the relationship between parties as well as their own relationship to parties. There is no necessary contradiction in finding that the respondents are knowledgeable about the relative position of parties with respect to some basic "ideological" dimensions, and the finding that the same respondents do not know very much about the parties' stands on specific issues or questions. Nor need there necessarily be a contradiction in finding that the respondents are able to locate themselves in terms of some basic "ideological" dimensions, but that nevertheless they need not be very consistent in their opinions on specific political issues.

What our results indicate is that the scope of validity which can be claimed for the social-psychological theory's picture of the generally uninformed or poorly informed voter is severely restricted: Finding lack of stability and consistency with regard to attitudes on specific issues and items does obviously not allow us to jump to the conclusion that the voters lack relevant political knowledge at all.

Another striking feature which emerged from the preceding chapters is the stability found in the respondents' perception of the party system throughout the period. In a number of respects, the perception of the party system shows surprisingly little change, especially when compared to the big changes in party preference (as witnessed by the ups and downs in the parties' proportion of the vote).

One important aspect of this stability concerns the dimensional structure of the perceived party system. Throughout the period, the party system has been found to be perceived basically in terms of the same two ideological dimensions: A left-right dimension, reflecting to some degree the time-

---

[5] Thus the highest correlation between two items reported by Worre (1987, p.68) is a meager r=0.50 between the attitude towards NATO and the attitude towards the EEC, meaning that our ability to correctly predict the attitude of an individual towards NATO is improved by 25 pct. if we know his or her attitude towards the EEC.

honored social cleavage between labor and capital, and a "backlash"-dimension that bundles a number of different anti system-attitudes and that on two occasions shows itself to be related to a social cleavage between those working in the private sector of the economy and those deriving their means of livelihood from the public sector, be it as wages or as transfers.

Our analysis does not support the interpretation of the 1973-election as implying, i.a., a shift from unidimensionality to twodimensionality in the perception of the party system.[6] The second dimension is discernable in the voters' perception of the party system in 1971 already. The difference between the elections of 1971 and 1973 was mainly that in 1973 there were two parties which identified themselves with a number of attitudes and opinions belonging to the second dimension, thus allowing it to become manifest in voting behavior; in 1971 there was no such outlet.

Another aspect of the stability in the respondents' perception of the party system concerns the issue-content of the "ideological" dimensions used to structure this perception. Table 7.3. shows the clear tendency for issue positions on the same items to be systematically related to the location of the respondents' "ideal points" throughout the whole period.

Table 7.3.: Issue content of 'ideological' dimensions in the respondents' perception of the party system 1971-79.

Items	1971	1973	1975	1977	1979
Economic equality	H	H	H	H	H
State control with investments	÷	H	H	÷	H
Harder taxation of high income	H	H	H	H	H
Interference with tariff negotiations	•	•	H	H	H
Stop for wage raises	•	•	H	H	H
Leave NATO	H	HV	H	H	H
Membership of EEC	HV*	HV*	H	H	H
Politicians make right decisions	•	÷	HV	V	÷
Politicians care too little	V	V	÷	÷	÷
Pol. spend money too lavishly	V	HV	HV	HV	V
Politicians give up principles	V	HV	÷	÷	÷
Strong man take power in crisis	•	V	V	V	V
Social benefits without need	•	HV	HV	HV	HV
Indoctrination in schools	•	•	H	HV	V
Worry about moral development	•	•	V	HV	V
TV-censorship of extremist views	•	•	÷	HV	V

Item belongs to:
H: Horizontal dimension; V: Vertical dimension; HV: Both horizontal and vertical dimension;
÷ : No pattern; •: Not asked.

*Battery of items

---

[6] Cf. Worre (1975).

But Table 7.3. also reveals a clear difference between the two dimensions with regard to content-stability, the left-right dimension standing out as the most stable one. With only few exceptions the positions taken by the respondents on a number of predominantly economic items can be seen to be consistently related to the horizontal distribution of their "ideal points" on the maps of the perceived party system throughout the whole period.

With the "backlash"-dimension, stability is somewhat lower. The only items consistently bringing out positions that are systematically related to the vertical distribution of the respondents' "ideal points" on the map are the item on a strong man taking power in a situation of economic crisis, the item on the politicians spending the taxpayers' money too lavishly, the item on too many people getting social benefits without really needing them, and the item on the moral development being a cause for concern. Other items, especially the ones on trust/distrust in politicians, do occasionally fail.

It thus appears that the most stable and in general most salient "ideological" dimension in the respondents' perception of the party system in the seventies was the left-right dimension. The saliency of the "backlash"-dimension, on the other hand, varied. It was apparently rather strong in the middle of the period and somewhat weaker at its beginning and its end.

Finally, the preceding chapters have revealed a much stronger perceptual continuity to exist in the respondents' perception of the location of the parties in the party system than might have been expected from the massive voter movements between the parties in the seventies. Clearly, the respondents perceived the parties to move in the party system; but in most cases these perceived movements are found to be restricted to fairly small regions of the space, and movements towards a new position to usually proceed in small steps rather than in large leaps. This agrees remarkably well with the Downsian assumption that parties are reliable and responsible in the sense of being consistent over time in word and deed - or at least that seems to be how they appear to the voters.

As an example of restricted movement one may look at the perceived position of the Socialdemocrats in the party system. If the different maps are compared, it can be seen that throughout the whole period the party is perceived to circle in a rather narrow center-left region.[7] A parallel example is provided by the socialist parties (SF, DKP, and VS): From 1973 onwards, they can be seen to be located in a rather stable, crescent-shaped formation on the left side of the perceived party system, and the changes in their relative positions are small.

Gradual movement is nicely exemplified by the Radical Liberals. In the beginning of the period (1971) the party is perceived as belonging to the liberal-conservative cluster of parties which held power from 1968 to 1971. But, starting in 1973 and gaining momentum from 1975 onwards, the party can be seen to be on its move away from its former partners in government

---

[7] It might be worth contemplating the fact that the party seems to be strong when it succeeds in occupying the center of the party space (as in 1971, 1977, and 1979), while it loses when it is perceived to have taken up a more leftist position, as in 1973 and 1975.

and towards the center of the party system, until in 1979 it ends up in its "classical" position close to the center in the vicinity of the Socialdemocrats. Also moving gradually is the Christian Peoples' Party: From a position close to the top of the map of the perceived party system in 1971, it can be seen to move gradually towards the opposite position, which it arrives at in 1979.

The main exception to the rule that changes in the perceived position of the parties occur gradually is provided by the Center-Democrats. From a position just a bit right of center in 1973 it changes to a position in the bottom-right region of the perceived party system in 1975, leaps upwards towards the center again in 1977, and back to the bottom once more in 1979. These rapid changes in the perception of the position of the Center-Democrats are in marked contrast to the gradual development in the perceived position of the Progress Party which is seen as gradually moving into ever deeper isolation.

Thus, as a whole, the electorate obviously did not change its perception of the parties in the party system of the seventies either dramatically or rapidly (except - to some degree - for the Center-Democrats). The changes that did occur, occurred at a measured pace, making for continuity rather than for disruptive changes.

This raises the question how such modest changes in the perceived position of the parties might possibly have translated into the high volatility of voters experienced in the elections from 1973 onwards, if it is assumed that voters vote for the party closest to their own position. The answer to this question is provided by the position of the voters relative to the parties: As can be seen from the various maps of the perceived party system (those including the respondents' "ideal points" as well), the bulk of the respondents is regularly found at or close to the center of the perceived party system. Given such a concentration of voter positions, even modest changes in the location of a party may lead to heavy losses or gains. Thus, paradoxically, it appears that it was the absence of strong - and strongly felt - divisions and polarizations in a large part of the electorate, rather than the presence of such a divisiveness, that made possible the electoral instability of the seventies.[8]

Thus in the seventies the voters were generally not floating because of lack of orientation. Neither were they just succumbing to various (and varying) "short term factors" like specific issues, the personality of candidates, or the special effects devised for them by the directors of various electoral campaigns. On the contrary, in the preceding analysis they have been found to exhibit a strong tendency to simply react to perceived changes in party positions, largely moving between parties as one would predict from combining the perceived changes in party positions with the as-

---

[8] This interpretation may even have some relevance to the discussion of Denmark as a consensual democracy, cf. Elder et al. (1988). It also runs counter to an interpretation of electoral behavior in the seventies in terms of an increasing "ideologization" of the electorate.

sumptions that voters do not change their own positions between two successive elections and that voters always vote for the party closest to their own position.

Obviously this interpretation rests on the assumption that the perception of the party system precedes the choice of a particular party on election day. Such interpretation might be contended, however, by claiming that the relationship is the other way around, i.e. that party preference determines the voter's perception of the party system.

But this contention is contradicted by two - related - findings of our analysis. In the first place, the influence of party preference (alongside with party identification and social class) on the perception of the party system has been found to be marginal. Secondly, the perception of the party system and of changes in it has been shown to closely reflect the legislative party system and changes within that system. These findings suggest that the voters' perception of the party system is indeed positioned as an intermediate variable between what goes on in the parliamentary arena and their vote decision.

In the present study the relationship between the perception of party positions in the party system and the reported vote has been established by means of a simplified model of "reactive voting", based on the above-mentioned assumptions. Table 7.4. summarizes the goodness of fit of this model with data from 1973 to 1979, measured by the index of non-similarity between the table of reported voter movements from the surveys and the table of voter movements as "predicted" by the model. Obviously the model does not "tell the whole story". There are shortcomings, two of which appear important.

In the first place, the model does not fit all voter movements equally well. The most spectacular failure occurs with data for voter movements from the other parties to the Progress Party in 1973, but there are other instances, like the upsurge of the Agrarians in 1975, where the predicted pick ups by a party are off the mark.

Table 7.4.: Values of index of non-similarity between tables of reported and predicted voter movements

	1971-73	1973-75	1975-77	1977-79
NS-index	0.10	0.14	0.12	0.13

In this context the discussion (sect. 1.5. above) of the distinction between 'position issues' and 'valence issues' should be recalled. As has been pointed out, valence dimensions cannot be constructed in the same way as policy-related dimensions in the spatial models we have been using . To the degree 'valence issues' influence the voters' perception of a party, prediction of voter movements based on 'position issues' only must be expected to fail.

'Valence issues' may hence constitute part of the explanation in cases where substantial deviations between observed and reported voter movements were found.

Secondly, the importance of the same independent variable in the model was found to vary strongly, both between parties in the same election and between elections.[9] We have not attempted any substantive interpretation of such differences, but clearly they call for further investigations.

Despite these reservations, Table 7.4. shows that, as a whole, the hypothesis of reactive voting, as embodied in the model, allows us to reconstruct fairly accurately voter movements in the seventies from data on perceived changes in party positions. Thus to a considerable degree the voter volatility of this period can be accounted for as a simple reaction to perceived shifts in party positions relative to the two 'ideological' dimensions found in the voters' belief system, even under the assumption - known in advance to be unrealistic - that the voters themselves do not change their positions[10] relative to these 'ideological' dimensions.

7.2. Some theoretical implications: The role of party behavior and the return of politics

It has been one of the aims of this study to investigate the "explanatory bite" of a rational choice framework when applied to Danish electoral behavior in the seventies. Though many relevant aspects have been left untouched altogether, and many details remain to be filled into the frame in order to complete the picture, it seems safe to conclude by now that it is possible to arrive at a consistent interpretation of Danish voting behavior in the seventies as the expression of reactive choice.

Adopting this perspective on voting behavior opens further perspectives and triggers off further questions. One of the most obvious theoretical consequences of the point of view adopted here is that the parties are brought back to the center of the scene on which the electoral combat is staged, not just as objects for psychological identification and ego-extension, nor just as the originators of residual "short-term factors" upsetting the "normal vote", but as central actors: After all, it is their activities - as seen by the voters in

---

[9] The same lack of stability in the models' coefficients can also be found in various applications of the "responsibility-hypothesis".

[10] The reactivity of the vote decision may even have lent extra momentum to the electoral instability following the initial shock of the 1973-election. Since this election resulted in a highly fragmented Folketing, new and unusual patterns of cooperation between parties became necessary to keep the parliamentary system functioning. This in turn led to the positions of some parties being perceived as having changed, triggering off new voter movements in the following election. Thus part of the electoral instability from 1973 onwards might well have been a "propagation" of the initial shock in the sense of a negative (destabilizing) feed back loop.

the coarse grid of their structuring "belief system" - that is voted upon. Thus party behavior in general and party strategies in particular suddenly (again) become central independent variables in the explanation and understanding of electoral outcomes. This, of course, is also true for the results of the Danish general elections in the seventies.

In arguing for the reactivity of the voters' decision, one may appear to just be shifting the onus of irrationality from the Danish voters to the Danish parties. Clearly, the idea of having voters reacting rationally to a-rational parties does not make much sense. But if parties were rational actors too, why would they ever move to positions in the party space that entail the loss of votes and seats, as some of them obviously must have done in the seventies? Why do they not uniformly rush to where the voters are?

Thus interpreting voting behavior within a rational choice framework drags with it the problem of the rationality of party behavior. It is far beyond the scope of this study to embark on the ambitious project of developing a rational theory of party competition in a multiparty system,[11] or even the meekest beginnings to one. Here we shall only point to some factors that, by restraining the freedom of movement of parties, may at times lead them to move to positions that do not appeal to their voters, or to keep them away from positions that could have been advantageous in terms of votes and seats, and indicate how they may possibly have influenced relevant aspects of the behavior of Danish parties in the seventies.

In the Downsian model, parties are allowed almost total freedom of movement along the ideological continuum in their attempt to maximize votes. They are only restricted by not being allowed to leap over each other. In real life, parties may find their ability to maneuver more limited in several respects. They may well find themselves maximizing under constraints.

One such constraining factor is party ideology and/or tradition: Parties do normally not feel free to move to every conceivable location in the party space, regardless of possible gains in votes. Some locations relative to the 'ideological' dimensions are "off limits" to certain parties or can be approached at best via a succession of small steps only. Concern for consistency and respectability limits freedom of action. The surprisingly small movements of the parties in the perceived Danish party system in the seventies may seem to provide some empirical evidence in that direction.[12]

Some parties may also be restricted by their affiliation with organized interests. In the Danish party system the Socialdemocrats' relationship to the trade union movement and the Agrarians' ties with organized agricultural interests naturally come to mind. While such affiliations need not hinder the party's movement in certain directions altogether - after all, Socialdemo-

---

[11] For such a theory (within the spatial model-tradition) see Robertson (1976). It is developed with respect to a two-party system, and hence not directly applicable to the Danish case. A conceptual model for this situation is given in Sjöblom (1968).

[12] In this connection the close resemblance between the perceived party space and the legislative party space should be kept in mind.

crats and Agrarians did form a coalition in 1978, despite strong resistance from trade unions - the organizations involved may be able to make such movements very costly to the party, be it in terms of material support or in terms of intangibles.

At least to a certain degree, parties have to take into consideration the position of their members and activists, as pointed out by Hirshman (1970). Thus there are some internal pushes and pulls influencing the movements of the parties as well. Damgaard and Kristensen (1982) have shown that, in terms of location with respect to the 'ideological' left-right dimension, Danish party activists tend to be more extreme than both party members and party representatives. Thus, for internal reasons, parties located on the left of the political spectrum may find it difficult to move further to the right, and vice versa.

The forces mentioned so far are all forces that may primarily be expected to restrict the movements of the parties by tying them to a particular position in terms of 'ideological' dimensions, or by confining them to a narrow region in the party space at best. There is, however, a factor that may work in the opposite direction, at least with some parties, compelling them to move, even some times at the cost of voter support.

As strongly pointed out by Robertson (1976), governments have to try to solve social problems. In a competitive democracy, the parties will present their envisaged solutions to the electorate for decision, and in a two party-system, the winning party will be able to implement its solutions. This ability, and not just power for power's own sake, is what the parties compete for.

In a multiparty system like the Danish, with a long tradition of minority governments, things are more complicated. Normally the government will not be able to solve social problem in its own way; it has to rely on support from other parties. Solving social problems thus can no longer be the responsibility of the government only; part of the responsibility rests on the parties in the Folketing as well. In the strongly fragmented Folketing that resulted from the 1973- and subsequent elections this was ostensibly the case.

A number of parties, admittedly, may not feel under any such obligation, or may reject it. Others, however, feel more or less strongly compelled by it to participate in trying to establish solutions by bargaining with the government and - as often - several other parties. The more urgent the problem, the greater becomes the pressure on such parties.

In the economic recession following the first and the second oil crisis in the seventies, the need to act on the weaknesses of the Danish economy became obvious at numerous occasions. Thus various parties, primarily the four "old" parties (SD, RV, KF, and V), and two of the new ones (CD and Krf), were forced to come together in varying combinations to work out compromise solutions. They were forced to "move" by sheer necessity, and at times paid a heavy toll in votes and seats in the following election. The fate of the Center-Democrats in the 1975-election may serve as an illustrative example.

The latter leads naturally to one final implication of interpreting voting behavior in a rational choice framework: A consequence of succumbing to the "perverse and unorthodox" argument that voters are neither automatons nor fools becomes the heretical position that obviously politics must matter, even to electoral behavior and to electoral outcomes: In order to understand why people vote the way they do, one cannot ignore political variables like policies and policy outcomes. The importance ascribed by a theory of reactive voting to political variables thus marks the most clear-cut difference to social-psychological or structural theories of voting which regularly can be found - in their theorizing as well as in their practice - to relegate politics to a very marginal position.[13]

---

[13] Looking at the writings on Danish electoral behavior in the seventies one cannot possibly avoid noticing how little they have to say about the actual political developments and events of that period.

List of party names and abbreviations

Socialdemocrats	(Socialdemokratiet)	SD
Radical Liberals	(Det radikale Venstre)	RV
Conservatives	(Det konservative Folkeparti)	KF
Justice Party	(Danmarks Retsforbund)	DR
Socialist Peoples' Party	(Socialistisk Folkeparti)	SF
Communists	(Danmarks Kommunistiske Parti)	DKP
Center-Democrats	(Centrum-Demokraterne)	CD
Pensioners' Party	(Pensionistpartiet)	Pens
Christian Peoples' Party	(Kristeligt Folkeparti)	Krf
Communist Workers' Party	(Kommunistisk Arbejderparti)	KAP
Agrarians	(Venstre)	V
Left Socialists	(Venstresocialisterne)	VS
Progress Party	(Fremskridtspartiet)	Frp
Schlesvigian Party	(Slesvigsk Parti)	Slp

References

Aldrich and Nelson (1984): John H. Aldrich and Forrest D. Nelson, *Linear Probability, Logit, and Probit Models*, Beverly Hills: Sage Publications.

Andersen (1982): Harald Westergård Andersen, *Dansk politik i går og i dag*, 3.ed., Copenhagen: Fremad.

Andersen (1980): Johannes Andersen, *Vælgerne, de politiske partier og staten*, Ålborg: AUC Forlag.

Andersen (1981): Johannes Andersen, "De politiske partiers krise", *Politica*, vol.13, 1981, pp.87-107.

Andersen (1982): Johannes Andersen, *Politiske partier og politisk magt i Danmark*, Copenhagen: Gyldendal.

Arendt (1964): Hannah Arendt, *Eichmann in Jerusalem*, München: Piper Verlag.

Barry (1970): Brian M. Barry, *Sociologists, Economists and Democracy*, London: Collier-Macmillan.

Buchanan (1972): J.M. Buchanan, "Towards Analysis of Closed Behavioral Systems", in Buchanan, J.M. and Tollison, R.D., *Theory of Public Choice*, Michigan: Michigan Press.

Burnham (1941): James Burnham, *The Managerial Revolution*, New York: John Day.

Borre (1974): Ole Borre, "Denmark's Protest Election of December 1973", *Scandinavian Political Studies*, vol.9, 1974, pp.197-204.

Borre (1977): Ole Borre, "Recent Trends in Danish Voting Behavior", in Cerny, K.H. (ed.), *Scandinavia at the Polls*, Washington: American Enterprise Institute.

Borre (1981): Ole Borre, "Den ustadige ligevægt - forskydninger i de danske partiers vælgerstyrke", *Politica*, vol.13, nr.2, 1981, pp.46-86.

Borre (1982): Ole Borre, "Ideologi og partivalg i Danmark 1979", in Anckar, D., Damgaard, E. and Valen, H. (eds.), *Partier, ideologier, väljare,*, Åbo: Åbo Akademi.

Borre (1983): Ole Borre, "Ideologi og partivalg", in Borre, O. et al. (eds.), *Efter vælgerskredet*, Aarhus: Politica.

Borre (1984a): Ole Borre, "Hvad siger teorien?", in Elklit, J. and Tonsgaard, O. (eds.), *Valg og vælgeradfærd*, Aarhus: Politica.

Borre (1984b): Ole Borre, "Træk af den danske vælgeradfærd 1971-84", in Elklit, J. and Tonsgaard, O. (eds.), *Valg og vælgeradfærd*, Aarhus: Politica.

Borre and Katz (1973): Ole Borre and Daniel Katz, "Party Identification and Its Motivational Base in a Multiparty System: A Study of the Danish General Election of 1971", *Scandinavian Political Studies*, vol. 8, 1973, pp.69 - 112.

Borre and Stehouwer (1968): Ole Borre and Jan Stehouwer, *Partistyrke og social struktur 1960*, Aarhus: Akademisk Boghandel.

Boyd (1972): John P. Boyd, "Information Distance for Discrete Structures", in Shepard, R.N., Romney, A.K., and Nerlove, S.B. (eds.), *Multidimensional Scaling*, vol.1, New York: Seminar Press.

Budge, Crewe and Farlie (1976): Ian Budge, Ivor Crewe and Dennis Farlie (eds.), *Party Identification and Beyond*, New York: John Wiley & Sons.

Campbell, Converse, Miller and Stokes (1960): Angus Campbell, Philip E. Converse, Warren E. Miller and Donald E. Stokes, *The American Voter*, New York: John Wiley & Sons.

Carroll (1972): J. Douglas Carroll, "Individual Differences and Multidimensional Scaling", in Shepard, R.N., Romney, A.K., and Nerlove, S.B. (eds.), *Multidimensional Scaling*, vol.1, New York: Seminar Press.

Converse (1964): Philip E. Converse, "The Nature of Belief Systems in Mass Publics", in Apter, D.E. (ed.), *Ideology and Discontent*, New York: The Free Press.

Converse (1966): Philip E. Converse, "The Problem of Party Distances in Models of Voting Change", in Jennings, M.K. and Zeigler, I.H. (eds.), *The Electoral Process*, Englewood Cliffs: Prentice-Hall.

Converse and Dupeux (1966): Philip E. Converse and Georges Dupeux, "Politicization of the Electorate in France and the United States", in Campbell, A., Converse, Ph.E., Miller, W.E., and Stokes, D.E., *Elections and the Political Order*, New York: John Wiley & Sons.

Converse and Valen (1971): Philip E. Converse and Henry Valen, "Dimensions of Cleavage and Perceived Party Distances in Norwegian Voting", *Scandinavian Political Studies,* vol.6, 1971, pp.107-152.

Coombs (1964): Clyde H. Coombs, *A Theory of Data*, New York: John Wiley & Sons.

Damgaard (1977): Erik Damgaard, *Folketinget under forandring*, Copenhagen: Samfundsvidenskabeligt Forlag.

Damgaard (1980): Erik Damgaard (ed.), *Folkets veje i dansk politik*, Copenhagen: Schultz.

Damgaard and Kristensen (1982): Erik Damgaard and Ole P. Kristensen, "Party Government under Pressure" in Anckar, D., Damgaard, E. and Valen, H., *Partier, ideologier, väljare*, Åbo: Åbo Akademi.

Damgaard and Rusk (1976): Erik Damgaard and Jerrold G. Rusk, "Cleavage Structures and Representational Linkages: A Longitudinal Analysis of Danish Legislative Behavior", in Budge, I., Crewe, I. and Farlie, D. (eds.), *Party Identification and Beyond*, New York: John Wiley & Sons.

Dich (1973): Jørgen S. Dich, *Den herskende klasse*, Copenhagen: Borgen.

Downs (1957): Anthony Downs, *An Economic Theory of Democracy*, New York: Harper & Row.

Easton (1965): David Easton, *A Systems Analysis of Political Life*, New York: Wiley & Sons.

Elder et al. (1988): Neil Elder, Alastair H. Thomas and David Arter, *The Consensual Democracies?* (Rev. edition), Oxford: Basil Blackwell.

Elklit (1984): Jørgen Elklit, "Det klassiske danske partisystem bliver til", in Elklit, J. and Tonsgaard, O. (eds.), *Valg og vælgeradfærd*, Aarhus: Politica.

Elklit et al. (1972): Jørgen Elklit, Ole Riis and Ole Tonsgaard, "Local Voting Studies of Total Electorates: The Danish General Election of 1971, *Scandinavian Political Studies*, vol. 7, 1972, pp.191-213.

Enelow and Hinich (1984): James M. Enelow and Melvin J. Hinich, *The Spatial Theory of Voting*, Cambridge: Cambridge University Press.

Farlie and Budge (1976): Dennis Farlie and Ian Budge, "Placing Party Identification within a Typology of Representations of Voting and Party Competition and Proposing a Synthesis", in Budge, I., Crewe, I. and Farlie, D. (eds.), *Party Identification and Beyond*, New York: John Wiley & Sons.

Fiorina (1981): Morris P. Fiorina, *Retrospective Voting in American National Elections*, New Haven: Yale University Press.

Fryklund and Peterson (1981): Björn Fryklund and Thomas Peterson, *Populism och misnöjespartier i Norden*, Malmö: Arkiv.

Glans (1984): Ingemar Glans, "Fremskridtspartiet - småborgerlig revolt, högerreaktion eller generell protest?", in Elklit, J. and Tonsgaard, O. (eds.), *Valg og vælgeradfærd*, Aarhus: Politica.

Goul Andersen (1979): Jørgen Goul Andersen, *Mellemlagene i Danmark*, Aarhus: Politica.

Goul Andersen (1984a): Jørgen Goul Andersen, *Kvinder og Politik*, Aarhus: Politica.

Goul Andersen (1984b): Jørgen Goul Andersen, "Udviklingen i de sociale modsætningsforhold frem mod år 2000", in *Konflikt og tilpasning*, Copenhagen: Aschehoug.

Goul Andersen (1984c): Jørgen Goul Andersen, "Aspekter af den politiske kultur i Danmark efter 1971", in Damgaard, E., Goul Andersen, J., Buksti, J.A. and Kristensen, O.P., *Dansk demokrati under forandring*, Copenhagen: Schultz.

Haarder (1974): Bertel Haarder, *Institutionernes tyranni*, Copenhagen: Bramsen & Hjort.

Hansen (1981a): Erik Jørgen Hansen, *Levekår og placering i det politiske spektrum*, Copenhagen: Socialforskningsinstituttet, meddelelse nr. 35.

Hansen (1981b): Erik Jørgen Hansen, "Fremskridtspartiet er et klasseparti - men hvilken klasse?", *Økonomi og Politik*, 1981, nr.3, pp. 206-217.

Hansen and Nannestad (1975): Peter Hansen and Peter Nannestad,"Measuring Prejudicial Attitudes in a Situational Context", *International Journal of Comparative Sociology*, vol.16, 1975, pp.207-227.

Heath et al. (1985): Anthony Heath, Roger Jowell, and John Curtice, *How Britain Votes,* Oxford: Pergamon Press.

Heiser (1981): Willem J. Heiser, *Unfolding Ananlysis of Proximity Data*, Leiden: Reprodienst Psychologie RUL.

Henriksen (1978): Per Henriksen, *Småborgerskabets deklassering - myte eller realitet*, Aarhus: Institute of Political Science (Master's thesis).

Hirshman (1970): Albert O. Hirshman, *Exit, Voice, and Loyalty*, Cambridge (Mass.): Harvard University Press.

Jensen (1979): Ulla Skovgaard Jensen, *Michiganprogrammet*, Aarhus: Institute of Political Science (Master's thesis).

Kaarsted (1988): Tage Kaarsted, *Regringen, vi aldrig fik*, Odense: Odense University Press.

Key (1966): V.O. Key, Jr., *The Responsible Electorate*, New York: Vintage.

Kruskal and Wish (1978): Joseph B. Kruskal and Myron Wish, *Multidimensional Scaling*, Beverly Hills: Sage Publications.

Kruskal, Young and Seery (1977): Joseph B. Kruskal, Forest W, Young and Judith B. Seery, *How to Use KYST-2, A Very Flexible Program to Do Multidimensional Scaling and Unfolding*, Murray Hill: Bell Laboratories.

Lantermann and Feger (1980): Ernst D. Lantermann and Hubert Feger (eds.), *Similarity and Choice*, Bern: Hans Huber Publishers.

Lazarsfeld et al. (1944): Paul E. Lazarsfeld, Bernard Berelson and Hazel Gaudet, *The People's Choice: How the Voter Makes up his Mind*, New York: Duell.

Lindrup and Pedersen (1984): Kurt Lindrup and Jørgen Pedersen "Politiske holdninger og partivalg", in Borre, O. et al. (eds.), *Efter vælgerskreddet*, Aarhus: Politica.

Lipset (1960): Seymour M. Lipset, *Political Man*, London: Heineman.

Madsen (1980): Henrik J. Madsen, "Electoral Outcomes and Macro-Economic Policies: The Scandinavian Case", in Whiteley, P. (ed.), *Models of Political Economy*, London and Beverly Hills: Sage.

Margolis (1977): Michael Margolis, "From Confusion to Confusion: Issues and the American Voter", *American Political Science Review*, vol. 71, 1977, pp.31 - 43.

Meyer (1984): Poul Meyer, *Dansk Politik 1944-1984*, Copenhagen: Gad.

Miller (1976): Warren E. Miller, "The Cross-National Use of Party Identification as a Stimulus to Political Inquiry", in Budge, I., Crewe, I. and Farlie, D. (eds.), *Party Identification and Beyond*, New York: John Wiley & Sons.

NAG (1980): Numerical Algorithms Group (Lim.), *GENSTAT 4.03*, Harpenden: Lawes Agricutural Trust.

Nannestad (1981): Peter Nannestad, *Combining Observations When Individuals Have Different Response-Functions: A Different Look at Individual Difference Scaling*, Aarhus: Institute of Political Science, Working paper nr.20, Den politiske beslutningsproces.

Nannestad (1984): Peter Nannestad, "Dimensioner i vælgernes opfattelse af partisystemet", in Elklit,J. and Tonsgaard, O. (eds.), *Valg og vælgeradfærd*, Aarhus: Politica.

Nannestad (1985): Peter Nannestad, *Geometriske repræsentationer af relationelle datastrukturer*, Aarhus: Politica.

Nannestad and Gaasholt (1982): Peter Nannestad and Øystein Gaasholt,"Denmark", in Andrews, W.G. (ed.), *International Handbook of Political Science*, Westport: Greenwood Press.

Nie and Andersen (1974): Norman H. Nie and Kristi Andersen, "Mass Belief Systems Revisited: Political Change and Attitude Structure", *Journal of Politics*, vol. 36, 1974, pp.540-587.

Nielsen (1979): Hans Jørgen Nielsen, *Politiske holdninger og fremskridtsstemme*, Copenhagen: Forlaget Politiske Studier.

Nielsen (1983): Hans Jørgen Nielsen, *The Reality of Distrust*, Copenhagen: Institut for samfundsfag (unpublished ECPR-paper).

Nielsen and Sauerberg (1976): Hans Jørgen Nielsen and Steen Sauerberg, "The Uncivic Culture", *Scandinavian Political Studies*, vol.11, 1976, pp. 147 - 163.

Nilson (1977): Sten Sparre Nilson, "Kryssende konfliklinier i norsk politikk", *Statsvetenskaplig Tidskrift*, vol.80, 1977, pp.93-103.

Page and Jones (1979): Benjamin Page and Calvin Jones, "Reciprocal Effects of Policy Preferences, Party Loyalties and the Vote", *American Political Science Review*, vol.73, 1979, pp.1071-1089.

Paldam (1979): Martin Paldam, *Economic Conditions and 145 National Elections*, Aarhus: Institute of Economics.

Paldam (1987): Martin Paldam, "Den økonomiske faktor i regeringens popularitet - en oversigt", *Økonomi og politik*, vol. 60, 2, 1987, pp.83-93.

Paldam and Schneider (1980): Martin Paldam and Friedrich Schneider, "The Macro-Economic Aspects of Government and Opposition Popularity in Denmark 1957-78", *Nationaløkonomisk Tidsskrift*, vol.118, 1980, pp.149-170.

Pedersen (1967): Mogens N. Pedersen, "Consensus and Conflict in the Danish Folketing", *Scandinavian Political Studies*, vol. 2, 1967, pp.143-166.

Pedersen (1977): Mogens N. Pedersen, "Om voteringsanalysens muligheder og begrænsninger - bemærkninger til en anakronistisk debat om brugen af kvantitative metoder", *Statsvetenskaplig Tidskrift*, vol.80, 1977, pp.259-263.

Pedersen et al. (1971): Mogens N. Pedersen, Erik Damgaard and Peter Nannestad, "Party Distances in the Danish Folketing 1945-1968", *Scandinavian Political Studies*, vol.6, 1971, pp.87-106.

Petersen and Elklit (1973): Nikolaj Petersen and Jørgen Elklit, "Denmark Enters the European Communities", *Scandinavian Political Studies*, vol.8, 1973, pp.198-213.

Poulsen (1979): Jørgen Poulsen, "Demokratiforståelse i det liberale konstruktørprogram", *Politica*, vol.11, 1979, pp.121-147.

Rasmussen (1987): Erik Rasmussen, *Complementarity and Political Science*, Odense: Odense University Press.

Rasmussen (1976): Gunnar Rasmussen, *Det småborgerlige oprør*, Copenhagen: Demos.

Robertson (1976): David Robertson, *A Theory of Party Competition*, New York: John Wiley & Sons.

Robertson (1976): David Robertson, "Surrogates for Party Identification in the Rational Choice Framework", in Budge, I., Crewe, I. and Farlie, D. (eds.), *Party Identification and Beyond*, New York: John Wiley & Sons.

Rusk and Borre (1976): Jerrold G. Rusk and Ole Borre, " The Changing Party Space in Danish Voter Perceptions, 1971-73", in Budge, I., Crewe, I. and Farlie, D. (eds.), *Party Identification and Beyond*, New York: John Wiley & Sons.

Rusk and Weisberg (1972): Jerrold G. Rusk and Herbert F. Weisberg, "Perceptions of President Candidates: Implications for Electoral Change", *Midwest Journal of Political Science*, vol.16, nr.3, 1972.

Schelsky (1975): Helmut Schelsky, *Die Arbeit tun die anderen*, Opladen: Westdeutscher Verlag.

Schönemann and Carroll (1969): Peter H. Schönemann and Robert M. Carroll, *Fitting One Matrix to Another under Choice of a Central Dilation and a Rigid Motion*, Ann Arbor: University Microfilms

Shepard (1974): Roger N. Shepard, "Representation of Structure in Similarity Data: Problems and Prospects", *Psychometrika*, vol.39, 1974, pp.373-421.

Siune (1982): Karen Siune, *Valgkampe i TV og radio*, Aarhus: Politica.

Sjöblom (1968): Gunnar Sjöblom, *Party Strategies in a Multiparty System*, Lund: Studentlitteratur.

Stokes (1966): Donald E. Stokes, "Spatial Models of Party Competition", in Campbell, A., Converse, Ph.E., Miller, W.E., and Stokes, D.E., *Elections and the Political Order*, New York: John Wiley & Sons.

Taylor (1971): Michael Taylor, "Review Article: Mathematical Political Theory", *British Journal of Political Science*, vol.1, 1971, pp.339-382.

Thomsen (1987): Søren Risbjerg Thomsen, *Danish Elections 1920-79*, Aarhus: Politica.

Tonsgaard (1984): Ole Tonsgaard, "Vælgerlune eller vælgerfornuft?", in Elklit, J. and Tonsgaard, O. (eds.), *Valg og vælgeradfærd*, Aarhus: Politica.

Wahlke (1971): John C. Wahlke, "Policy Demands and System Support: The Role of the Represented", *British Journal of Political Science*, vol.1, 1971, pp.271-290.

Valen (1981): Henry Valen, *Valg og politikk*, Oslo: NKS Forlaget.

Veblen (1899): Thorstein Veblen, *Theory of the Leisure Class*, London: Allen & Unwin (3. impr 1957).

Wendt (1978): Frantz Wendt, *Besættelse og atomtid 1939-1978*, vol.14 in Danstrup, J. and Koch, H., *Politikens Danmarkshistorie*, 3.ed., Copenhagen: Politikens Forlag.

Weisberg and Rusk (1970): Herbert F. Weisberg and Jerrold G. Rusk, "Dimensions of Candidate Evaluation", *American Political Science Journal*, vol.64, 1970, pp.1167-1185.

Wickman (1977): Wickman, Jane, *Fremskridtspartiet. Hvem og hvorfor?*, Copenhagen: Akademisk Forlag.

Worre (1987): Torben Worre, *Dansk vælgeradfærd*, Copenhagen: Akademisk Forlag.